Something More

G·K
Hall
&C°.

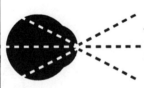 This Large Print Book carries the
Seal of Approval of N.A.V.H.

Something More

Excavating Your Authentic Self

Sarah Ban Breathnach

G.K. Hall & Co. • Thorndike, Maine

A portion of this work was originally published in *Good Housekeeping*: pages 65–69; 91–95; and 293–296.

The following authors, their agents, and publishers have graciously granted permission to include the following excerpts:

ABKCO Music Inc.: From "Sitting On a Fence" written by Mick Jagger and Keith Richards. © 1966 Renewed 1994 ABKCO Music Inc. All rights reserved. Reprinted by permission.

Artisan: From *Late Bloomers* by Brendan Gill. Text copyright © 1996 by Brendan Gill. Used by permission of Artisan, a division of Workman Publishing Co., Inc. New York. All rights reserved.

I would like to gratefully acknowledge all the writers I have quoted from for their wisdom, comfort, and inspiration. An exhaustive search was done to determine whether previously published material included in this book required permission to reprint. If there has been an error, I apologize and a correction will be made in subsequent editions.

Published in 1999 by arrangement with Warner Books, Inc.

G.K. Hall Large Print NonFiction Series.

The text of this Large Print edition is unabridged.
Other aspects of the book may vary from the original edition.

Set in 16 pt. Plantin.

Printed in the United States on permanent paper.

Library of Congress Cataloging in Publication Data

Ban Breathnach, Sarah.
    Something more : excavating your authentic self /
Sarah Ban Breathnach.
        p. cm.
    Originally published: New York : Warner Books, 1998.
    Includes bibliographical references.
    ISBN 0-7838-8652-7 (lg. print : hc : alk. paper)
    1. Spiritual life. 2. Women — Religious life. 3. Self-realization —
Religious aspects. I. Title.
    [BL625.7.B353   1999]
    291.4′4′082—dc21   99-23296

Those who live passionately
teach us how to love.
Those who love passionately
teach us how to live.

For
Katie Brant
and
Larry Kirshbaum

Soul friends.

Contents

Shattered   281

Sensing   341

A book must be the axe for the frozen sea inside us.

FRANZ KAFKA

Our Authentic Lives

*I have a sense of these buried lives
striving to come out through me
to express themselves.*

MARGE PIERCY

Our Authentic Lives

Our birth is but a sleep and a forgetting:
The soul that rises with us, our life's star,
Hath had elsewhere its setting,
And cometh from afar:
Not in entire forgetfulness . . .

WILLIAM WORDSWORTH

Human beings, as far as I can tell, seem to be divided into two subspecies — the resigned, who live in quiet desperation, and the exhausted, who exist in restless agitation. The quiet and resigned believe that our time on this Earth is random, a roll of cosmic dice, completely beyond our control. You know these folks when you hear them; their sighs speak volumes.

The rest of us — the restless agitators — sense that there's got to be Something More to why we're here, something other than discovering what money, love, and sex have to do with the Meaning of Life. We grow our own organic vegetables, take our vitamins, drink mineral water, meditate, start study groups. We work out five days a week, treat ourselves to low-fat

15

sorbet the other two, and then wonder why we're perpetually cranky. *So what's the rest of it?* we want to know (preferably by the end of the afternoon). This question distracts and disturbs us and keeps us worn to a raveling.

But then, perhaps figuring out what money, love, and sex have to do with the texture and truth of our lives is the rest of it. Certainly the little face staring out from a vintage black-and-white photograph of me as a two-year-old seems determined to find out something. Hands grasping both arms of her high chair, chin set in defiance, jaws clenched, and dark, solemn eyes reveal an indomitable will *to get it right,* a will that's unnerving in one so small. This is not the face of an ingenue; this is an old soul in a new body — wary, wise to her own long past, on to the wiles of the world, and having miles to go before she sleeps. An experienced guerrilla, she's taking no prisoners this time around.

I unearthed the photograph after my mother died. Like an archaeologist searching in the sand, I was sorting and sifting through the most amazing collection of paper shards from two women's lives, my mother's and my own — vintage greeting cards, old bankbooks, mass cards, Irish sweepstakes tickets, and old (but new to me) photographs. For all the reasons that drive historians crazy — flooded basements, moves, lapses in memory — there are only a few pictures of my childhood. Most of them are lost. But as I relived every family Hallmark moment I could find, I unearthed myself. I was as thrilled, I imagine, as the famous Egyptologist Howard Carter was when he found the tomb of the Egyptian boy-king, Tutankhamen.

A picture is not just worth a thousand words, it's worth a Jungian personality inventory; for there, in black and white, are my personality assets or deficits (depending on the circumstances and who's making the assessment): strong, dogged, tenacious. Courageous. Steadfast, purposeful, unflinching. Stubborn — a defining trait summed up in a single snapshot.

I wish I'd known from the beginning that I was born a strong woman. What a difference it would have made! I wish I'd known that I was born a courageous woman; I've spent so much of my life cowering. How many conversations would I not only have started but *finished* if I had known I possessed a warrior's heart? I wish I'd known that I'd been born to take on the world; I wouldn't have run *from* it for so long, but run *to* it with open arms.

Flash forward nearly five decades later. A new photograph accidentally captures the same pose. Same heart-shaped face, same tilt of the head, same straightforward gaze, but a completely different aura surrounds the camera's subject. The steely stubbornness has become spiritual moxie; the child of the world has grown up to become a savvy innocent. The wariness has been transformed into a *knowing*, as in, *Relax, I know what I'm doing.* Better yet, all the tension is gone; the burden of the assignments her soul chose to tackle in this lifetime has been lifted; she's learned her lessons well. Her karma's been erased, an enormous divine debt has been paid off. Can this be possible? Perhaps I'm looking at the photos of two women related by blood from different eras, but I know better.

Surprised by Joy

The soul is here for its own joy.

RUMI

The writer Cynthia Ozick believes that "after a certain number of years our faces become our biographies." I hope she's right. If she is, then the woman in the photograph is *prima facie* evidence to support my theory of *re*embodiment, a variation on the ancient spiritual principle of reincarnation.

Reincarnation is the belief that, after our physical deaths, our souls are born again in another time, another place, and another body in order to continue our journey to peace and perfection by mastering spiritual lessons. The ancients believed that this deeply personal, *authentic* journey takes many lifetimes. But once the lessons are mastered, we get to move on, promoted, in a sense, to the next grade.

But what if we're awake and willing to take an accelerated course during *this* Earthly visit? Why can't we ask Spirit right now to teach us the particular lessons that we need to speed up our journey to authenticity? Perhaps we can reach a state of enlightened reembodiment — *here and now* — in which we enrich and transform our lives by remembering and reexamining the dreams, loves, and fears of our own past.

Yes, even the fears. I fully believe that we can alter the course of our destiny in wondrous ways when we invite into our lives the very lessons that frighten us most. This is because spiritual law transcends the laws of karma. We are meant to work our way through the fears; that's our karma. But we overcome them through Spirit. When we extend an invitation to meet our fears, even as our knees are knocking and our stomachs are churning, Heaven admires our mettle, applauds our audacity, and gifts us with Amazing Grace. Always remember, never forget: *first the gesture, then the grace.*

In his book *Crisis Points: Working Through Personal Problems*, the English writer Julian Sleigh explores the idea of looking at the demons in our lives who make "us shrink in fear and revulsion" as bearers of gifts hidden under their wings. "If we challenge them and make them yield up their gifts," he says, "they will be satisfied and will fly away, leaving us to benefit from what they brought."

Regardless of how we choose to look at our fears — whether we have caused our own problems or are simply caught in the snares of others', whether we are blindsided by a sudden crisis or have been running from one for a long time — Sleigh reminds us that we only have three choices:

1. *Ignore it and hope it will go away.* It won't.
2. *Try and live with it.* Not forever.
3. *Look for the gift within our fear and benefit from it.* When we do, we emerge on the other side of life, surprised by joy.

"Be joyful," the poet Wendell Berry encourages us. "Because it is humanly possible."

When the
Student Is Ready

If you can learn from hard knocks,
you can also learn from soft touches.

CAROLYN KENMORE

Our spiritual lessons are the myriad life experiences that come our way, especially the ones we don't understand. Our masters are soul-directed events.

Soul-directed events push us past the perimeter of comfort and the safety of old patterns. Soul-directed events defy logic and ridicule reason. But soul-directed events — authentic moments — never betray us. It's true that frequently they leave us in a daze or catapult us into confusion. But, as with driving through a patch of fog that comes upon you suddenly, if you keep your heart steady in the same way you'd firmly hold the steering wheel, you can make it until the fog lifts. Suddenly you can see the road again. You can see where you're headed. You are returning to your Self.

Reembodiment is not easy; if it were, everybody would be doing it. It's been my observation that only women of great discernment, women with no time to lose or squander, and women who frequently feel too close to the edge for comfort, are the best candidates. Women very much like you and me. We choose reembodiment not as a way out, but as a way to get on with it. To jump-start the process. Do you remember the 1980s expression "Get a life"? Well, reembodiment is how you get a love life — a life you love.

Because the life you get is *finally* your own, not your mother's, not your sister's, not your partner's, not your best friend's life. And isn't this the miracle you've been praying for for as long as you can remember? I know because it was mine. Now when I look at the photograph of the woman I am, the woman I've become, the woman I always was but never knew, I am surprised by joy and astonished by awe. For the first time in my life I am not wanting, for I have finally come into my own.

So can you.

This is the miracle I would like to midwife for you. The reembodiment of your Self. We need to go back to the moment you lost your Self. For while you were almost certainly unaware of it at the time, there is a place where you veered off your authentic path. Fortunately for us, life's highway has as many on ramps as it does off ramps.

On the way to authenticity, on the way to our soul-driven need to discover Something More, each of us has lived seven past lives, lives in which we have been: starting over, surviving, settling, stumbling, shattered, sensing, and searching for Something More. As in the psalmist's prayer, we must pass through the Valley of the Shadow of discouragement, denial, doubt, and darkness — before we emerge into the light of Something More.

The soul of *Simple Abundance* was its first principle, *gratitude*. The soul of *Something More* is the last *Simple Abundance* principle, *joy*. Just as gratitude helped us move from lack to abundance in all facets of our lives, joy will help us as we move from imitation to authenticity.

Many of us confuse happiness and joy. Happiness is often triggered by external events, events we usually have no control over — you get the promotion, he loves you back, they approve your mortgage application. Happiness camouflages a lot of fears.

But joy is the absence of fear. Joy is your soul's knowledge that if you don't get the promotion, keep the relationship, or buy the house, it's because you weren't meant to. You're meant to have something better, something richer, something deeper, Something More. Joy is where your life began, with your first cry. Joy is your birthright.

However, reclaiming joy as your birthright

requires a profound inner shift in your reality. Most of us unconsciously create dramas in our minds, automatically expecting the worst from every situation, only to have our negative expectations become self-fulfilling prophecies. Inadvertently, we become authors of our own misfortune. And so we struggle from day to day, careening from crisis to crisis, bruised and battered by circumstances, without realizing that we have a choice.

Imagine this scene. A woman arrives at Heaven's gate with more baggage than she can carry. "Why are you still hauling all this nonsense?" the angel at Celestial Control asks. "You were supposed to get rid of most of it this time around."

"I know, but I could never kick the misery habit. It's a real drag, but misery loves company down on Earth. Besides, if you'd been born into my family, and married the four carbon-based life-forms I did . . ."

"Repeat and return, Sweetheart," the angel says sarcastically, stamping the woman's traveling papers. "Repeat and return. Into the Recycling Center until a counselor goes over your case."

"How long will that be?"

"Not a clue — could take a week, could take a couple hundred years. Depends on whether or not you'll be classified as hard-core. The hard-core boneheads get shipped out almost immediately."

"What's a hard-core case?"

"The lowest rung in Divine Devolution. Every time you go back, life keeps getting harder and harder. At some point your core gets shattered, and you hit rock bottom. Finally you look up, asking for help. Maybe even being grateful. You're grateful you're still alive to work through whatever spiritual assignment you brought with you into the world. Being grateful. That's the first step to the path of joy."

Hold that thought.

Something More:
A Site Map

*What would happen if one woman told the truth
about her life? The world would split open.*

MURIEL RUKEYSER

To be one woman, truly, wholly, is to be all women.

KATE BRAVERMAN

It would seem to be an easy thing, really, the
reading of a book. You pick a book up, open it,
fix your gaze, and begin. Well, maybe so and
maybe not. As a reader, I'm hard on books and
other writers. A passionate woman, I like my
men and books to knock my socks off. It's got
to be love at first sight. I need to be bowled
over by an author's insight, to wonder how I
lived before the book explained it all to me, or
how the author knew me so well.

In reality, while there is often a mystical bond
between writer and reader, the author is just
trying to figure out his or her own life, on the

26

page, not mine. But as the Irish poet W. B. Yeats once told an admirer of his work, "If what I say resonates with you, it's merely because we are both branches on the same tree."

So it is with this book. The wonderful writer Katherine Paterson has observed that part of the magic of books is that "they allow us to enter imaginatively into someone else's life. And when we do that, we learn to sympathize with other people. But the real surprise is that we also learn truths about ourselves, about our own lives, that somehow we hadn't been able to see before."

This was a very difficult book to write, and there were many times when I didn't believe I had the courage to finish it. Over a year and a half, I threw out three versions. Why? Because when I read what I'd written, there was no emotional connection. I had tried to tell the stories, especially my own, from a distance. But our souls long for communion and connection. I knew what I wanted to say, but I wasn't saying it; I was frightened to put myself out there in an even more honest and intimate way than I had in *Simple Abundance*. But as Jessamyn West tells us, "Talent is helpful in writing, but guts are absolutely necessary."

To be very frank, I was afraid that you'd read too much into every woman's story I recounted in this book and imagine that I was really writing about myself. "Good Lord, are they going to think that's me?" I'd ask. Finally, the page told me to stop stalling and get over it. The truth is that some of the stories are mine, but most are other women's. They are women in the public eye and women who have lived their lives far from the camera's gaze. But it shouldn't matter whose stories these are, because some might resonate with you so deeply they could be yours. They are. They are *all* our stories.

We are all branches on the same tree.

I've told you before that authenticity pushes us past our comfort zone — it's meant to. Reading this book will do the same. "No tears in the writer, no tears in the reader," the poet Robert Frost confided, "No laughter for the writer, no laughter for the reader." I laughed and cried as I wrote this book, just as women laugh and cry when we give birth. And I sense that this will be your experience as well. We are giving birth: to our Authentic Selves. That's why I want to urge you to go slowly. If you get to a passage that's just too tough, save it for another day.

At the end of each chapter are some enjoyable exercises intended to prime your well of inspiration and give you some psychic breathing space between the sections. They're called Field Work. Archaeology is our frame of reference, and as the archaeologist of your Self, it will be necessary for you to do some digging in the verdant field of your past, in order to aid the excavation process. I've placed various Field Work suggestions at the ends of specific chapters because I felt that the questions asked in the exercises complemented the journey undertaken in them. But if you're in the midst of a chapter that's difficult and want to turn ahead to the next set of excavation exercises, go ahead. And if you're a gal who likes to skip ahead, please be my guest. But at some point, if the reembodiment process intrigues you, you'll need to go back and pick up where you left off.

That's really what this book is about anyway. Picking up where we left off on our deeply personal journey to Wholeness.

I recommend that you read *Something More* once through and then go back and take your time rereading each chapter. There's a lot to think about when we invite the reembodiment process to begin — a lot to ponder in our hearts.

You may be used to reading books that have creative exercises promising "Here's how to change your life."

This is *not* one of those books.

This is a book meant to be read, absorbed, and then mulled over until it begins to make sense with your own authentic interpretation. And whether you agree with me or not as we have a conversation on the page, please be willing to think about your life in a new way.

Transformation is a slow process, so don't be discouraged. Take as long as you need. Do be gentle with yourself and allow your heart, mind, and spirit to process the stories and lessons you've read before you return for more. Don't worry — your Authentic Self will guide you. And your search will be all the more fulfilling.

I hope your search for Something More is just that — more bountiful, more exciting, more exhilarating, more joyous, more miraculous than any personal journey you've ever been on before. Blessings on your courage. Your buried treasure lies within.

Romancing
the Soul

*She had been forced into prudence in her youth.
She learned romance as she grew older — the
natural sequence of an unnatural beginning.*

JANE AUSTEN

Facing Your Future by Excavating Your Past

The past is never where you think you left it.

KATHERINE ANNE PORTER

The Quaker writer Jessamyn West believed the past was almost "as much a work of the imagination as the future." Any archaeologist will agree. Archaeology is humanity's humble attempt to understand the meaning of life by looking at how civilizations and cultures lived before us.

The word *archaeology* comes from the Greek *arkhaiologia,* which translates as "the study of the ancient." But as archaeologist Dr. Paul Bahn points out, the term "has come to denote the investigation of the remains of the human past, from the very first artifact all the way to yesterday's garbage."

Whether you realize it or not, you also have lived many lives, and I'm not talking about your past romps as Cleopatra or mine as the Queen of Sheba. I'm referring to the episodic

33

ways in which our lives evolve: childhood, adolescence, college years or early jobs, career, marriages, motherhood, perhaps life as a single mother, or as a single woman in midlife through divorce or death, and onward. Each life experience has left an indelible mark on our souls as well as a layer of memory like a deposit of sediment.

I've spoken of the *Simple Abundance* journey as a safari of the Self and Spirit. In *Something More* you're embarking on an archaeological dig to excavate your Authentic Self. Our journey has brought us to the sacred site of your soul. The choice of archaeology as our fantasy is very deliberate, because women are born incurable romantics. Plumb the female psyche and you will find an elegy of romantic remorse. Melancholy fragments of unrequited love stretch from our cradles to our graves. Regrets not necessarily caused by lovers who chose to live without us, so much as by recollections of the things we loved once but learned to live without.

Life is supposed to be a romantic adventure. Is yours? Didn't think so. There might be a few things in a woman's life that a romantic interlude won't cure, but I don't know any of them. Well, if romance won't come to us, we'll just have to go to romance.

"Gold-laden pharaohs . . . long-forgotten civilizations mantled in swirling mists: the world of archaeology evokes adventure and romance,"

34

archaeologist and writer Brian M. Fagan reminds us. Going back and excavating our past won't always be easy. It will be fun. It will be fascinating. It will be thrilling. But it won't always be easy.

Excavating is not glamorous work on an archaeological dig. It demands painstaking effort under often harsh conditions. Tons of dirt must be removed carefully from the site if the search to uncover treasures from the past is to be successful. The thrill of discovery wouldn't be half so sweet if time didn't have to be invested in slowly digging through the dirt. No matter how impatient everyone on the dig is, the excavation process cannot be rushed. And when we hit a bedrock of disbelief and discouragement, the undeniable romance of the treasure hunt will always save the day.

There are other reasons for us to begin to think of ourselves as archaeologists. The qualities that lead excavators to their spectacular finds are the same qualities that we must hone to reach our own breathless discoveries. According to Dr. Fagan, archaeologists need sheer persistence, endless patience, the ability to recognize patterns, keen powers of observation, curiosity, and "a conviction, nay, a passion, that their instincts are correct. An archaeologist's instinct is powerful, compelling, perhaps best described as an overwhelming sense that one knows where to find

35

what one is searching for."

What *we'll* be searching for are the moments that have made a difference in the trajectory of your life. To do that we'll need to dig deep: through the assumptions and expectations that have shaped you; through the successes and failures that have defined you; through the loves and hates, gains and losses, promises and pain that have bound you; through the risks and ruins, tumults and triumphs that set you free. We'll exhume all the perfectly reasonable choices that derailed your dreams and brush off the clinging soil hiding the half-truths that have haunted you for all these years.

Pay dirt.

The Book of Love

Unfulfilled desires are dangerous forces.

SARAH TARLETON COLVIN

Sometimes when we awaken from the bad dream of disowning ourselves, we think that the sojourn to self-discovery is a new one. But it is an ancient quest. When you close your eyes, your Authentic Self picks up your story where you left off during the day, and it's always been this way.

Just as paintings can be impressionistic or abstract or can appear to be so real they jump off the canvas, so can our dreams. Dreams can also be like a *collage,* an artistic composition made up of various materials such as paper, fabric, and wood. Our dream collages can be as illogical as snippets of conversation spoken by a woman balancing a tepee on her head as she's chased by a pack of llamas. Most of the time there seems to be no rhyme or reason to them, but if we're willing to reflect on them, they make perfect sense. Eventually, dreams are our spiritual illustrated discovery journals.

Simple Abundance introduced you to my favorite self-discovery tool, the illustrated discovery journal. In keeping a discovery journal, you'll be creating an authentic book of love that reveals your passions on every page. "I dote on myself," the poet Walt Whitman confessed. "There is a lot of me, and all so luscious."

There's a lot that's luscious about *you,* although *you're* probably bound to disagree. Why do you play down all your assets and call attention to your deficits? We've got to change that. Invest in a blank, spiral-bound artist's sketchbook today, and in a month you'll be amazed by the wondrous attributes you've unearthed.

In *Simple Abundance* we used the illustrated discovery journal as our explorer's log as we expanded your horizon of what's possible. Here, in *Something More*, this astonishing insight tool is transformed into an archaeologist's site report as you document discoveries while excavating your past lives, loves, losses, and longings.

If you've never kept an illustrated discovery journal before, you're in for a delightful surprise. For our excavation purposes, you'll also need these tools: a stack of magazines and mail-order catalogues from which you'll cut images of anything that pleases you — from clothing, lush home furnishings, and travel adventures to children's faces, gorgeous landscapes, and wacky ads; a pair of small, sharp scissors, glue sticks, nine large (9" x 12") manila envelopes, colored pencils (the watercolor ones are fabulous because, after you draw, you can go over your work with water on a paint brush and, voila! you're a painter!). Don't forget to peruse foreign publications, particularly British women's magazines (which you can often find at large newsstands), for some of your images, because they are so completely different in layout and design from our home-grown ones. Their fresh visuals and witty headlines always get my creative juices flowing.

Now, how often should you get out your illustrated discovery journal? Reveling in this pastime twice a week will produce remarkable results. One night you cut, the next night you paste. I suggest you do this in the evening because, after the house is quiet, you're better able to unwind. Besides, this pastime is more effective if you're in a drowsy, relaxed, and receptive state as you glean visual clues. Create a ritual around your musing. Focus on the pictures that move you. I always light a beautiful scented candle, listen to some favorite music, and enjoy a glass of wine or a soothing cup of ginger tea as I'm working on my discovery journal.

When you see an image you love or one that elicits a visceral reaction, cut or tear it out. But don't stop to analyze why you ripped out pictures of a tiger with bared teeth one minute and an undulating velvet recamier with silk fringe the next. The logic of it all will be revealed in the by-and-by.

Now label the nine large manila envelopes:

- Authentic Success
- Authentic Style (includes fashion, beauty, fitness)
- Return to Self
- Relationships
- Spiritual Journey
- Someday
- The House of Belonging (includes decorating, cooking, gardening)
- Entertainment
- Mystery

You'll notice that these envelopes each bear the name of an exercise you will find at the end of one of this book's chapters. As I mentioned in my introduction, these exercises are your Field Work — mental and physical archaeological assignments meant to help you apply and absorb the ideas presented in the chapters. Your journal work — play, really — may be used in tandem with these exercises to help you get at the heart of your Authentic Self. However, don't let this format confine you. Take out your journal whenever the urge seizes you and excavate away.

As you select your images, pop them into whatever envelope you think fits them best. The tiger could be a subconscious message concerning your spiritual journey or a relationship. Then again, you might not have a clue as to what it means; it's a Mystery, and that's the envelope it belongs in. Follow your instincts; no assessing allowed. The French painter Georges Braque confessed, "There are certain mysteries, certain secrets in my own work which even I don't understand, nor do I try to do so."

Certain mysteries *we'll* leave alone as well, and with others, we'll be on the case until they're solved. But now is not when we unravel mysteries. Now is when we discover them. And we do that by getting reacquainted and reconnected with our imagination and intuition, the soul's telecommunication uplinks.

You'll be happy to know that, unlike any other area of your existence, *you cannot do the illustrated discovery journal incorrectly.* In my workshops I have seen many women get into a dither because they don't know how to begin and are afraid they'll do it wrong. You can't. It's impossible. Why? Because I said so. I'm the one who made this up; I should know.

But here are a few suggestions to get you started. The bigger your artist's sketchbook, the better — preferably 9″ x 12″, because you need to have plenty of white space on which to dream, reminisce, and play. And really, that's what our illustrated discovery journals are — vehicles for us to begin playing with our Authentic Selves.

Think fun. Think delight. Think seven years old and paper dolls. This is not an intellectual exercise. Let me say this again so that I'm sure you understand: *You cannot do this wrong!*

Your magazine and catalogue pictures are just the beginning. You'll also be collecting and adding favorite quotes, sketches, greeting cards, photocopies of photographs (you don't want to glue down the real thing), feature article headlines, travel brochures, art post-cards, ribbons, menus, pressed flowers, mock-ups of magnificent events you want to occur in the future — and any other darn thing you want that triggers a memory, whether it's past, present, or to come. The idea is to craft with paper what the poet W.

H. Auden calls a map of your planet.

After you've spent a month gathering images, it's time to create collages. I know you're eager, but try to resist the temptation to create nine different ones at one sitting. Do one only.

Why? Because this is a meditative insight tool as well as a playmate, which means you want to bring your full concentration to your collage. Remember that these are the illustrated versions of the book your soul is writing for and about you. This is the first rough draft of your *magnum opus*, which is Latin for "great work," the most important work in a person's life. As far as I'm concerned, that's discovering who we are and why we are here at this point in eternity. It's for a reason. But what is that reason?

Hold that question.

Small Things Forgotten

There are no little things. "Little things"
are the hinges of the universe.

FANNY FERN

A lovely concept in the excavation process is searching for "small things forgotten," as archaeologist James Deetz calls it. Because so much of our life is spent in a variety of commonplace activities, the search for small things forgotten is "central to the work of historical archaeologists. . . . Chipped-stone hand axes made hundreds of thousands of years ago and porcelain teacups from the eighteenth century carry messages from their makers and users. It is the archaeologist's task to decode those messages and apply them to our understanding of the human experience," Deetz says.

Which is precisely what we will be doing — decoding the messages of all the things that have made you happy in the past and that you've forgotten. You're going to rediscover the books, films, clothes, furnishings, pets, playthings, vacations, holidays, food, com-

43

forts, comic strips, fantasies, music, and magazines that first spoke to you as a young girl — the things that, when recalled, still have a special meaning for you. Your passions communicate with you through emotional touchstones — those eccentricities that give expression to your essence and trigger what Emily Dickinson called "the ecstatic experience": what excites us or moves us to tears, what makes the blood rush to our heads, our hearts skip a beat, our knees shaky, and our souls sigh.

Our authenticity is found hidden in the small details of our daily round — home, family, work, pleasures. We think that it's the big moments that define our lives — the wedding, the baby, the new house, the dream job. But really, these big moments of happiness are just the punctuation marks of our personal sagas. The narrative is written every day in the small, the simple, and the common. In your tiny choices, in these tiny changes. In the unconsidered. The overlooked. The discarded. The reclaimed.

When I think about my father, the first image that comes to mind is holding his hand as he drove me to the train station six weeks before he died; I had never noticed how beautiful his hands were until I saw them, for the first and last time, entwined in mine. "As often as not our whole self . . . engages itself in the most trivial of things, the shape of a particular hill, a road in the town in which we lived as children, the movement of wind in grass," the English writer Storm Jameson wrote in *That Was Yesterday* back in 1932. "The things we shall take with us when we die will nearly all be small things."

What small things are you taking with you from the life you're leading right now? Select one today with care, and savour it.

The Authentic Dig

Direct your eye right inward, and you'll find
A thousand regions in your mind
Yet undiscovered. Travel them and be
Expert in home-cosmography.

HENRY DAVID THOREAU

An excavation site needs to be selected, marked out, and meticulously prepared before the dig begins. That's the job of the expedition director. As I write, archaeological teams are being recruited to search for Etruscan treasures, unearth lost cities on the Silk Road to China, and reconstruct the mystical Mayan ruins of Tikal and Caracol. I know this because I have a stack of their very exotic, very alluring invitations to throw my lot in with them for two unforgettable weeks. The temptation is great. But my daughter's softball practice ends in about forty-five minutes and then I have to make dinner. You might have similar conflicts of interests — in other words, everybody else's needs.

What is needed then is an accessible archaeological adventure for women who do too much and live too little. A perfectly plausible but unpredictable locale full of mystery, intrigue, fascination, and romance. One that will captivate us and hold our attention for as long as the excavation process requires, which could take several "seasons," as archaeological forays were known to those pith-helmeted darlings in khaki ankle skirts, pearls, and long white chiffon scarves, who dug in the sands of Arabia during the 1920s and 1930s.

Besides the fact that your soul is one of the last unlooted sources of the miraculous, with discoveries as spectacular as any ever found in the Delta of Venus or Egypt's Valley of the Kings, you can embark on a soul trip and be back before anyone even notices you're missing. They might be curious about that gleam in your eye and the flush on your cheeks, but I'll never tell if you won't.

Are you game?

We're heading to the sacred site of your soul.

The Chain of Chance

How can you say luck and chance are the same thing?
Chance is the first step you take,
luck is what comes afterwards.

AMY TAN

What a pleasant surprise to find you here —
and alone! Where'd you leave them? Outside
the bathroom door? Good. A perfect ruse.

Well, here we are. Take a look around. You
look surprised. You didn't think your soul
would look like this? What were you expecting? (Write in the margin the first thing
that comes to mind.)

One of the mysteries of archaeology is the
role that chance plays in the discoveries of
the past. Just as so many of us are unaware of
our own worth, so has the past hidden her
treasures beneath the mundane, visible only
for those with "eyes to see." It was chance
that led the Queen of Naples to relics from
Pompeii under a backyard garden. A Bedouin
youth found the Dead Sea Scrolls while
looking for a lost goat. A find in an Athens

flea market led to the discovery of the ancient Palace of Minos that had long been thought to exist only in Greece's mythical past.

Of course, the chain of chance can only *lead* us to our destiny. It is entirely up to us to choose to transform chance into luck through courage, risk, leaps in the dark, and what-the-hell moments. The boy who found the Dead Sea Scrolls in clay jars buried in a cave, didn't realize their value; the cobbler in Bethlehem to whom the Bedouin sold the scrolls only bought them because he thought they might make sturdy *soles* for shoes. But something stopped him before tearing them apart. Curiosity made him scratch beneath their leathery surface. Although the writing he discovered on the scrolls was meaningless to him, he was a religious man and followed Spirit's prompting to take them to his Syrian confessor. One can imagine the priest's astonishment at the thought that someone could have been wearing the lost Old Testament's Book of Isaiah on his feet. "Thus strangely are our souls constructed," wrote Mary Shelley, "and by such slight ligaments are we bound to prosperity or ruin."

Suddenly-Seen Things

*Most new discoveries are suddenly-seen things
that were always there.*

SUSANNE K. LANGER

According to *The Archaeology Handbook* by Bill
McMillon, once the boundaries of an excavation
site have been established, other preparatory
steps must be taken before the dig can begin. A
site map must be drawn delineating the scope
of the dig; the site *topography,* or surface
appearances, must be charted so that there is a
reference point of what the area looked like
before it was dismantled. A screening area
must be established where the artifacts can be
brought for examination.

Archaeologists search for two types of
evidence; physical and documentary. For
example, if a ring were found, it would be
physical evidence. If a diary were discovered
that offered information about who owned
the ring, the diary would be known as *documentary* evidence.

We'll adapt these procedures and references

for your authentic dig. Your site map will lay out the different time periods you'll be retracing. Your site's topography will be a description and visual depiction of who you are today. Your screening area can be an accordion folder with several compartments to hold your documentary evidence, and a standard paper file box can be the repository of your physical evidence until after the dig is completed.

For now, it is time to begin the search.

"The pages are still blank," the Russian writer Vladimir Nabokov tells us, "but there is a miraculous feeling of the words being there, written in invisible ink and clamoring to become visible."

Starting Over

*We are always afraid to start something that we want
to make very good, true, and serious.*

BRENDA UELAND

The Sacred Adventure

An adventure is a transgression you don't regret.

KATE WHEELER

The search for Something More is a sacred adventure, one that will provide you with all the amusing anecdotes, profound turning points, and provocative choices you'll ever need to be able to live this life without regrets. "True adventures start with desire, an inclination to enter the unknown," the travel writer Kate Wheeler tells us. "In hopes of finding what? More of yourself, or of the world? Yes . . ."

Are you with me? If you are, you've got to make a conscious choice every day to shed the old — whatever "the old" means for you — old issues, old guilt, old patterns, old responses, old resentments, old rivalries. We no longer have the luxury of wallowing in what's held us back; this is the emotional baggage we're supposed to be getting rid of this time around.

This is the choice standing between your dream of living authentically and its coming true. This is the choice that is not optional if you want to discover your Something More. Both authenticity and adventure require a point of departure, the willingness to shed what's safe and predictable in order to embrace the new — people, places, predicaments, pleasures, and passions. Your new, authentic life.

A Tale of Two Lives

You don't get to choose how you're going to die.
Or when. You can only decide how
you're going to live. Now.

JOAN BAEZ

Do you remember the scene in the movie *The Natural*, when Robert Redford is lying in a hospital bed, sick, discouraged, and about to give up? It's the play-offs, and he's not playing because he's been poisoned by the woman he loved. Glenn Close, his childhood sweetheart, comes to visit him. Bob's feeling pretty sorry for himself. The doctor has told him that he can't ever play baseball again or it will kill him. But baseball, or more specifically, the pursuit of a career in the major leagues, is the only life he knows; he's thirty-nine and he's just made it to the top. Everything is riding on the next game, and he's afraid if he doesn't play, his life is over. And he's right. His life *is* over. His life, that is, as he's known it up until now.

But Glenn knows better. Knows there's Something More because she's living it. "I believe we have two lives," she tells him. "The life we learn with, and the life we live after that."

So how do we get to this second life?

Starting Over

We must be willing to get rid of the life we've planned, so as to have the life that is waiting for us.

JOSEPH CAMPBELL

"On this narrow planet, we have only the choice between two unknown worlds," the French writer Colette instructs us. "One of them tempts us — ah! what a dream to live in that! — the other stifles us."

Take a deep breath.

What if I told you that one year from today, you could be living your dreams, but (there's always a "but") it would mean that every day between now and then you would have to choose your destiny; in other words, that there are at least 365 choices standing between your dream and its coming true?

That's all. Just 365 choices.

Hey, where'd everybody go? Before you flee, I didn't say they had to be *big* choices. Parting-of-the-Red-Sea choices. Mt.-Everest choices. Before-and-After choices.

Little choices count, too. In fact, little ones can often be more life-altering than big ones. Little ones, such as, *Oh God, I'm just too tired to argue about this tonight,* so you choose to swallow your anger, walk away in silence, throw in a load of laundry, tune out with a sitcom, eat a pint of ice cream, drink a bottle of wine, or track down your high school sweetheart just to see how he's doing after twenty-five years.

Trust me, tiny choices — day in, day out — shape your destiny just as much as deciding to run away to be an elephant girl with the circus rather than turn fifty. "True life is lived when tiny choices are made," Leo Tolstoy believed. "Tiny choices mean tiny changes. But it is only with infinitesimal change, changes so small no one else even realizes you're making them, that you have any hope for transformation."

Designing Women

*It's when we're given choice that we sit with
the gods and design ourselves.*

DOROTHY GILMAN

Many of us don't think of choice as a spiritual gift. We believe choices are burdens to be endured, not embraced. And so they become burdens. But after breath, is there a more precious gift than free will?

Consider for a moment that there are only three ways to change the trajectory of our lives for better or worse: crisis, chance, and choice.

You may not realize it, but your life at this exact moment — it doesn't matter who you are, where you are, or who's getting ready to jerk your chain — is a direct result of choices you made once upon a time. Thirty minutes or thirty years ago.

Did you balk at the thought of having to make 365 choices in order to span the distance between your dreams and their coming true? It seemed an enormous obstacle to overcome, didn't it? But actually, if you just decide to get out of bed, show up to make breakfast, get the kids to school, and get to work on time, you've already made more than three choices, and it's not even nine o'clock in the morning. I would conservatively estimate that most women make a dozen choices a day — 4,380 decisions a year. Now, don't you think that 365 of those choices can be ones that move you toward an authentic life? I know they can.

Our choices can be conscious or unconscious. Conscious choice is creative, the heart of authenticity. Unconscious choice is destructive, the heel of self-abuse. Unconscious choice is how we end up living other people's lives. "The most common despair is . . . not choosing, or willing, to be oneself," the nineteenth-century Danish philosopher Søren Kierkegaard warns us, "[but] the deepest form of despair is to choose to be another than oneself." This is how we always hurt the one we love. The one we shouldn't hurt at all. Our Self.

We live in a world defined by duality — light or dark, up or down, success or failure, right or wrong, pain or joy. This duality keeps us in perpetual motion. Like a pendulum in an old clock, we swing back and forth through our emotions. But creative, conscious choice gives us the power to stop swinging and remain in balance, at peace. Be still, woman, and know who you are.

Most women are petrified of making choices.

This is because we don't trust our instincts. It's been so long, we've forgotten how. We'd opt to clean the kitty litter or work for our passage to the Congo if it meant we never had to make another choice again other than deciding what's for dinner, which is hard enough. (How many times have you had chicken this week?) Having to decide what to wear to a cocktail party or which of forty-seven different shades of white to paint the dining room trim have been known to trigger the kind of emotional response that puts women behind bars — or on the floor of one.

The reason we're terrified of making choices, even little ones, is that we're convinced we'll make a wrong one. *Again.* Maybe you're too tired tonight to have that conversation, although you know it's long overdue. Maybe you can choose to put it off until tomorrow night. *Again.* If you're anything like me, a lot of wrong choices got you where you are today and continue to keep you there.

But a wrong choice isn't necessarily a *bad* choice.

You married the wrong man. Became a teacher instead of a country and western singer. You didn't finish college, join the Peace Corps, or move to New York. If you had, your life would have been different. But *not necessarily better.* That's because *we,* not our outer circumstances, are the catalysts for the quality of our lives. Not then. Not now. Not ever.

We don't know if a choice is wise or wrong until we've lived it. We can't ever really know where a choice will take us, though we may sense its direction. We're torn between the agonizing should's and shouldn'ts. An inner debate begins to rage. Writer Jeanette Winterson describes our dilemma beautifully: "I have a theory that every time you make an important choice, the part of you left behind continues the other life you could have had."

So you gather as much information as you can. You weigh the options. You ponder the possibilities. You brood. You probe the probabilities with your best friend. You ask your heart. You pray for guidance. Then you take a leap in the dark and hope you land on your feet. You live your choice. You don't look back for a long time. Eventually, with hindsight, you'll glance back and see which it was, wise or wrong. But at least it's a calculated risk, and you did the best that you could. Spirit asks nothing more. Neither should you.

Bad choices should *never* be confused with wrong choices. Bad choices — and we have all made them — happen when we embark on sinuous stretches of self-destruction, usually with a smile. You don't ask your heart or a pal for advice. You don't ponder, and you certainly don't pray. Why? Because on the deepest intuitive level you know you shouldn't even be entertaining the thought of this choice. But you want to do it so badly that even its badness doesn't daunt you. In fact, it eggs you on.

Quite frankly, my dear, we don't give a damn what *anyone* thinks at times like that, do we?

If we close our eyes, we can honestly say that we never saw disaster coming. How could we? Bad choices are made while we're sleep-walking. From now on, let's call them *coma choices*. Before we even make them, we know that when we wake up, we'll ask, "How could I have been so stupid?"

But our lives are not entirely shaped by wrong or bad choices, thank God. There have been wise choices, good choices, strong choices, courageous choices, happy choices. Brilliant decisions. We just don't remember many of them. That's because we shrug off any good thing that arrives in our lives as if it were a fluke, a lucky break, a mis-delivery. Certainly we don't give ourselves credit. Only when things don't work out, only when we make mistakes, or stumble on missteps, do we feel we're responsible. Then we claim all the blame.

So it should hardly be surprising if our primary reaction to any choice is to avoid it. Put it off as long as possible. Postpone the inevitable. But by not choosing, we allow others to decide for us. It doesn't matter how well-meaning or wonderful they are. It doesn't matter *who* they are. Just remember: if you didn't make the choice, you can't blame someone else if you're unhappy.

Today, as you start to retrace your journey,

be willing to reflect on the choices you've made in the past, as well as on your style of choosing. Are you deliberate? Impulsive? Comatose? Do you make choices with your heart, your mind, or your gut? Are you comfortable with your style of decision making, or do you cringe? What about trying a different approach? Whatever your style, I'll bet that your life, like mine, is a direct result of choices you never even considered.

Scary, isn't it?

Choice is destiny's soul mate. In her novel *Avenue of the Dead*, Evelyn Anthony exquisitely evokes the moment of recognition: "Long afterwards, she was to remember that moment when her life changed its direction. It was not predestined; she had a choice. Or it seemed that she had. To accept or refuse. To take one turning down the crossroads to the future or another."

Starting from Scratch

Not all horses were born equal.
A few were born to win.

MARK TWAIN

Sometimes we are compelled to start our lives over "from scratch." Like one of the Four Horsemen of the Apocalypse in the Bible's Book of Revelation, either death or divorce or debt or disaster gallops into our lives, and suddenly our familiar world comes to an abrupt end. We lose our home, or our health. We lose our partner, or our job. We lose our way. And we must start over. From scratch.

"Starting from scratch" is a familiar saying, but do you know where it comes from? Surprisingly, not from the kitchen, but from the rules of eighteenth-century English horse racing, which permitted gentlemen to "fix" races so that, in theory, all the horses could cross the finish line together, with the winner only beating his competition by a nose. Of course, this never happened. Nonetheless, in order to perpetuate the illusion of "a jolly good show," the horse considered the finest was sent to the back and had to start the race from behind a line scratched in the turf or gravel.

In modern horse racing, the champion doesn't start from behind but is loaded down with heavy saddlebags in order to equalize the competition. Incredibly, the more races a horse wins, the more weight it has to carry. There are wonderful stories about Secretariat — arguably this century's greatest thoroughbred — leaving other horses with dust in their nostrils despite his being saddled with fourteen pounds of lead bars as he sped across the finish line, not by a nose, but by thirty-one lengths. After Secretariat died, an autopsy revealed that his heart was larger than those of other horses. Doctors were fascinated by this finding, and many hypothesized that the horse was born with this vital organ enlarged and had simply gone on to fulfill his natural promise. Others swore that the horse's will and determination to compete had strengthened his heart muscles to the point of enlargement. The truth? I don't know. In the final analysis, though, does it matter whether the champion was born with a large heart or grew one to live up to his destiny?

A Continuous Thread
of Revelation

Things come suitable to their time.

ENID BAGNOLD

Did you ever see the film *National Velvet*? Based on the heartwarming book written by Enid Bagnold, the film starred a teenage Elizabeth Taylor in her first leading role as Velvet Brown, a young English girl determined to transform an ordinary horse she'd won in a raffle into a racehorse. Every time she rides him, she sees herself trotting triumphantly into the winner's circle of the world's greatest steeplechase, the Grand National. Velvet believes that she and "The Pie" share a special destiny — that underneath his plain horsehide exterior beats the heart of a champion. But Velvet has a few obstacles in her path: she's fourteen, her parents think her dream is nonsense, and The Pie is actually unruly and untrained. Even if there were a trainer in the small English country village where she lives, there's no money for one, or for the race entrance fee or to hire a jockey, since girls are not permitted to ride in England's most illustrious horse race. However, as all dreamers know, these are but minor hurdles when a determined young lady is taking fate for a ride.

Remember Velvet Brown the next time you've got a few obstacles to overcome. If you do, you'll be delighted to discover, as I have, that there are few things in life more satisfying than accomplishing whatever "they" tell you can't be done.

Since first grade I've held very firm convictions about money, fame, dreams, and destiny. The origins of these opinions or how I formed them so early was always a mystery to me, especially since they bore no resemblance to the philosophical fare served up at home. I discovered one of the sources soon after I embarked on my own deeply personal excavation process, as I recalled cherished books from my childhood. Prominent among them was *National Velvet*. It had been given to me by my favorite aunt, who loved horses and wanted to share her enthusiasm with me. I'd finished the book practically in one sitting and declared, "If Velvet Brown can do it, so can I." It didn't matter that I hadn't a clue as to what my authentic *it* would be, but horseback riding seemed like a good place to start.

My parents couldn't afford horseback riding lessons and with then three children in the family, wouldn't let Aunt Em "play favorites" and pay for them. Coincidentally, a local Girl Scout troop was sponsoring a contest for the most enterprising Brownie, and first prize was free horseback riding lessons. I spent most of that entire year earning extra merit badges. All my hard work was worth it the day Aunt Em took me shopping for my new riding gear, followed by a celebratory lunch. We were both so proud of me; it was one of the happiest days of my life.

Two weeks later, Aunt Em died suddenly of a brain aneurysm; she was only thirty-four. The morning of her funeral I was supposed to take my first riding lesson. I was crushed, heart-broken, incredulous; it was like the Fall from Paradise. Now, suddenly, I knew that at any moment life, happiness, security, safety, and most of all, love, could be snatched away without warning. I refused to go to her funeral; I insisted that she couldn't be dead, that some dreadful mistake had been made.

And the riding lesson? The prize? Finally I had to make my first conscious choice, an act of self-assertion grounded in my own sense of what was right. I took the lesson. I knew in my heart that Em would have approved, but secretly I wondered what kind of wicked girl would go horseback riding on such a sad oc-casion. With the earnestness that only the young can bring to any serious endeavor, I threw myself into my first lesson. But as soon as it was over and I walked away from the barn, the tears started and in some ways haven't stopped yet.

Later, when I was twelve and just learning to jump, I fell off my horse; I was shaken but not badly injured. I should have gotten back on the horse immediately, but I didn't. The next week's lesson came and went, but I became afraid and never rode again. I never talked about it, just shrugged it off as if I'd lost interest.

Many years later I took my daughter to her first horseback riding lesson. While walking from my car to the barn, my sense memories kicked in and it all came flooding back to me: my beautiful aunt, her unconditional love for me, the comfort of our close companionship, her belief in me, my determination to win that contest, our celebration. And then, of course, the memory of my loss. In an instant I realized for the first time that I had buried my love of horseback riding beneath layers of fear, a little girl's guilt, and the recasting of a courageous choice into something shameful. Finally I could untangle the twisted truth of an ancient lie that had robbed me of so much joy.

Thirty-five years after I fell off a horse, I got back on one, starting from scratch in a beginner's class with seven-year-olds. It didn't matter. I was seven years old once again, too, grateful to be back in the saddle, thrilled to have recovered a precious portion of my relinquished Self. On my way home I stopped off at a bookstore and got myself a brand-new copy of *National Velvet*.

Even though you are searching for a pattern of personal, authentic pleasures and preferences, be prepared; you can't know what memories will be triggered as you reacquaint yourself with the girl you were once upon a time. But remember, you're not alone. Your Authentic Self is with you, a loving spiritual companion ready to help you unravel the tangled threads of memory, promise, and abandonment. I had no idea that the aromatic alchemy of warm leather, sweat, hay, and horses would act as conduits of such powerful soul memories for me. But, thanks to them, I could bring gentle emotional closure to a pivotal life experience.

Pain is part of the past. There isn't one of us who doesn't still carry childhood wounds. Some are more horrific than others, but no matter how painful your young memories are, there were also glorious moments that kept you alive, or you would not be here today. "The events in our lives happen in a sequence in time, but in their significance to ourselves they find their own order," writer Eudora Welty confides. With patience and quiet observation, these events will provide your authentic archaeologist with a "continuous thread of revelation" that will reassuringly lead you back to your Self.

Back to the Beginning

The past is not only that which happened but also that which could have happened but did not.

TESS GALLAGHER

We will be taking many backward glances throughout our journey, so we ought to accept at the outset that no life retraced ever really begins at the beginning, especially a woman's life. For while the past asks only to be remembered, a woman's memory alters on her behalf and in her best interests. Memory — the vain old biddy — cannot resist penciling a few slight, cosmetic revisions in the margins of the past. Memory is also fickle. She must be wooed and courted if she is to succumb to our charms. Sometimes she surprises us with her generosity, and we recall moments with astonishing clarity. Most of the time, however, our memories are fragmented, like shards of pottery found during archaeological excavations. When this happens, we need to let patience do her perfect work as we piece back together the girl we left behind.

"The past is such a subtle thing," the writer

Natalie Barney tells us. "[But] in the end, nothing else exists, everything is made of the past, even the future."

Having It All

Longing is all that lasts.

JENNIFER STONE

Simple Abundance reassured you that "all you have is all you need" and showed you how to come to that awareness by using the mystical power of gratitude. Hopefully, thanks to gratitude, your life, like mine, was changed in wondrous ways for the better.

But now it might seem that I'm contradicting myself by saying that it's okay if you still find yourself longing for Something More, even after being grateful, making positive changes, and growing into your authenticity.

There is no paradox here. Remember the notion that, if we want to live fulfilling lives, we must learn to distinguish between our wants and our needs? We still do. An example of a *need* is food; if this need is not met, we

71

die from hunger. A *want* is a different thing: having it contributes to the enjoyment of our lives, but we could live without it or be satisfied to wait for it.

When we talk about Something More, it isn't wanting a fancier car, a bigger house, or a designer dress. Something More is what we need to fill our spiritual hunger.

You don't *want* Something More. You *need* Something More. You feel deep within that something crucial is missing. You're constantly looking for it, but since you don't know what it is, the best you can hope is that if you run across it, you'll recognize or remember it. In defending your life you might say, "I know I should be happy. I am, really. Don't misunderstand me. I've got a great husband and fabulous kids, and we're all healthy. I've got a good job, wonderful friends. Mom's doing well in the nursing home. Our finances are okay, the credit cards are under control, and we've even started to save a little money. Next spring we're going on a cruise to the Bahamas. We're comfortable and content. And every day I'm grateful for my blessings. So why do I feel so empty?"

You're not alone. Reba McEntire, one of country music's superstars, ponders, just as we all do: "No matter what you achieve in life, you're always wondering, 'Is there something I should be doing? Is there something I'm missing?' "

Words can't begin to express my gratitude for my wonderful life. I'm living most of my dreams. Every day I say aloud, "I'm the most blessed woman on Earth," and I mean it. Which is why I was as confounded as I was comforted after I discovered the English novelist Vita Sackville-West's despair during what was supposed to have been the happiest time of her life. In 1930 her book, *The Edwardians*, was an enormous critical and popular success, providing her with financial security after a lifetime of being one of the educated, genteel poor. Her success enabled Vita and her new husband Harold Nicolson to purchase the romantic but rundown Sissinghurst Castle and begin turning it into a renowned showplace. At thirty-eight she felt at the height of her creative energies and was in the throes of writing *All Passion Spent*, the novel that would be hailed as her finest work. Still, she confessed to her best friend, Virginia Woolf: "If I, who am the most fortunate of women, can ask, 'What is life for?' how can other people live at all?" Not long after she confided her distress, she began a love affair which temporarily masked her depression but didn't alleviate it.

So here we are — you, Reba, Vita Sackville-West, and I — a group of talented, eclectic, even brilliant women. But at the end of the day, when we're finally alone, we're peering down into the black hole in our hearts.

Our insatiable, inexplicable longing probes the emptiness much the same way you do when you can't keep your tongue out of the sensitive, empty spot that once held a decaying tooth.

"Many women today feel a sadness we cannot name. Though we accomplish much of what we set out to do, we sense that something is missing in our lives and — fruitlessly — search 'out there' for the answers," writer Emily Hancock observes. "What's often wrong is that we are disconnected from an authentic sense of self."

Divine Discontent

[If] there were none who were discontented with what they have, the world would never reach for anything better.

FLORENCE NIGHTINGALE

Because we can't articulate this emptiness, we secretly feel, even in the midst of plenty, anywhere from mildly embarrassed to downright shameful, to enormously guilty. We shouldn't.

What we should be feeling is an enormous sense of relief.

Divine Discontent is about to get us moving again. This is how the spiritual world inevitably gets our attention. Heaven knows it tries with all the fun prompts: imagination, intuition, coincidences, synchronicity, daydreams, reveries, and delightful hunches. But after we ignore them for years, just as little grains of sand, or "sleep," are left in the corners of our eyes at night, little grains of grit are deposited in the cavities of our souls, where they will begin to irritate the lining of our lives, much the way one grain of sand does to the oyster before it produces a pearl. As the English historian Dame Cicely Veronica Wedgewood points out, "Discontent and disorder [are] signs of energy and hope, not despair."

Divine Discontent can manifest itself in many different ways. You can be washing your face and not recognize the woman staring back at you. "Who's this?" you ask the mirror. No reply. She looks vaguely familiar but bears little resemblance to the woman you were expecting to see there. Psychologists call this phenomenon a "displacement of self," and it usually occurs during times of great stress (which for many of us is an everyday occurrence).

Then there's an extreme psychological condition known as the "borderline personality." Clinical symptoms include feeling "no real identity," the need to look constantly outside oneself for assurance and comfort, and the need for control at any cost. Usually the victims are women who can find no value or sustenance within and so begin to feed on themselves, literally or figuratively, often developing eating disorders or becoming disciplined drinkers (to mask their despair) but emotional drunks. Why this condition should be considered "extreme" is beyond me; it sounds very ordinary, very familiar. Very hidden to some, perhaps, but very obvious to us.

Often when you're coming down with Divine Discontent, you feel extremely fragile and exposed. You're left with no protective covering, so you find yourself bursting into tears at the oddest or most inconvenient moments, like in the middle of a business meeting, or when a friend asks "How are you?" For a man, Alfred, Lord Tennyson described it pretty well:

Tears, idle tears, I know not what they mean.
Tears from the depth of some divine despair
Rise in the heart, and gather in the eyes.

With Divine Discontent, everything is out of kilter. You eat too much; you eat too little. You can't get to sleep or you sleep for days. A glass gets knocked over; you erupt. "It's only spilt milk," your husband says. "Exactly!" you scream back, scaring him, the children, the animals, but especially yourself. Suddenly you can't stand one thing about your life, from the living room curtains to your job. You're accident-prone. You get in the car and find yourself on the other side of the city with not a clue as to how you got there or why. You can't shake the flu or remember to take a shower until you grow pungent. None of your clothes fit or look right. You're bored with the meals you're cooking, the crowd you cook for, the company you're keeping. You can't remember the last time you were happy. Were you ever? And sex? Not even with Rhett Butler. Is it a megalith migraine coming on, or do you just need an intravenous drip of Midol?

That's because everyone assumes you're experiencing a severe case of PMS or having one of those "going through the change" episodes. Well, you're getting ready to undergo a change all right, but it's not menopause or the beginning of your menstrual cycle.

It's your pre-magnificent stage. "You sit here for days saying, *This is strange business,*" the Sufi poet Rumi admonishes us. "*You're* the strange business. You have the energy of the sun in you, but you keep knotting it up at the base of your spine. You're some weird kind of gold that wants to stay melted in the furnace, so you won't have to become coins."

The Mortal Wound

Regrets are as personal as fingerprints.

MARGARET CULKIN BANNING

So which is worse, regretting what you did —
or regretting what you didn't do?

Which comes first, the despair or the
longing? Either way, the Russian novelist Ivan
Sergeyevich Turgenev tells us that to be human
means that we must journey through a
profound passage of reckoning — experience
"days of doubt" and "days of sad brooding" —
when we must acknowledge, honor, and mourn
"the regrets that resemble hopes" and "the
hopes that resemble regrets."

Wanting Something More is really wanting a
life of no regrets. Or at least no more regrets
than we can die with peacefully.

Because the truth is — and we know it — we
were born to die without regrets. Regret is the
only wound from which the soul never re-
covers. In the wee small hours of the darkness, we can faintly hear the last words Spirit
whispered to our souls as we made our descent

to the Earthly realm.

Next time, come back without regrets. For the sake of all that is holy, my love — Live!

Being Willing to
Live for the Last Time

What an interesting life I had. And how I wish I had realized it sooner!

COLETTE

Wouldn't it be wonderful to declare to destiny: "I warn you, I am living for the last time," as did the Russian poet Anna Akhmatova?

Go ahead. Say it. *I am living for the last time.*

I know that I am. And it's the most thrilling choice I've ever made. Why? Because I have no more time for regrets. Every morning when I awake, I ask my soul this question: "If I died tonight, what would I regret not having done today?" Do I need to say "I love you," "I forgive you," "I'm sorry"? If I do, it's the first telephone call I make.

Is there one small action that I can take to nurture my new dreams toward their fruition?

If there is, it goes at the top of my To Do list.

If I should be blessed with tomorrow, is there a choice that I *can* make, *need* to make, or *want* to make that could enhance the quality of my life? Is there one I'm postponing because it's difficult or painful? If I ignore it, will it be the regret I take with me? If there's a chance it will, then I make room in my heart and schedule to think about it. I call this reflective interlude time out for Something More. A pause to get grounded in the Real. Fifteen minutes of soul divesting. I know life holds no guarantees for me. I am not promised a tomorrow. I no longer take anything for granted.

Could there be anything more important than living without regrets?

No. You know it. And so do I.

But what you might not know yet is that you don't have to have a bad marriage to want a better one.

You don't have to have a bad job to want to find your calling.

You don't have to be miserable before you feel you deserve to be truly happy.

All you need to know is that searching for Something More is settling for nothing less than you deserve. And admitting that you want Something More in your life is the first step in starting over, in discovering what that Something More is for you.

Introducing Your Life

Her work, I really think her work
is finding what her real work is
and doing it,
her work, her own work,
her being human,
her being in the world.

URSULA K. LE GUIN

Here we are, ready to begin retracing your life. Have you chosen the site for our excavation? How about that old chest of memorabilia from childhood that stands in your bedroom or in the attic of your parents' home? Or in the hall closet or garage? (If such memorabilia aren't available, you can do the excavation in your imagination.)

Put your blank artist's book — your illustrated discovery journal — nearby so you can write down your thoughts, memories, and responses to the artifacts you uncover. Or make notes in this book. As Piero Ferrucci tells us in his book *Inevitable Grace*, a fascinating exploration of spiritual and creative breakthroughs, "We all have moments of inspiration — a sudden flash of understanding, the solution to a problem, a state of grace, a brilliant thought about a future project, a witty remark. These are the moments in which we experience original thoughts accompanied by euphoria and energy, sometimes even by manic agitation: we forget about the tiredness, and spontaneity puts an end to doubt and tension.

"Inspiration comes whenever it wants," Ferrucci writes, "even at the most unlikely times and in the most inappropriate situations. Often it arrives bit by bit. Therefore it must be anchored, and this is where a most valuable item makes its appearance: the notebook."

Using our illustrated discovery journal, we will employ the three levels of study — *observation, description, explanation* — that Bill McMillon describes in his *Archaeology Handbook*. "Observation occurs during the excavation of a site," he explains, "and is central to all archaeological study." This means keeping your sharp eyes open, not only to the whole area of your life, but also to small things, the unexpected. "Description occurs when archaeologists analyze the materials collected during an excavation, and explanation when they draw conclusions based on the analysis of the collected material."

On a fresh sheet of paper, draw your site map, which will be a time breakdown of the various stages of your life (future as well as present and past). I'd suggest the following grouping of years, but you can combine these into larger entities if you want (e.g. your twenties, your thirties — whatever time frames have significance for you): years 1–5, 6–10, 11–14, 15–20, 21, 22–29, 30, 35, 40, 45, 50, 55, 60, 65, 70, 75, 80, 85, 90, 95, 100. (Think positively! You have only just begun to live!)

Louis Pasteur tells us that, "In the fields of observation chance favors only the prepared minds." So let's approach our site and concentrate our attention!

Claiming the
Events of Your Life

You need to claim the events of your life to make yourself yours. When you truly possess all you have been and done, which may take some time, you are fierce with reality.

FLORIDA SCOTT-MAXWELL

Florida Scott-Maxwell ought to know, for she claimed the events of her life and went on to reinvent herself many times. At age sixteen she went on the stage; at twenty she began a career as a short story writer. After her marriage she moved with her husband to his native Scotland, where she worked for women's suffrage, wrote plays, and raised her children. At fifty, irrepressibly she began still another career as an analytical psychologist, studying under Carl Jung. Later, she practiced in clinics in Scotland and England. When she was 84, she wrote *The Measure of My Days*, a journal and meditation on old age.

I love her phrase "fierce with reality." I think she means for us to say, "Okay, reality, you took my [husband? mother? job? youth? health?], but that's all. You haven't taken my spirit, my essential Self. I can peel away layers, like a good archaeologist, and the unique and strong can be revealed. I can reclaim all of these qualities. Fiercely."

Let's keep her spirit in mind as you turn now to those nine manilla envelopes you've prepared, and fill them with thoughts, notes, photos, mementos, drawings.

FIELD WORK

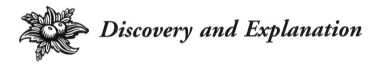 *Discovery and Explanation*

Discovery

Discovery consists of seeing what everybody has seen and thinking what nobody has thought.

ALBERT SZENT-GYORGYI NAGYRAPOLT

Open the lid of the trunk under a good light. What's in that small box in the corner? Your baby shoes? Your christening gown? The scrapbook of your first two years? Did your mother note that you took your first steps at twelve months? Record this in your discovery journal and reflect on your daring and courage, your skill at balancing, your sense of adventure, your reaching out, even then, for Something More. Which three or four of the artifacts especially reveal who you were in these early years? Describe or draw them in your journal.

As for that dusty black photo album — is that you in long braids, sitting in an oak tree with your best friend? Celebrate your physical agility and love of nature, the sense of tranquility that the tree gave you, and the feeling of connection with people long ago. Where is that friend today? Can you call her? Or can you propose an expedition to a friend or family member now? "Let's go on a hike, a nature walk. Let's sit in a tree!"

Reflect on some of those timeless moments spent with friends or with nature when you were a child. Where were you? In the mountains? At the seashore? In your backyard?

Carol Gilligan, psychologist, professor at Harvard, and author of *In A Different Voice*, believes that many women lose in adolescence the daring sense of adventure and confidence they had when they were younger. As you think of yourself in that tree, concentrate on regathering your power.

Explanation

The simplest explanation is always the most likely.

AGATHA CHRISTIE

If your parents are still living, show them that baby dress, the scrapbook, and ask now, as an adult, "What was I like as a child?" Listen to what they say, maybe even tape-record it, for a fresh angle on your own memories. If they're gone now, or if their memories are failing, talk with other relatives — aunts, uncles, cousins. You might want to invite your own children to accompany you on your oral sentimental journey. We tend to tell more detailed stories to others, especially if we've got a curious audience.

Who are the people in your photo album? Tell your children as you turn the pages and remember them.

Is that your silver baby cup tucked away to the side? Writer and designer Alexandra Stoddard believes in pulling out such beautiful artifacts, enjoying them, and integrating them into our daily lives now. You can do this both physically and psychologically. The silver cup can be polished and used by your own child. Or you can use it for paper clips, small flowers, for sipping juice; or just place it on your shelf and admire it each day.

A friend has taken the little bead necklace spelling out her name that was put around her neck in the hospital when she was born, and has hung it over her computer. She wanted to make a kind of grid line, showing her evolution from "there" to "here," reminding herself that she is the same person now that she was then.

Site Report

When you think of the word *discovery*, what image of yourself comes to mind? Where are you? How are you dressed? Is there anyone there with you? Can you visualize your Authentic Self?

Were there events in your childhood that seemed very mysterious when they occurred? Could you recreate the scenario and see if you could discover what was really happening and give the events an *explanation?* Pretend you're telling a story. This is a very good exercise because, when we learn to fill in the gaps in our past, we can use this insight to help us understand events that are unfolding in our lives today.

Do some of your keepsakes seem quite ordinary to you now? Can you remember what their significance was and can you try to recapture the feelings of pride, wonder, or curiosity you associate with them?

Why not take a blank page in your illustrated discovery journal and create a one-page autobiography of yourself as a child. Make it multimedia, using visual images from magazines or your own drawings as well as words. Place the images first and then see what written thoughts want to accompany them.

Surviving

Surviving meant being born over and over.

ERICA JONG

Near-Life Experiences

We tell ourselves stories in order to live.

JOAN DIDION

Every day we experience death. The death of dreams, misconceptions, illusions. The death of vibrancy and enthusiasm. The death of hope. The death of courage. The death of confidence. The death of faith. The death of trust. More often than any of us ever expect, life stuns us with the sudden wrenching away of a loved one, a devastating diagnosis, a conversation that begins with the chilling words, "There's something I've got to tell you."

We feel as if life is over, and we are right. Life as we knew it *is* over.

Twice the life I took for granted ended abruptly; once when my health was threatened and again when my marriage of nearly two decades ended. "Death in its way comes as much as a surprise as birth," the Irish writer Edna O'Brien laments, surely for us all. In each instance, when I regained consciousness months later, I was someone else. I died to myself, and a stronger, wiser, and more passionate woman was resurrected in my place. Although this woman answered to my name, she was profoundly different. So different, that her DNA — what scientists describe as a string of genetic molecules, but what I know is really our *Destiny, Nature,* and *Aspirations* — had changed.

Ironically, both of these "deaths" occurred when everything finally seemed to be coming together for me at home and at work. During the mid-1980s, I was a freelance writer and radio broadcaster who had devised a way to work and stay at home with my then-two-year-old daughter. I decided to take one afternoon off to treat Katie to lunch at her favorite fast-food restaurant. I remembered returning her ketchup-smeared smile before taking the first bite of my sandwich, when a large ceiling panel overhead dislodged, fell, and knocked me on the table. No one else in the restaurant was hit.

Thank God I took the brunt of the blow and my child was spared harm. But I sustained a severe concussion that left me bedridden, confused, and disoriented for months, and partially disabled for a year and a half. During the first three months of recuperation, my senses were all skewed. My eyesight was very blurry and I was extremely sensitive to light, so the shades had to be pulled at all times. Even seeing the different patterns of the quilt on our bed disturbed my sense of equilibrium, so much so that we had to turn it over to the plain muslin backing. I couldn't listen to music because it made me dizzy; nor could I carry on telephone conversations because, without visual clues such as reading lips, I could not process the sounds coming through my ears and rearrange them into meaningful patterns in my brain. The accident threatened to deny me (forever, I thought) the consolation of my keenest companions, the written and spoken word — not to mention my livelihood. For a long time I was unable to read with comprehension or speak articulately.

These unsettling side effects lasted for quite a while. They were dark months, both emotionally and physically. I lost track of time, my sense of rhythm, my identity (if I wasn't a wife, mother, and writer who was I?), and my feeling of safety. My isolation was acute; it was as if I were imprisoned in my own body, sentenced to solitary confinement for an unspecified duration, with no chance of time off for good behavior. I wasn't dead. I wasn't alive. I was suspended in a near-life experience. Eudora Welty has written that "the fantasies of dying could be no stranger than the fantasies of living. Surviving is perhaps the strangest fantasy of them all." She is right.

In order to get through this purgatory, I would lie in the dark and tell myself stories — discombobulated sagas, to be sure — as I wove in and out of wakefulness. Clarissa Pinkola Estes believes that "Stories are medicine." They certainly became my homeopathic remedies. Although I had been a journalist for ten years, I had never thought of myself as a storyteller. But snatches of stories — fairy tales I'd heard as a child, adventures I'd lived as a young woman — would float to the top of my distress and hang in midair until I retrieved one and recast it as a personal parable. Each starred my own romantic heroine, an extraordinary woman who triumphed over her travails with courage, grace, and grit — a person who bore no resemblance to me at all. This woman was beautiful and radiant, with a strong, healthy, vibrant aura. Her eyes sparkled and she laughed uproariously. She was mysterious, magnetic, accomplished, powerful, irresistible, confident, smart, sassy, funny, and sexy. She was passionate. She possessed verve, but more important, she reflected, even in the worst situations, the essential characteristic of all romantic heroines — repose of the soul. I couldn't remember having an imaginary friend as a child, but now I did and I adored her company.

I looked forward to my alter ego's daily dose of *diva-gation* — her wandering, straying, but always pulling through with pluck to live and love again. Of course, I didn't possess the knowledge then that she was my Authentic Self — my soul made visible. I needed, as will you, time and space to grow into my authenticity and to accept myself — not for what is wrong, but for what is gloriously right. Excavating is a lifelong peeling away of layers and cannot be forced. Owning our spectacular finds takes longer still.

Keeping Body and
Soul Together

*There is no agony like bearing an
untold story inside you.*

ZORA NEALE HURSTON

Misfortune sprinkles ashes on the head of the man, but falls like dew on the heart of the woman, and brings forth [gems] of strength of which she herself had no conscious possession," Anna Cora Mowatt wrote in *Autobiography of an Actress, or Eight Years on the Stage* in 1854. Anna never intended to be an actress. To begin with, this was a scandalous occupation for a woman during the nineteenth century, and Anna was a proper lady, the wife of a well-to-do attorney. But her husband became ill, and then a

series of bad investments left the couple home-
less and in debt. Suddenly they had no means of
keeping body and soul together. With her husband sick, it was up to Anna to figure out a way
to survive. As she wondered what she could do,
she asked herself, "Were there no gracious gifts
within my nature? Had I no talents I could
use? Had a life made up of delightful
associations and poetic enjoyments unfitted
me for exertion? No — there was something
strong within me that cried out, It had not!"
and so Anna began her next life behind the
footlights as a trouper.

When we think of "surviving," the immediate connection we make is with money. Trust
me, you can have a million dollars in the bank,
but if your first conscious thought on waking
is how to make it through another day — or
whether you really *want* to — then, my dear,
you're existing at survival level. We all desperately want to believe that money makes
all the difference. But when your heart is
broken, it doesn't matter whether the pillow
you sob into is cotton or silk damask.

Like an understudy waiting for her big
chance to strut the stage of our lives, survival
disguises herself in various and often surprising roles. There's one perfectly suited for
each of us. Our personal scenes are
specifically rewritten so they can be performed on the pulse point of our vulnerability,
that delicate membrane of ancient memory

where emotionally, psychically, and spiritually, our soul is weakest. We need to learn endurance. We need to become strong. The scar tissue needs to be built up. Only the strong survive.

"When you are living at a survival level," Sanaya Roman comforts us, "do not feel like you are a failure. This is simply the way you have chosen to learn many important lessons and experience the essence of who you are."

The Realm of
the Unspeakable

[The history of most women is] hidden either by silence, or by flourishes and ornaments that amount to silence.

VIRGINIA WOOLF

On the journey to authenticity it can be difficult for us to identify with women whose lives seem seamlessly pulled together. When we ourselves are existing at survival level, it's virtually impossible for us not to be sick with envy and jealousy over another woman's good fortune,

97

especially if we know her. We say we're happy, we smile and exclaim, "Isn't that wonderful!" and then we slink away and slowly poison ourselves on the bile of disbelief that anything good will ever come our way again. We are in pain, and while we don't consciously wish others ill, we do wish they'd keep their happiness to themselves. It's not that we don't want our friends to have _____ (fill in the blank). It's just that when we ourselves are starving and scrounging for a few crumbs of contentment while *they* seem to be grazing at life's all-you-can-eat buffet, their breezy good cheer robs us of the last residue of stoicism — our pride. Mum's the word for those of us currently dwelling in the realm of fear and loathing. And we have all been tenants there at one time or another.

"There was a time when my life seemed so painful to me that reading about the lives of other women writers was one of the few things that could help," Kennedy Fraser confesses in her luminous collection of essays, *Ornament and Silence*. "I was unhappy, and ashamed of it; I was baffled by my life." During this time Kennedy Fraser was covering the world of fashion for *The New Yorker*, and her elegant grace and acute intelligence were evident on every page of her prose. I deeply admired her aplomb — the way she could turn a phrase and look utterly fabulous with her hair pulled slick back. This was during the 1970s, when I was a freelance fashion hack and her brilliant career was on the ascent.

Kennedy Fraser nestled comfortably at *The New Yorker* until it was sold in 1985. When her mentor there, editor William Shawn, left, followed by the tight group of writers whose identity, like her own, had been wrapped up in the allure of the elite, Kennedy had to begin all over again, from scratch. Naturally, this incarnation was frightening; it required her "to summon up new courage and explore new forms of speech."

As always, survival knew just where to tighten the screws on her soul. Not only was she displaced professionally, but at the same time she sustained a blow to her self-worth as a woman in the very vulnerable area of age and sex appeal.

It is hard not to love and admire a woman who confesses the devastating moment when a man her age "withdrew his attention from me to look hungrily over my shoulder at a pretty young woman many years my junior. As a younger woman I had relied on the attention of older men and depended upon their approval. I saw very clearly, in that instant when the man's gaze shifted, that one kind of power had passed from me."

During the 1970s, while I was envying Kennedy Fraser, she began a passage in her life that she calls her "armchair period," a detour of dormancy, survival's partner in our spiritual growth. Dormancy visits all of us, but our fallow time can take place lying in bed or standing in front of the refrigerator.

"I felt very lonely then, self-absorbed, shut off" — a perfect description of a near-life experience — and so she sought refuge in the private lives of other women, perusing their journals, letters, memoirs, and autobiographies. "The successes gave me hope, of course, yet it was the desperate bits I liked best. I was looking for direction, gathering clues. I was especially grateful for the secret, shameful things about these women — the pain: the abortions and misalliances, the pills they took, the amount they drank."

Whatever it was, these women's stories "seemed to stretch out a hand" that helped pull her through her abyss. When I have been wrenched and wrung out, other women's distress stories, their *jeremiads* (an exquisite word derived from the Old Testament Prophet Jeremiah who wrote the Book of Lamentations) have been a source of word-to-word resuscitation. Often, when going down for the third, fourth, or fifth time, it was what I glimpsed between the lines of other women's stories — both their triumphs and their cautionary tales — that pulled me back to the safety of my own sanity.

The Silent Hemorrhaging
of the Soul

No [woman] was ever ruined from without;
the final ruin comes from within.

AMELIA E. BARR

Is there a vein of misery that runs deeper in all
our lives than self-loathing? A fault line that
guarantees our failure ever to be truly happy,
no matter how much we accomplish or accumu-
late, or in whose arms we lie?

I have run away from the life lesson of
self-loathing for the last twenty-five years.

But unconsciously, my better half — my
Authentic Self — knew that the day would
come when I would have to face my strongest
weakness and wrestle the demon down on the
page in order to save my soul. And so she has
been on the alert, a spiritual and savvy
ghostwriter, jotting down phrases and glimmers of insight and then burying them between the lines of my private journals, memos,
and love letters. Especially my love letters. All

my life, thorny knots of understanding have unraveled themselves on scraps of paper: napkins, newspaper margins, the backs of recipe cards, and Post-it notes. Sometimes I have been awakened in the dead of night after a dream by the insistent voice of a superior: *Write this down.* I did as I was told.

The exquisite writer Katherine Paterson tells me this morning that I must write the story within myself "that demands to be told" at this particular point in my life. I don't want to, but I *must.*

If I were to assign a color to self-loathing, it would be the bluish black and purple of an ugly bruise. This is what self-loathing is, an ugly bruise that erupts on the surface of our lives or on our bodies; a warning sign that something serious is happening on a deeper level. We bruise when we bleed within.

This may be hard to read, but its truth is crucial for us to process if we are to move beyond survival, if we are to live.

One of the more horrific ways to die is through internal *hemorrhaging,* the uncontrollable bleeding buried in the body's cavity. What makes this particular exit route even more insidious is that internal hemorrhaging is most often painless to the victim. There are no visible clues signaling the tiny trickle that starts when a small blood vessel begins to leak until it's become a fatal flood, "a blood-stemmed tide," as the Irish poet W. B. Yeats so beautifully describes destiny.

Self-loathing is the silent hemorrhaging of the soul. You don't feel or see the life force fleeing until it's no longer there, and then, of course, it's too late.

Self-loathing.

Do not confuse loathing with hatred. It would be healthier if we hated ourselves because, as Annie Lennox sings, "There's a thin line between love and hate." If only we could still just slam the door, heave our bodies across the bed, and scream, "I hate myself," the way we used to when we were coming of age. Did you know that the word *hate* comes from the Greek word *kēdos,* meaning grief? When we hated ourselves as teenagers, we were grieving for our loss of identity — for the childhood that was slipping beyond our reach while true adulthood was not yet quite within our grasp.

Loathing is grief that has festered; the rampant infection of self-pity. To *loathe* something or someone is "to detest" with just enough disgust and intolerance to make the feeling the emotional equivalent of roiling rot. This is what self-loathing is, although we never call it that. It's easier and safer to tell ourselves and others, "Oh, I'm a bit hard on myself."

How do we loathe ourselves? Let me count the ways. Reasons that have nothing to do with our appearance, age, or weight. Some of the world's most famous beauties can't stand the sight of themselves. Self-loathing is an equal-opportunity oppressor.

In short, we may loathe our human frailties, flaws, and foibles in a world that only approves perfection; loathe our oddities, eccentricities, and ugly habits; loathe our inability to avoid insidious comparisons; loathe our buying into the illusion that good men would save us because that would be easier than striving to save ourselves or believing that we could.

We loathe ourselves for constantly capitulating to the needs of others by disavowing our own; for ignoring the careless cruelties of loved ones in order to keep the peace; for struggling to live up to the expectations of people we don't even care about; for denying the validity of our own unrequited desires. "The ingenuity of self-deception is inexhaustible," Hannah More wrote in an essay entitled "Self-Love." She wrote that in 1811.

You tell me. Is it nature or nurture? Does it matter?

We loathe ourselves because we don't look quite like the multi-orgasmic sex goddesses we thought we'd be when we were twenty-five; or because we're not quite the natural, totally bonded mothers we hoped we'd be when we held that baby in our arms for the first time. And perhaps most of all, we loathe ourselves because we haven't quite fulfilled the promise of our astonishing authentic gifts. The truth is, we didn't even try — not because we were afraid we'd fail, but because we were terrified we would succeed.

We loathe ourselves because she who excused so much or asked too little has learned only to mask the stalking shame that comes from being successful at things she doesn't respect, from failing to defend that which she knows is true. We loathe ourselves for living and lying every day in little ways that devalue and dishonor us.

When was the last time you started off a conversation with "I'm sorry" when you weren't? I did it yesterday.

"She had developed a passionate longing for making other people comfortable at her own expense," Phyllis Bottome wrote in 1934 about a woman we all know all too well. "She succeeded in getting other people into armchairs . . . with nothing left for herself but something small and spiky in a corner."

Looking-Glass Shame

We live in an atmosphere of shame. We are ashamed of everything that is real about us; ashamed of ourselves, of our relatives, of our incomes, of our accents, of our opinions, of our experience, just as we are ashamed of our naked skins.

GEORGE BERNARD SHAW

From the time we are small, we pick up the signals that will mark us for life — other people's impressions of whether or not we're acceptable, whether or not we're pleasing in their eyes. It's conveyed in the cuddling and the cooing, the compliments and the little songs they sing as they wash us, dress us, and show us off. Or not.

Oh, you must have been a beautiful baby,
You must have been a wonderful child.
When you were only startin' to go to kinder-
*   garten,*
I bet you drove the little boys wild.
And when it came to winning blue ribbons,
I bet you showed the other kids how.

106

I can see the judges' eyes
as they handed you the prize,
I bet you took the cutest bow.
Oh, you must have been a beautiful baby,
'Cause, baby, look at you now.

Yeah, baby. Let's look at ourselves now. Are you pretty? Are you plain? I've got my good days, and I've got my bad. We all do. But the reality doesn't matter. If your mother or father thought you were plain, one way or another, you still reflect the image they bestowed upon you. This is the origin of self-loathing, or our *looking-glass shame,* which is what the English novelist and critic Virginia Woolf called the malady that breaks all our hearts.

We are marked in many ways, as you will discover as we excavate the memories that have to do with our self-image. A friend cannot forget the memory of her beautiful mother slipping quietly to her bedside when she was twelve. Thinking that she was sleeping, her mother lifted a slender, lacquered finger to her daughter's misproportioned nose. There in the dark she tilted my friend's head first to the left, then to the right to admire what she imagined would be the result of a surgeon's scalpel.

Sure enough, on the eve of her sixteenth birthday, my friend's mother asked the surgeon if he could make my friend look like Vivien Leigh. He couldn't, but whatever he did somehow fits my friend's face. Nonetheless, she wonders today if her mother would have been happy to have a daughter who looked like Barbra Streisand now that Barbra's proved that success, money, and fame are pretty good cosmetologists.

It was a photograph that marked me. When I was ten there was a garbage strike in our town. For weeks the garbage piled up in front of trim suburban homes. One day a newspaper photographer drove up in front of our house and asked if any children lived there. He wanted to photograph children near the garbage pile to emphasize how much had accumulated. When he came to the door, I was standing shyly behind my mother, so I was selected and propped up on piles of garbage for the photograph. "Just think," my mother exclaimed, "you're going to have your picture in the newspaper." And I certainly did. On the front page. When I went to school the next day, I was taunted by classmates who called me "a pile of garbage." I was marked. In order to handle this public humiliation, I became numb to my own beauty for a very long time. For years I wouldn't have my picture taken; I was terrified at what would be reflected there. To this day I still don't feel comfortable being photographed — and I'm always amazed (and so grateful!) when they come out well. I'm dumbfounded when I can say "Now there is a beautiful woman." It is nothing less than miraculous that I am no longer blind to my own radiance; it has been a lifelong struggle. You must believe this: if I could do it, so can you.

We like to think that the reason we loathe our bodies is that we're sure others secretly do. (Haven't they been talking behind our backs since high school?) Forget other people; it's really we who are most disturbed by our cellulite thighs and lined faces. We can't believe that anyone could possibly love a woman with a little flesh on her bones. Of course they could — and the right ones do! We may be blinded by our own perceived flaws, but others have clearer visions. I love the relationship in a popular television show between an older woman and her lover who is twenty years younger than she. He adores her "wattle," the loose skin under her chin. It's a riot — and quite reassuring — to watch him become aroused by something that would have me wearing a bag over my head. I have a man friend who swears that once men pass their "breeding years" — after forty-five or so — they become blind to a woman's physical defects, especially if the woman respects her body, has a healthy sense of self-esteem that's not based on her looks alone, and loves sex. "What could be better?" he asks. It is we who insist on thrusting a magnifying glass into the hands of a potential lover so that we can point out the minuscule hair growing out of a mole on our chin. Why not just cut to the chase and say instead, "Please find my flaws quickly so you can reject me and be done with it?"

Women have always tried either to flee from the looking glass or to fool it. Archaeologists in Asia Minor have found the burial sites of women filled with elaborate cosmetic enhancements. It seems the ancients, too, from Egypt's first female pharaoh Hatchepsut to Helen of Troy, felt compelled to conceal their true images, camouflaging themselves even into the next world, comfortable neither here nor in the Hereafter with who they really were.

Our Pilgrimage Places

There is more here than meets the eye.

LADY MURASAKI

We think in youth that our bodies are identified with ourselves and have the same interests," reminisced Rebecca West toward the end of her life, "and later [realize] they are heartless companions who have been accidentally yoked to us." But if our bodies rebel and act merciless and unyielding as age begins to shut us down and beauty fades, who abandoned whom? Where did the betrayal begin? Weren't the battle lines drawn years before, when we first began to echo the opinions others had of us? And didn't we make matters worse by upping the ante with our own faultfinding? We've taken our bodies for granted, abused and dishonored them with too much hard living, with our excesses, and with too few compliments or cherishing caresses. How would you react if you had to live day in and day out with Cruella de Ville harping at you? Well, guess what? That's exactly what your body has been up against. If she's tired of the abuse, don't blame her; applaud her spunk. Thank her. One essence — body, mind, or spirit — has to stand up for you if you're going to survive. Oddly enough, but also regrettably, this is what happens when we become seriously ill. Our bodies call a spiritual time-out until we can make a lifesaving attitude adjustment.

Starting today, if you can't be with the body you love, love the body you're with.

"The body is wiser than its inhabitant," Erica Jong reminds us. "The body is the soul. We ignore its aches, its pains, its eruptions, because we fear the truth. The body is God's messenger."

It's time to declare a détente with our imperfections, to lay down the artillery of self-abuse we aim at ourselves — the potions, prayers, and punitive diets, cosmetic artifice, and extreme, customized correction. I'm not suggesting that there isn't a place for hair

111

color, makeup, and cosmetic nipping and tucking on your way to authenticity if it's going to help you awaken to your own inner beauty. I *am* telling you that nothing will help you get over looking-glass shame if the transformation doesn't begin from within. You first have to be willing to seek holistic and holy ways of renewal that honor your body and restore her to her rightful place as the "sacred garment" of your soul. "The body must be nourished physically, emotionally and spiritually," Carol Hornig tells us. "We're spiritually starved in this culture — not under-fed but undernourished."

One of the truths I learned on the *Simple Abundance* journey is that you cannot begin the search for authenticity, you cannot embark on a spiritual path within, and not see it reflected on the outside. A Gnostic axiom teaches, "As is the inner, so is the outer." Time well spent in meditation gives you more serenity and it shows on your face. A half hour of walking every other day increases your vitality and energy level and you find yourself less depressed. Suddenly you become more relaxed and fun to be around. You smile, maybe even laugh. You catch a reflection of yourself in a mirror and you're pleasantly surprised. "Who's that babe?" you wonder. As Rosalind Russell points out, "Taking joy in life is a woman's best cosmetic."

A plastic surgeon once told me that he will

not perform cosmetic surgery on women he knows are in shaky marriages or those he suspects have severe self-esteem problems. Instead, he gently advises them to seek therapy and come back to him in six months. Why? Because he can't promise that a face-lift will save a marriage or that breast implants will attract Mr. Right.

Learning to accept ourselves exactly as we are today gives us the motivation to move forward to the next step, whether it's searching for a healthier way of eating or finding an exercise program that's fun to do alone or with a pal. For years I starved myself in a desperate battle to stay at a certain weight. I didn't exercise. I said I didn't have the time, but the truth was that the very thought made me want to hit the snooze button. Then, out of desperation to relieve stress that couldn't be alleviated with self-medication, I started walking around the block a few times a week. Oddly enough I began to notice that the days I walked, I felt better. What's more, I could eat food without feeling guilty or bungee-jumping off the scale. My suburban saunters became such a pleasant part of my daily round that my daughter and I began going to a gym twice a week. Suddenly, sleeveless dresses! Sleep, instead of tossing and turning. The benefits of being kind to one's body are astounding.

Diana Roesch, a fitness expert, assures us:

"With enlightenment and self-awareness, we can re-guide and realign our *whole* selves: our bodies, by finding new ways of moving and celebrating them and by adding good food in amounts they tell us they need; our souls, our sense of ourselves as good and worthwhile, by connecting them to the earth and to each other."

Now, when I reflect on my body-ography, something surprising happens. Like the archaeologist who just has unearthed a priceless porcelain fragment from a lost civilization, I can only feel appreciation for all the places my body has taken me, and for the memories it stores, and for the secrets it keeps. For the children it has carried, nourished and nurtured, for the lovers who have found solace and joy within my hills and valleys, for the exquisite pleasure my body has bestowed on me, for the exultation of passion it has expressed through me. My journey to reveal my Authentic Self has become a romance, for I have begun to fall in love with my own reflection. Blessed am I among women to live in such a beautiful temple. So are you. Say this softly to yourself upon awakening and retiring: *Blessed am I among women to live and love in such a beautiful temple.*

Today, at the sacred site of your soul, make peace with your present reflection as you go in search of the body and face you were born with and excavate the many extraordinary faces that have evolved during your many lives. You will learn to love them all. I promise!

Embrace the lines that stare back, the parts that sag in the middle or stick out where you think they shouldn't, the hair that never keeps a curl or never loses it. Invoke the Tibetan poet Saraha's psalm of praise: "Here in this body are the sacred rivers; here are the sun and moon as well as all the pilgrimage places. . . . I have not encountered another temple as blissful as my own body."

When we learn to love our pilgrimage places, we begin to understand that it is because Spirit loved beauty in so many exquisite guises that He created each one of us unique and authentic. We are the ones who try to copy and clone others so that we fit in. But fit in where exactly?

We're not meant to fit in. We're meant to stand out. As Marianne Williamson says, "We ask ourselves, who am I to be brilliant, gorgeous, talented, fabulous? [But] actually," she goes on, "who are you *NOT* to be? You are a child of God. Your playing small does not serve the world. There is nothing enlightened about shrinking so that other people won't feel insecure around you. [You] were born to make manifest the glory of God that is within [you]."

Spirit is the ultimate womanizer, basking in the glow of our matchless beauty and incomparable perfection, no matter how our outer packaging appears to the world. Beauty, indeed, is in the eye of the beholder. As you journey toward Something More, you'll know you're headed in the right direction when, as the Talmud tells us, you start to see things not as they are, but as you are.

Here's looking at you, kid!

Your Own Natural
Selection Process

She endured. And survived. Marginally, perhaps, but it is not required of us that we live well.

ANNE CAMERON

There are many ways to survive, many ways to have near-life experiences. But the natural selection process, which is what biologists call the survival of the fittest, is covert and unconscious. There's survival by smoke and mirrors (pretense), by subsistence, by sacrifice, by substitution, by subterfuge, by stonewalling, by sedition, by surrender. Just as we each weave in and out of the seven lives of authenticity, so too, at various times, do we all move in and out of survival's guises until we can't fool ourselves anymore. When we are finally willing to relinquish the need to live through others and acknowledge that we deserve a life of our own choosing, we are ready to move on and be born again through the reembodiment journey.

Smoke-and-Mirror Survival

Into how little space can a human soul be crushed?

OLIVE SCHREINER

In 1862, eighteen-year-old Sophie Behrs made the catch of the season when she married the dashing, romantic Count Leo Tolstoy who was then thirty-four. The following year she gave birth to the first of their sixteen children (thirteen of whom survived). When they first married, Sophie was filled with hope, enthusiasm, and passion. Theirs was going to be a creative partnership of equals, not just husband and wife, and she threw herself into helping her husband with his writing career, juggling the many difficult roles of copyist, editor, and tactful critic, even as she was struggling with the demands of being a new mother.

In an effort to live up to the lofty ideal of being equals, her husband suggested that they regularly read each other's diaries so that they might get to know each other's deepest inner thoughts.

Sophie, always wanting to please, agreed. *Bad idea.* Our diaries and journals are often our last defenses when fighting for survival, dispatches from behind the front lines of life's skirmishes. *They are not supposed to be shared with anyone.* What we write when we record our most intimate feelings, fears, and fantasies are sacred love letters to Spirit.

Because her constant pregnancies depleted his wife's physical and psychic reserves, Tolstoy hired another literary aide without consulting her. This seriously undermined Sophie's confidence and left her deeply wounded. She was demoted from partner to spouse, and soon her unused intellectual energies found their expression in nasty quarrels and bouts of self-pity. Being authentic, her diary entries careened from her profound grief at the deterioration of a relationship that had begun with so much promise to her feeling of being trapped by the constant responsibility for so many children, and then to more fanciful musings — self-deceptive smoke-and-mirror projections about how wonderful her life really was (usually written after her husband offered the slightest nod of approval in her direction). Together, extracts from a few of her diary entries reveal how Sophie's spirit began to starve when she was forced to draw comfort from half-truths rather than from genuine emotional nourishment. Between the lines of her own pain, she speaks volumes about the way we women learn to subsist on the random crumbs of affection haphazardly tossed our way — all the time deluding ourselves into thinking that everything is as it should be. We're happy, really happy, aren't we? Shouldn't we be?

Read Sophie's reflections slowly, meditatively. Do any of them resonate with you? Why?

I can't find any occupation for myself. He is lucky to be so clever and talented. But I'm neither the one nor the other. . . . One can't live on love alone.

★ ★ ★

I suddenly felt that we would gradually drift apart and each live our own lives. . . . And it begins to hurt me that this love of mine, my first and last, should not be enough for him.

★ ★ ★

In a few years I shall have created a woman's world for myself, which I shall love even more, for it will contain my husband and my children, whom one loves even more than one's parents and brothers. But I haven't reached that stage yet. I am still wavering between the past and the future. My husband loves me too much to [allow me to work on my own writing] just yet; it is difficult anyway, and I will have to work it all out for myself. . . . With a little effort I can again become what I was before, although no longer a maiden, but a woman, and when this happens, both he and I will be satisfied.

★ ★ ★

I am to gratify his pleasure and nurse his child, I am a piece of household furniture, I am a woman.

★ ★ ★

Now I am well once again and not pregnant; it terrifies me to think how often I have been in that condition . . . [When I was young I thought] I both can and want to do everything, but after a while I begin to realize there is nothing to want and that I can't do anything beyond eating, drinking, sleeping, nursing the children, and caring for them and my husband. After all, this is happiness, yet why do I grow sad and weep, as I did yesterday?

★ ★ ★

It makes me laugh to read over this diary. It's so full of contradictions, and one would think I was such an unhappy woman. Yet is there a happier woman than I? It would be hard to find a happier or more friendly marriage than ours. Sometimes, when I am alone in the room, I just laugh with joy, and making the sign of the cross, say to myself, "May God let this last *many, many years."*

★ ★ ★

The sheer force of my suffering and my passionate love for him has broken the ice which has recently separated us. Nothing can resist the power of this emotional bond — we are joined by our long life together and our great love for one another. I went into his room as he was going to bed and said: "Promise me you won't ever leave me on the sly, without telling me." And he replied: "I wouldn't ever do such a thing — I promise I shall never leave you. I love you." And his voice trembled. I burst into tears and embraced him, saying how afraid I was of losing him, that I loved him so much, and that despite some innocent and foolish passions in the past I had never stopped loving him for a moment, and still in my old age loved him more than anyone else in the world. [He said] that he felt exactly the same, that I had nothing to fear, that the bond between us was far too strong for anyone to destroy and I realized that this was true and I felt so happy.

★ ★ ★

I am so tired of problems, plots, secrets, cruelty — and my husband's acknowledged "growing indifference" to me! Why should I be perpetually in a fever, loving him to distraction? My heart too can change and cool towards a man who does all he can to let me know of his indifference. If one has to live, and not kill oneself, one has to find some comfort and hap-

piness in life. I cannot live like this. I shall say, "You give me your cold heart, and [others] your passion."

★ ★ ★

I am so physically and emotionally exhausted that my mind is blank and I don't feel like writing. I would desperately like to know what my husband is writing in his diary. His present diaries are like works of literature, from which people will extract the ideas and draw their own conclusions. Mine are a genuine cry from the heart, and a true description of everything that happens to us.

Survival by Surrender

Then she knew that whatever power she might have had was . . . wasted and gone.

REBECCA HARDING DAVIS

The jolted gentlemen readers of the April 1861 issue of *The Atlantic Monthly* — including such illustrious men as Ralph Waldo Emerson and Nathaniel Hawthorne — needed to wash the "soot" off their hands after finishing an anonymous work of fiction entitled *Life in the Iron*

Mills, which depicted, with gritty realism, the "thwarted, wasted lives . . . mighty hungers . . . [and] unawakened powers" of the white working-class slaves toiling in the dark, satanic mills of nineteenth-century industrial America. Who in Heaven's name wrote this social and spiritual wake-up call? When it was discovered that the author was an unknown *woman* from Wheeling, West Virginia, the literary world reeled — and then rolled out the red carpet. Rebecca Harding became a classic overnight success story.

Life in the Iron Mills was Rebecca Harding's first published work, and it's hard to imagine a more auspicious beginning for what should have been a brilliant career. Famous Victorian men of letters paid her homage; she was invited to contribute to the country's most prestigious publications; and she was paid handsomely. However, on her death in 1910 — and despite the fact that in forty years she had produced over 275 short stories, a dozen novels, 125 children's stories, and over 200 essays — she disappeared without a trace.

So how did this happen?

Reader, she fell in love.

There was no more ardent fan of Rebecca's than a young Philadelphia attorney named L. Clarke Davis, who was captivated by Miss Harding's authenticity. According to writer Tillie Olsen, who tracked down Rebecca's story after seeing a reference to her in one of Emily Dickinson's letters, Clarke "was attracted by what would have made most men shun her: her very achievement, seriousness, power; her directness and sardonic eye for sham; the evidence of a rich secret life." After Rebecca and Clarke had corresponded for a year, he invited her to visit him. She did, and within a week she had agreed to marry him.

Clarke was a charming fellow, agreeable but lazy. Not shiftless, really, just selfish. He meant well. Early on, they both realized that his income from various part-time jobs would never be enough to allow them to live in the manner to which Clarke aspired. One of Clarke's pursuits was as a literary editor for a popular women's magazine, *Peterson's*. There was easy money if Rebecca could put aside her serious literary work for a little while and "write for her Boy." What her Boy wanted was heartfelt women's stories that paid more than serious "art." Rebecca agreed to try. In "The Wife's Story," written in the final months of her first pregnancy, Rebecca touched a chord in the hearts of American women but foreshadowed her own fate. As the story's protagonist confesses: "I was so hungry for affection that night! I would have clung to a dog that had been kind to me . . . [for] the need with which I, an adult woman, craved a cheering word, and a little petting." The more Rebecca wrote for Clarke, instead of for herself, the more petting she got.

A year after the birth of their second child,

Rebecca wanted to put the pulp fiction aside and begin her next book, this time about righting the wrongs of slavery. Clarke was skeptical — now he wanted to pursue a political career, and that meant they'd need plenty of money coming in. Would it be worth taking time away from the family for art rather than commerce? Rebecca promised to do it all — tend the family, make money at writing, *and* write the book she was dreaming of.

Don't we all recognize the impossible task she set for herself? When she'd written *Life in the Iron Mill*, she'd been single and she'd had her days to call her own and her wits about her. But now, with two young babies and a self-centered, demanding husband who expected his wife not only to fry the bacon but to bring it home, too, the only time for "the Book" was stolen, exhausted moments at night after cranking out the stories that paid their rent. She was desperately burning the candle at both ends. Tillie Olsen tells us, in her book *Silences*, that Clarke, for all his love, his initial recognition of her potential greatness as writer (her first attraction for him), settled easily into what Rebecca, too, accepted unquestioningly: the "ordained man-wife pattern of *his* ambitions, activities, comforts, needs coming first."

Then Rebecca received an offer to write her novel as a monthly serial for a new magazine hoping to cash in on her name and following.

125

Even though she was smart enough to know they were taking advantage of her, the offer was too great to pass up.

The result: an unrecognizable version of her book, virtually rewritten by her editors as a romance novel. "Mutilated" was what she called it.

Waiting for the Verdict was not a critical success. Though in her soul she had set out to write something profound, she was unable to swim against the tide of her circumstances. She had failed to write her great novel and she knew it. *"A great hope fell, you heard no noise, the ruin was within,"* was all Rebecca Harding Davis would say about her failure, but that said it all. Self-loathing set in.

And so she buried her Authentic Self with denial and surrendered to her husband's choice for her life, a choice that meant the death of her dream "to fulfill her mission in life to change the world," but one that made Clarke's dreams come true. Rebecca resumed writing popular fiction, scraping out the marrow of her soul in weekly and monthly installments.

The sighs she must have uttered as he greeted her each evening with "How is it going?" drive a stake into one's heart.

For, like her readers, even in her desperate moments it was only on the page that Rebecca Harding Davis left — or thought about leaving — her marriage. Eventually, Tillie Olsen recounts, Rebecca "no longer believed in, acted upon, the possibility of high achievement for herself. It was the price for children, home, love. . . . [But] was part of the price, too, that there was no one to whom she could speak" of the enormous dimension of her pain and loss? Certainly not to her husband, who now was prominent enough to be one of President Grover Cleveland's fishing buddies. Nor to her children. Not even to herself.

But she did convey to her readers that they were not alone in their struggle to survive. In another of her stories, a woman in her sixties named Anne tries to run away from home, only to be brought back after the train on which she is making her getaway is wrecked. She is forgiven for her temporary lapse of insanity and quietly lives out her days in inconsolable silence:

> *Yet sometimes in the midst of all this comfort and sunshine a chance note of music or the sound of the restless wind will bring an expression into her eyes which her children do not understand, as if some creature unknown to them looked out. . . . At such times [she would] say to herself, "Poor Anne!" as of somebody whom she once knew that is dead.* **Is** *she dead?*

Toward the end of her life, in a note to a friend that accompanied one of her later novels, she begged the recipient to "Judge me — not by what I have done, but by what I have hoped to do."

Rebecca Harding Davis hoped to change the world. It is heartbreaking that she did not realize that she had done so, not as the social reformer she'd expected to be, but as a source of comfort, compassion, and companionship for thousands of nameless women who found their own voices by reading her words. Perhaps they survived because she seemed to do it so well.

But aren't the saddest of all stories the ones in which the heroine cannot save herself?

Survival by Substitution

We too must be afraid and awed and amazed
That we cannot live forever and that our
Replacements are eager for their turn, indifferent
to our wishes, ready to leave us behind.

ANNE ROIPHE

As long as women have borne daughters, they have attempted to live through them. The noted anthropologist Ruth Benedict described the survival instinct by proxy or proximity this way: "It's very simple: this is my daughter's life that's posing as mine. It's my daughter's love life which shall be perfect; it's my daughter's abilities which shall find scope; it's my daughter's insight that shall be true and valid; she owes it to herself to speak out her beliefs. It is she who shall not miss the big things of life."

Don't you find it fascinating that an anthropologist made this astute observation? Anthropology is the study of human behavior. Maybe it started with Eve. Maybe she mused, "It's my daughter who will figure out a way to get us back into Paradise. She'll marry well." You know what they say: "The apple doesn't fall far from the tree."

Is there a crueler way to survive than by feeding off your young?

My friend Lily was just twenty when her mother pushed her into marrying into the Wall Street world of privilege, comfort, and inherited wealth that she herself had married into. The night before her wedding, Lily broke down and begged her mother to let her call it off. She was not in love. "One doesn't marry for love," her mother told her. "One marries to survive in class — first class, of course."

Christopher was nice, congenial, and unexciting in every way. In four short years they had two children, a Park Avenue penthouse, a sailboat moored alongside a summer cottage in Martha's Vineyard, and a marriage that only seemed to come alive when they partnered in their regular Sunday tennis game. It was at the Vineyard house one hot night, after too many vodka tonics, that Chris and Lily and their weekend houseguests, Sam and Kelly, decided to swap spouses to break the boredom that comes only to those who can do anything they want except be happy. For Chris and Kelly, the evening was a novelty and only that; for Lily and Sam it was something altogether different, igniting a passion that Lily, so young and inexperienced when she married, had never known. Within months, each had left their spouse and planned to marry. The ensuing scandal was society-page fodder, as the men were partners at the same brokerage house and the women's mothers were distant cousins. When Lily's mother asked how she could do this to her husband, to her children, but above all to *her* (threatening to disinherit Lily if she went ahead with the divorce), Lily replied, "So my life will finally be my own."

But the love affair with Sam flamed out after less than a year. Lily realized that she'd launched herself into this new relationship in order to escape the life her mother had chosen for her the first time around. Walking away from one marriage into another wasn't the answer; this time, she would walk to no one except to *herself.*

The last few years have not been easy. In her

haste to leave her marriage, Lily gave up custody of her children and agreed not to contest the meager property settlement proposed by Christopher's attorneys. The breach with her mother has not healed, and while many of her old friends have been there for her, others have sided with Chris, or with Kelly, who eventually reconciled with Sam. Lily has had to fight to restart her life, and that has meant living frugally, carefully, and purposefully. There is no one in her life now; not parents, not a man to lean on, only the ashy memory of a choice that everyone around her still regards as selfish and misguided. But despite everything, Lily emphatically feels otherwise — and this defiance is what she lives on. She was dying inside the "to die for" marriage that had been a mirror of her mother's own loveless match. For all her husband's goodness, for all the comfort and ease of their life together, she had been lonely. As her mother had been before her. Lily says she shudders to think of the countless times her little girl found her weeping for no apparent reason and tried to comfort her. Now, at least, when her daughter visits, she sees her mother smiling.

"Sometimes you don't know that the house you live in is glass until the stone you cast comes boomeranging back," Jessamyn West tells us. "Maybe that's the actual reason you threw it. Something in you was yelling, 'I want out.' The life you saved, as well as the

131

glass you shattered, was your own."

Of course, not all mothers push their daughters into loveless marriages. But how many women continue to remain in them for the sake of their daughters?

"Don't be afraid your life will end," Grace Hansen warns us. "Be afraid that it will never begin."

When Survival Is Called Success

The literature of women's lives is a tradition of escapees, women who have lived to tell the tale . . . They resist captivity. They get up and go. They seek better worlds.

PHYLLIS ROSE

The weekend before her first baby was born, Helen, who was a rising editorial star at a large publishing house, arrived home from work laden with manuscripts, leaving behind in the office the baby gifts — some of them unopened — that she'd received earlier that day at a surprise shower. There was only so much she could carry.

Like it or not, many of us, like Helen, find too much of our worth in our work. Our careers become personal Richter scales, measuring the seismic and psychic value we place on ourselves. Close a sale? Make a deadline? Lose a case? The earth rumbles beneath our feet every day.

That fateful final weekend of Helen's pregnancy became a turning point for her. She knew she had found a potential best-seller among the stack of submissions she'd read over the weekend, and early Monday morning she pleaded her case to make an offer on it. As she waited anxiously for the editorial board's reaction, the baby would wait no longer and she went into labor. Her son arrived six weeks prematurely — fortunately healthy, though confined to the hospital for another month. One week to the day after she gave birth, she was back at her desk taking a meeting with the book's author and his agent. Helen's breasts were leaking; she was exhausted and still suffering from the postpartum short-term memory loss that no one remembers to mention. Never mind — she was where the action was, and while her company's offer was ultimately not high enough to win the publishing rights, everyone admired her dedication to her job, despite some snide comments about her being at work instead of in the hospital nursery. (Ironically, that very manuscript later became a classic how-to book for new mothers.)

For the next several years Helen's life became a frazzled, fragile, frightening balancing act — "Gidget Goes to Work" by the Brothers Grimm. (If this is Wednesday, where do I pick the baby up after 7:00 p.m.?) Years before, as a young editorial assistant, she'd studied her role models in the industry — dynamic and determined women who seemed to have it all, families plus careers — looking for clues on how to do it when her time came.

But one by one, like designer-dressed dominos, their lives had come crashing down around them, despite six-figure salaries, corporate titles, and personal drivers. There were marriages failing suddenly and acrimoniously, depressed and angry children in therapy and family court, and clandestine love affairs gone awry. The women she'd watched in awe were now constantly on the edge of nervous breakdowns and papering over their behind-the-scenes dramas with bravado. But soon Helen was busy acting out her own — a life that was chaotic and untidy, yet not without its successes and satisfactions. Smart and savvy, Helen was swinging from promotion to promotion like a gymnast moving across traveling rings.

As the ante cranked up — new job, second baby, more money, greater responsibility, intensive-care-level stress — she would wonder each night, not how she could enjoy the few precious hours she had with her children before bedtime, but how fast she could get them off to sleep and herself back to work.

One incident stands out in her mind as emblematic of her existence at survival level. She recalls, frame by frame, the morning she came rushing into her kitchen, a wind gust in Calvin Klein, picking up papers here and there, and barking instructions to the au pair who was making the children breakfast. When Helen arrived at the office, the phone was ringing as usual. It was the au pair.

"Do you have Tommy's homework? He can't find it."

"No, of course not. I put it in his backpack this morning," she snapped, reaching for her own briefcase. "Check his homework folder." There, where she expected to see the report she'd labored over until after midnight for an important meeting that morning, were the penciled spelling words her seven-year-old had carefully written out the night before. She burst into tears and the crying jag lasted for three days.

Not so long after that, Helen closed the biggest deal of her professional life. But between the handshakes and the signatures on the final contracts, something inside her had begun to wake up. One night she arrived home late and exhausted as usual to find a message on her answering machine from a hysterical author demanding delivery payment on a manuscript that was virtually unreadable. Helen had been quietly rewriting it because the publishing house, on her recommendation, had paid a bundle for it. Instead of calling the author to task for turning in unacceptable and sloppy work that needed rescuing, she heard herself, to her horror, *apologizing* for not saving the writer's face fast enough. She was shaking with fury when she got off the phone, but swallowed her anger.

Then, a month after saving that book and landing the big deal, Helen was terminated in an abrupt corporate takeover.

First came the shock waves, then the hurt, then the anger, then the anguish. Then the doubts. Then the recriminations. She had never failed at anything in her entire life. What hadn't she done right? Why was she singled out when there were others left in place who didn't have her track record or seniority?

But then, just as suddenly, came a tidal wave of relief: what new hell had she been saved from? How had she gotten it all so mixed up? She wasn't living. She was existing. Barely surviving. Enduring. Marginally. She wasn't supposed to live like this. There had to be Something More, and she would find it. She remembered what Alice James wrote: "The success or failure of a life. . . . seems to lie in the more or less luck of seizing the right moment of escape."

All mothers with responsibilities outside the

home — Helen, you, and I — have felt that terrible pull between our jobs and our children every day. The German poet Rainer Maria Rilke calls the challenge that confronts us the work of understanding. "Somewhere there is an ancient enmity between our daily life and the great work." Acknowledging it openly is the first step toward making courageous choices. That's why it's important, when we select role models in life and work, to remember that we're all human, even women who *seem* to "do it all." The truth is, *no one* can do it all at the same time, and we all know that. So why not start calling women who appear to have achieved a balance between the various demands on them our *reality* models, keeping in mind that even they don't walk the balance beams perfectly every day. It's just that, when they fall, they get back up and try again.

FIELD WORK

 *Authentic Success*

The real moment of success is not the moment apparent to the crowd.

GEORGE BERNARD SHAW

When you were a child, you got report cards filled out by teachers to tell your parents how you were doing in school. It's difficult to make the transition from external judgment to internal acceptance, but it's a journey we all must make to reach our essential selves as adults.

Authentic success is internal. Often, other people aren't even aware at first that you've reached it. The moment of success is the awareness that "I can do it" or "I have done it." And it's comforting to know that this can't be taken away from you by an external event. Not by someone divorcing you, not by someone firing you.

When we achieve authentic success, we don't compare ourselves to others quite so often. That awful force, envy, seems to diminish. In fact, we want others to have the same chances we've had, to do what they would truly love to do. We become generous of spirit.

"I believe talent is like electricity," says Maya Angelou. "We don't understand electricity. We use it. You can plug into it and light up a lamp, keep a heart pump going, light a cathedral, or you can electrocute a person with it. Electricity will do all that. It makes no judgment. I think talent is like that." Maya Angelou believes all of us are born with talent. She's right.

Site Report

What do you think are your talents, your authentic gifts? Are you using them in your work, your life, right now?

If you could have ten other career choices, what would they be, who would you be?

What was one of your "real" moments of success? What really happened before that photo was taken of you holding your trophy?

Joseph Campbell spoke of "following your bliss." What is your bliss? What activity makes you glow, makes the hours slip away, makes you lose track of time?

FIELD WORK

 *Authentic Style*

> *The Greek word for truth,* aletha, *means "not hidden."*

CATHERINE KOBER

As we continue removing layers of psychological and emotional sediment from the dig, take a moment to glance through some old photos. What were you wearing? What does that indicate about who you were at the time? What were you doing? Does that dress spark memories for you? A photo of me at six years old reminds me of a game I used to play as my mother emptied our laundry baskets in preparation for the wash. Sometimes I would throw a sheet over myself and become the Princess Suzette. When my mother took the sheet to be washed, Suzette transformed into an ordinary girl, able to mingle among her people incognito. The villagers did not realize that I was a princess, but *I* knew, and that knowledge transformed my everyday life into something exciting and exotic. Did you do something similar? What has happened to that sense of majesty and importance, that appetite for being dramatic? Why shouldn't you reclaim it? What about a creative excursion to a thrift shop to search for something different, offbeat, or dramatic to wear to your next party? (Ease into it by wearing it around the house first!)

I have a very tall friend who used to try to hide the fact. She always wanted to be petite like me. (I, on the other hand, wanted to be tall!) She would hunch her shoulders; she wore frilly clothes. Finally one day a special friend gave her a long, forest-green tunic that was perfect for a tall, stately woman. She looked stunning in it. So she began changing her wardrobe, wearing long jackets and blazers, long sweaters and skirts, large pins. She came to accept the fact that *she is tall!* Soon she moved differently, not taking small steps but "possessing the air around her" as her dance teacher used to say. She opened her eyes and saw who she really was, and found her authentic style, going *with* who she was instead of against it.

A friend who is a computer software designer came upon her authentic style of speaking in public when she had to address her first sales conference. She led off by trying to tell a joke — she thought all public speaking started out that way. But her joke fell flat, and she found it difficult to recover during the rest of the speech. My friend's experience taught her that being a comedian is not her style, that she should simply present the facts straightforwardly. If humor happened to emerge spontaneously between the lines, that was fine, but she realized she spoke best when she wasn't trying to play to the crowd. She realized she had to be herself.

Site Report

Have you discovered your own authentic style? Did someone help you in your quest? What was the first occasion on which you looked in the mirror and thought, "Now *you* I like! *This* is more like it!"

What colors make you smile? List them, color them in your book. It took me years to realize that gold was a color I should wear. I had ignored the fact that every time I put it on, I shined. What colors do you love?

List the physical activities that make you feel joyous.

In which photos in your scrapbook do you look like the essential you? Make photocopies of these and paste them in your illustrated discovery journal.

Settling

Stealthily and perpetually settling
and loosely lying . . .

ROBERT BRIDGES

O Pioneer

The world is full of partial stories that run parallel to one another, beginning and ending at odd times. They mutually interlace and interfere at points, but we cannot unify them completely in our minds.

WILLIAM JAMES

The first image that usually comes to mind when we think of the word *settler* is that of pioneers — those courageous, adventurous, and intrepid individuals who pushed past their well-padded perimeters of safety and security to seek better lives for themselves and those they loved. "Pioneers may be picturesque figures, but they are often rather lonely ones," Lady Nancy Astor once remarked, speaking about her own pioneering adventures in Africa.

But when we contemplate the word *settling*, loneliness is usually just the opposite of what we think of. That's because the first association with *settling* is staying put with someone, as in *settling down*.

I find it fascinating the way the ancient Chinese belief of yin and yang — the complementary opposite female and male energies inherent in the Universe — runs as a pattern through every aspect of our lives. Career and home, dark and light, cold and heat, sorrow and joy, intimacy and solitude, aggression and passivity, Earth and Heaven. Push past or stay put.

Actually the word *settle* is one full of stories that run parallel to each other; it just depends which adverb is telling the tale. For we can settle *down,* settle *for,* settle *up,* and settle *on,* and at some point in our lives we do all four. There's no way around it, only through; on our deeply personal journey to authenticity we must all become pioneers and make peace with settling before we can move on. "Woman must be the pioneer in this turning inward for strength," Anne Morrow Lindbergh tells us. "In a sense she has always been the pioneer."

Settling Down

All my friends at school grew up and settled down
Then they mortgaged up their lives . . .
They just got married 'cos there's nothing else to do.

MICK JAGGER AND KEITH RICHARDS

It was during the 1600s that the expression *settling down* came to be associated with marriage. Women have always longed to create stable, orderly, serene, comfortable, and safe surroundings in which to raise their children, and since Eden, have preferred not to do it alone. We'd like a little help from our darlings' fathers. Well, you know what they say about mothers inventing out of necessity. One day a brilliant woman thought of stuffing the soft downy feathers of ducks and geese into mattresses made of muslin and hay. (Now you know where the expression "making hay" came from.) "Don't sleep out in the cold and damp," said our woman sweetly. "Come inside and settle down here with me where it's cozy and warm." Thus began a pivotal chapter in connubial history. Soon feather beds and plump pillows became prize possessions in a new bride's dowry, and single men, eager to reap the multiple rewards offered with such bedding, flocked to marital unions.

Speak Now or Forever Hold Your Peace

One way or another, women have been telling each other, "If you want to get married, don't ask questions."

MARY KAY BLAKELY

We believe that there are only two kinds of marriages, good and bad. But really there are three: good, bad, and indifferent — and the last of the three is really the worst kind. Unfortunately, plenty of women who feel uncomfortable admitting it to the world will confide in private that their once-upon-a-time orange-blossom dreams of domestic bliss somehow became a downward spiral of surviving — making it through the day, the week, the year, a life. However, a woman doesn't usually mention this to her husband because she doesn't know how to pinpoint what's missing, and her complaint often merely gets voiced as, "You don't bring me flowers anymore." And even this feeble cry goes unanswered; he doesn't hear her — he's too busy trying to get the ball scores.

And so the unexpressed gets pushed down deeper and deeper — a splinter of silence wedged into the feminine soul that becomes sore, hot, and inflamed, continuing the surreptitious cycle of self-loathing that infects our relationships. And the more we grow to despise ourselves for not clearing the air, for not expressing our needs, for saying "All right," when it clearly isn't, for not pulling the damn splinter out, the more we begin to resent our partners, who become the unwitting, unmerciful, unforgivable reflections of our covert resignation.

Eventually, inevitably, settling *down* becomes settling *for* something less, something you both swore wouldn't happen: becoming your parents. "The word 'marriage' connotes for many the kind of life mother had, so lots of couples end up with an arrangement neither really wants," the Canadian writer Merle Shain observes in her luminous meditation on loving, *Some Men Are More Perfect Than Others*: "It is not possible to be the kind of wives our mothers were because the world is different and so, therefore, are our needs. Most of us are better educated than our mothers were and abilities that are not used clamor to be used, festering when they are not."

Furthermore, she points out, "There isn't any single formula for marriage which all couples should find right, and attempting to run your life by your parents' standards or your neighbors' is bound to run aground. Marriages should be as diverse as the people in them are, which means some will be of one kind, and some totally different still. And those who don't want to love, honor and obey, should be able to promise each other anything they choose, without having to ask anyone what they think of that, particularly themselves."

Two for the Road

I don't think marriages break up because of what you do to each other. They break up because of what you must become in order to stay in them.

CAROL MATTHAU

What kind of people just sit in a restaurant and don't even try to talk to each other?" Albert Finney asks Audrey Hepburn in the movie *Two for the Road.*

"Married people," she responds brightly. But this is just as their romance is beginning and hasn't been worn away yet by years of neglect, assumptions, expectations, disappointment, the loneliness of living with someone who is no more interested in your day than you are in his, the tedium of so much familiarity that you no longer have a clue as to who you're living with. There is no visibility at point-blank range. Eventually, twelve years into their movie marriage, Finney and Hepburn become that couple sitting in a restaurant without a word of conversation to share, having grown into "the intimacy of estrangement that exists between married couples who have nothing left in common but their incompatibility," as Nadine Gordimer so chillingly describes the desert of the heart — when benign neglect turns a good marriage into an indifferent one.

More Married
Than Happy

We marry for all the wrong reasons, and often we marry the wrong person as well. . . . We marry to grow up, to escape our parents and to inherit our share of the world, not knowing who we are and who we will become.

MERLE SHAIN

A poet friend of mine believes that all marriages are built on varying degrees of dependence and addiction, which I translate as *habit* and *need*. But the ties that bind two people together can be made of silk elastic or forged steel.

I once asked a new acquaintance, a man married for over twenty-five years, if he was happily married. Jack looked at me with astonishment.

"I suppose," he said, as if confused by the question. "As happy as anyone can be and still be married. My wife is a good woman and we have a life — you know, friends, summers at the lake, family vacations. We agree completely about the kids," his voice trailed off. As he sheepishly shrugged his shoulders with a shy smile, I wanted to reach over and feel for a pulse. "How long have you felt this way?" I asked, morbidly curious, as only a woman who had just ended a long marriage can be.

"I don't know, it's been so long now I can't remember. Maybe always." He began to laugh uncomfortably. "But don't get me wrong . . ."

I didn't get him wrong. I knew exactly what he was saying because of all he didn't say, couldn't say, wouldn't say. And while I felt sorry for him, I felt even sorrier for his wife. For many years I had been a settler and then a survivor in a virtual no-man's-land — the long-standing domestic arrangement — a barren place I suspected his wife now inhabited. As Dorothy Gilman pointed out, for a woman, "one of the more devastating kinds of loneliness . . . [was] being in close contact with someone to whom she was a nonperson, and who thereby rendered her invisible and of no consequence."

A year after our friendship began, Jack called and asked if we could get together for a drink. "I've fallen in love and I don't know what to do," he confessed, as if he were admitting the discovery of a terminal illness. "I can't leave and I can't stay. Every time I get ready to tell my wife, I walk around the house and see the family pictures, my books. I hear her in the kitchen the way I've heard her in the kitchen half my life and I think, 'What has this woman done to deserve my leaving her after all these years?' But there isn't a night while we're lying next to each other in the dark that I don't wish I were asleep in Anne's arms instead. Still, I can't do it — make the move. Not just yet. So I snap at my wife about anything and everything to push her away from me, make her hate me. If she hates me, it would be easier.

"Then I don't call Anne for days. I don't call because I can't bring myself to tell her that I can't leave, or that it's over between us, because I know it's not. It won't be over between us until our last breath. But I have to do something to regain control, so I push her away. Then, when I see her smile again, I think, 'How can I walk away from the love of my life? I'm fifty-two years old. How can I turn my back on my last shot at happiness?' I can't, so I ask Anne to give me a little more time, as she has before. But now she says there is no more time. She wants to get on with her life with or without me."

The level of panic and pain in Jack's voice caught me off guard. I am always so surprised to find a man courageous enough to be engaged in the full monty of emotion, so used am I to observing them live their lives and ours in nanosecond brain waves. He was deeply in love with this woman and deeply conflicted. Here was a man who wanted to do the right thing. I knew the road ahead for all of them was going to be rocky, at least for a little while. "Sometimes I wish they'd both just leave me. I'm going insane," he said.

I believed him. I also knew, from his breathless angst and red-rimmed eyes, that he'd probably never felt so alive before and never felt so frightened. It was clear to me that he would leave, sooner or later. The sooner, the kinder.

"Well, if you can't leave for yourself, leave for your wife," I told him.

"What do you mean? She'll be devastated."

"Yes. And she'll be furious. But there's a strong possibility that she'll also be secretly relieved. Grateful that her long captivity is over. A woman's husband cannot be unhappy for so long that he can't even remember when his indifference to her began, without her being acutely miserable as well. There's nothing lonelier than being the lesser partner in a loveless merger. I wouldn't be surprised if, when she comes up for air between sobs, she doesn't say, 'Thank you, God. The bastard.' "

"Whose friend are you?"

"Yours. I know you're in love with Anne. It sounds as if you're soul mates. I also know you're a man of integrity, Jack. But your children are grown and leading their own lives. We work out our karma through our choices. Isn't it possible that the truly moral choice, the courageous choice, the good choice, is to leave? If we want to be happy, I don't think life asks us to choose between doing what's right and what's wrong. I believe we're always asked to choose between loving and learning. Do you care about your wife at all?"

Jack bristled. "Of course I do."

"Then be generous. Find the courage to leave not just for yourself but for her. She deserves a man who loves her, who wants to hold her in the middle of the night. She deserves to be as happy as you want to be. You left years ago for whatever reason. All you're doing now is shutting the door behind you." And shutting the door to unhappiness is the crucial step we must take before opening the next door to joy.

Seeing Is Believing

There is a stage with people we love when we are no longer separate from them, but so close in sympathy that we live through them as directly as through ourselves. . . . We push back our hair because theirs is in their eyes.

NAN FAIRBROTHER

Since women view themselves through the prism of their love relationships, it's crucial that we take a closer look at the reflector we hold up to our eyes every day.

Please fill in the blank with the first word that comes immediately to mind.

_____ love affair.

Tragic love affair? *Doomed* love affair? *Disastrous* love affair?

Did I hear anyone say *happy* love affair? Of course not. That's because we don't believe there is such a thing as a happy love affair. Oh, there are moments of happiness, moments we all live for, and moments we'd mortgage our souls for, but you know as well as I do that most of those heart-to-hearts with your best

157

friend are about how badly he's treating you and the reasons you put up with it — punctuated by exclamations like, "You're not going to believe this!"

If we can't be happy when we're in love, what do we expect from marriage? A woman in Ellen Glasgow's 1911 novel *The Miller of Old Church* wryly observes that marriage is mostly putting up with things when it isn't make-believe. Let's face it, most women today — especially those who consider themselves happily married — would agree with her.

I wouldn't want to give you the impression that I don't believe in marriage. I do! I believe in the curative powers of marriage the way Joyce Johnson believes in "the curative powers of love, as the English believe in tea and the Catholics believe in the Miracle of Lourdes."

To love, honor, and cherish another person? To weave together your dreams? To promise to be there through all the changes of your life? Can there be anything better than waking up with a smile and a snuggle next to the person you want to grow old with? Knowing "the deep, deep peace of the double bed after the hurly-burly of the chaise longue," as the Victorian English actress Mrs. Patrick Campbell so perfectly described wedded bliss. The sweet days of marriage (and they can last for years or forever) are nothing less than Heaven on Earth. The bad ones strip you of the fear of death.

"Many of us settle for something less than love, even in our most intimate relationships," the contemporary spiritual writer and poet Kathleen Norris admits, surely for us all, in her exquisite book *Amazing Grace: A Vocabulary of Faith*. "Most of us know couples who despise each other and yet stay together, living as if in an armed camp."

The truth is, our marriages are only as emotionally healthy, happy, holy, and content as we are. We can divorce a man, but we can't divorce ourselves; we learn the truth about ourselves through our personal relationships.

"A relationship is more of an assignment than a choice. A powerful connection between two people is a potent psychic factor that exists regardless of either person's opinion about the relationship. We can walk away from the assignment, but we cannot walk away from the lessons it presents," Marianne Williamson tells us in *Illuminata: Thoughts, Prayers, Rites of Passage*.

If we do walk away from the lessons, they will only reappear in the next relationship until we recognize what's going on. Remember the woman who brought back to Heaven the spiritual baggage she was supposed to lose this lifetime on Earth? It's known as repeat and return. We marry, we divorce, we marry again. We divorce or we suffer by settling down, or settling for, or staying stuck. But until we learn whichever life lesson we're meant to at the time — self-acceptance, self-determination, self-discipline, self-esteem, self-forgiveness, self-interest, self-knowledge, self-respect, self-sufficiency or self-worth — our lessons will keep coming back to us.

You may find it interesting to note, as I have, that the majority of our life lessons have to do with ourselves before others. What about lessons of intimacy, communication, compassion? You don't hand a copy of Dostoevsky's *Crime and Punishment* to a child just learning to read. How can we convey our soul's most private thoughts, feelings, and truths to others if we don't have the courage to communicate confidentially with our Authentic Selves? The hardest, most heart-wrenching conversations I've ever had have been with myself.

The prism through which we view ourselves every day tends to be our love relationships. "I wonder why love is so often equated with joy when it is everything else as well," the writer Florida Scott-Maxwell reminisced toward the end of her life. "Devastation, balm, obsession, granting and receiving excessive value, and losing it again. It is recognition, often of what you are not but might be. It sears and it heals. It is beyond pity and above law. It can seem like truth."

When another's love for us or its lack becomes our truth, we see ourselves through that person's eyes and through the relationship that exists between us. Because our love relationships are often imperfect, emotionally manipulative, disappointing, sometimes even dishonest delusions, and because we see ourselves reflected in them, we often see ourselves as damaged goods.

If the relationship is lonely and unfulfilling; it must have been something you did or said. If it's been months since he's reached for you; it must be the way you look. No matter how many times you try to engage him, he shuts you out. You sit by the phone and wait for the call that never comes; you call him and immediately interpret the irritation or hesitancy you hear in his voice to mean there's something lacking in you. You cry yourself to sleep or roll over to your side of the bed in the dark and hug your pillow; you pretend nothing's wrong; you fake your pleasure. You begin to shut down, disown, diminish until you disappear. "How much of my true self I camouflage and choke in order to commend myself to him, denying the fullness of me," Sylvia Ashton-Warner wrote in 1943. "How I've toned myself down, diluted myself to maintain his approval."

That's why every woman must at some point in her life become courageous enough to turn away from the prism of her relationships as the reflector of her worth. "Women have served all these centuries as looking glasses possessing the magic and delicious power of reflecting the figure of a man at twice its natural size," Virginia Woolf observed. It's time we found a *mirror, mirror* to do that for ourselves. Married or single, you have to "go cold turkey." Pull away from *his* view of you until you can commit to an exclusive, inclusive relationship with your Authentic Self. The reembodiment process spiritually induces this life-altering, lifesaving choice. Today, pick up a mirror and look in it until you see Spirit's truth reflected back. You are a woman of great style and enormous substance. Did you know that? You are a woman of beauty, intelligence, vision, warmth, power, influence, strength, wit, generosity, compassion, and soul. And if you don't see this, you've been looking for your worth in all the wrong faces, and I don't care who you live with.

A Crime Against Nature

The opposite of love is not hate,
it's indifference. . . .
And the opposite of life is not death,
it's indifference.

ELIE WIESEL

A friend of mine who was so well organized she might have been born color-coding socks and towels, suddenly began having a difficult time getting her house in order. Overnight, it completely disintegrated as dramatically as the fall of the Roman Empire. One day she was on top of everything, the next morning she was engulfed. No matter how many drawers, closets, and shelves she uncluttered, the chaos returned with a vengeance. "It's the weirdest thing," she explained. "It's as if I suddenly have poltergeists coming in every night to undo whatever progress I make."

"Sounds like you need an exorcism," I joked.

"You know, you could be right," she said. "I'm so desperate, I'll try anything." And so she consulted a house doctor, an English psy-

163

chic who performed energy readings on houses to see if there were any metaphysical blockages. Remember the Gnostic axiom: "As within, so without."

We were both mystified when the psychic asked if the house had a history of violence; the readings she picked up were "very dark," she said. Had there been any murders, rapes, or beatings? She told my friend that the house was weeping; it was traumatized like a woman after a sexual assault. The psychic told us that the energy of the house had shut down and was not cooperating with my friend because it was grievously wounded. The disarray and clutter were an outward manifestation of the violations that had been committed in it. The spirit of the house was hiding from the "attacker" beneath the clutter and confusion.

Shocked by this analysis, my friend and I challenged the psychic's findings. To begin with, my friend was only the third owner of her house, had lived there for ten years, and knew of no violence that had ever taken place there. The psychic said that she was only reporting the aura reading she'd picked up. Did my friend want a healing ritual for the house or not?

Now, both of us are very open-minded women, but this was a bit far-fetched. I suggested that the next exorcism be performed by Goodwill. But my friend said, "Okay. Since you're here . . . Go ahead . . . Might as well . . . Who knows?"

A month later, my friend discovered her husband had been having an affair. She also learned that he had been bringing his mistress to their home to stay while my friend was away on business trips so that he'd be there to answer the phone if my friend called. It was my friend herself who'd been sexually violated on the ethereal level.

Human nature understands crimes of passion — heat-of-the-moment eruptions of righteous rage when a person catches a loved one breaking the bond between them with a physical indiscretion. In some sovereignties — France and Texas among them — a crime of passion is recognized as a perfectly understandable and reasonable defense to reduce the charge of murder to manslaughter, the killing of another without premeditation.

But indifference gets away with murder every day; soul slaughter that destroys countless lives at every level — physical, intellectual, emotional, and spiritual holocausts of the heart. For years, my friend had ignored the "problems" in her marriage — namely her misery and her husband's avoidance of conflict through silence. They had lived in an armed camp of a marriage except in social situations, where both could manage to be pleasant to each other for a few hours (one of the reasons why they had a very active social life). But eventually their private silence drove a wedge of indifference between them — so much so that he no longer even thought of his wife as a person. It never occurred to him that he was "violating" her when he invited another woman there. He was just being practical. Indifference breeds animosity.

If it's true that sometimes we marry for the wrong reasons, we convince ourselves to stay for even worse ones. We stay to be kind. We stay for the kids. We stay because we think we can't afford to leave and won't calculate the psychic cost of remaining. We stay because we put loyalty to others above loyalty to our own truth.

We stay because we're genuinely good and decent people. Good people do not walk out on marriages that are congenial enough to get through a dinner party, school conferences, a child's learning disability, a father-in-law's stroke, family holiday gatherings, ski vacations with friends, weekends at the beach and serviceable sex.

We stay because we're afraid to believe in true love. Because we don't believe we'll ever find the love of our lives. And you know what? We're absolutely right if we stay where we're not supposed to be but continue to deny it on every level — spiritual, intellectual, emotional, sexual, and creative. A year before my husband and I ended our marriage, I asked him one night, "Do you believe in soul mates?" "No," he said. "I believe in accommodation." It had taken me seventeen years to get up the courage to ask that question. It would take me another year to believe what I'd heard.

A courageous woman I know walked out on a perfectly congenial marriage of thirty years after undergoing a mastectomy. Her husband was stunned; her grown children and friends were aghast. Her support group wasn't. Time was no longer infinite. Life could not be taken for granted. She refused to become a martyr to other people's measurement of her goodness; she refused to stay in an unfulfilling marriage. Five years later she is cancer-free, remarried and reunited with her soul mate, and designing personal sacred spaces as a landscaper.

Conscious indifference in a marriage — by which I mean partnering on tax forms, greeting cards, and at cocktail parties, while seeking emotional connection, intellectual stimulation, and sexual solace elsewhere — dangerously undermines our sense of integrity, pawns our honor, siphons our creative energy, and buries both partners alive with resentment. It's not the illicit love affair that should seem so shocking; it's the fact that your authentic and unmet needs are so ignored, discounted, and disregarded by both of you that the soul feels compelled to search for something more in secret. This is the crying shame.

Do you remember a movie from the 1970s called *Lovers and Other Strangers*? It was a very funny movie about marriage seen through the eyes of a young couple and both sets of in-laws. My favorite scene is when the son tries to explain to his old-fashioned Italian father why he and his wife are getting a divorce after only a couple of years of being married. "You've got to understand, we feel there must be something more." His father just looks at him and retorts, "We all feel there's something more."

"But then, why don't you leave Mom and go out and get it, Dad?"

"Because there isn't something more!" the father roars back.

I know what both of them are trying to say, because I've been on both ends of that conversation. But on my own journey to authenticity, I swear there truly is Something More waiting for all of us. It's just hidden in all our relationships — the good, the bad, and the downright ugly. Just because you failed at a relationship doesn't mean it was a failure. Not if you learned something new about yourself (and you did, especially if it's vital information about your threshold of pain or your limit of patience). Not if you gleaned authentic glimpses of your Self even in your moments of anguish and acceptance. Not if you discovered what your authentic needs and passionate yearnings are.

Jane Austen believed that happiness in marriage is entirely a matter of chance. Perhaps. But I know it always involves choice. Little choices and whoppers. Every day you're together or apart. "Love cannot survive if you just give it scraps of yourself, scraps of your time, scraps of your thoughts," Mary O'Hara reminds us.

And you can't do it alone. It takes two people to keep love alive and well in a marriage, two to let it fail to thrive, and two to invite resignation to take room and board with them. It is only after the two allow these lapses to take place that room is made for a third-party intrusion.

Can This Marriage Be Saved?

What is missing in him is probably necessary for what is missing in you. Let us not to the marriage of true impediments admit minds.

JEAN KERR

Imagine this: imagine that you had been chosen by God to be the receptacle of grace. Imagine God had whispered . . . mysteries to you not in words but in flashes of splendor. Imagine that as God was with you a wondrous current had flown into you, gripping your heart tight and washing your spirit with tidal waves of love; imagine hearing the words "I am Yours and I love you." In this passage from their book *Judaic Mysticism*, Dr. Avram Davis and Manuela Dunn Mascetti seek to evoke the most intimate, mysterious, glorious, and unconditional love affair in the Universe: that between God and us.

Imagine feeling that way about your marriage. Imagine feeling that way about yourself. Imagine feeling that way about another person. You're meant to.

And if you can't, will you ask yourself, "Why not?"

"When we bury feelings, we also bury ourselves," Nathaniel Branden tells us in *The Psychology of Self-Esteem*. "It means we exist in a state of alienation. We rarely know it, but we are lonely for ourselves."

You know I'm not talking about bad patches. You know I'm not talking about a rough year or two. I'm talking about having awarded someone else sole custody of your happiness years ago without even asking for visitation rights.

"How complicated life can get when morality, sexuality, reputation, commitment, pleasure, pain, good, and bad are all inexorably mixed together!" Alexandra Stoddard reminds us in her thought-provoking book *Making Choices: The Joy of a Courageous Life*.

"Marriage counselors encourage people to work harder at the relationship," she writes. "Sex therapists suggest certain strategies, tips, tricks, and secrets. A Lawyer is professionally obligated to try to get the married couple back together. There are certainly many instances in which relationships can be turned around through professional help. But when someone isn't right for you, for either basic or exceedingly complex and mysterious reasons, you can't force a reconciliation. The marriage could have deteriorated to such an extent that parting may be the only solution. If a couple chooses to stay together to share the mortgage payments, the food bill, the car — that's their choice but marriages of convenience will never bring joy. The couple becomes locked into a dreary life of not-so-quiet desperation. When you consider that you only have so much time to experience the joy that can be shared by two people who deeply love and respect each other, you must choose wisely, even if it means making the decision to divorce."

This is awfully difficult to write, but I do believe with all my heart that marital indifference is so insidious, abusive, and destructive to ourselves, our partners, our children (no matter what their age), and to Life itself that it seems to be nothing less than a crime against love, because it brutalizes and bludgeons our better natures. Marital indifference is a silent scream of despair that cries out for the release, forgiveness, restitution, and absolution of the confessional — not the church's, but the soul's. Truth is the only thing that stands between broken hearts and Wholeness. And if

171

the despair that begins as a daily disquiet between two people is ignored in private, it will grow in strength and intensity until it becomes a roar of rage that will not be denied until despair gives outward, palpable expression to its grief: alcoholism, accidents, affairs, or heart attacks. When the silence becomes deafening and it's all over but the shouting, it should be all over.

Ask Spirit for grace, guidance, clarity, and peace. If you have and hold not, ask for help to hang on or let go. Ask for courage. Ask, *Can this marriage be saved?* Ask your heart if you should stay or leave. Ask to be shown how to leave with honor, integrity, and love. If you are meant to leave, you will be shown the path. If you are meant to stay, you'll not want to stray. "But mayn't desertion be a brave thing? A fine thing?" Susan Glaspell asked in her novel *The Visioning*, written in 1911. "To desert a thing we've gone beyond — to have the courage to desert it and walk right off from the dead thing to the live thing?"

Imagine You Don't Know Me

Some women wait for something
to change and nothing
does change
so they change
themselves.

AUDRE LORDE

For many years the energy between Judy and Dan gave credibility to the old adage that opposites attract. They couldn't have been more different: Judy, with her flaming red hair and dimples, was a fun-loving, can-do, adventure-seeking kind of woman. A dynamo. Openhearted, generous, and enthusiastic, it was she who planned the family's travel itineraries, making reservations up to a year ahead of time for their annual summer vacations; and it was she who organized the holiday bazaar and regularly rounded up their friends for an evening of theater and dinner in the city. Dan was solid: steady, reliable, hardworking, unflappable. In fact, the only bend in his otherwise straight-arrow demeanor was his dark wavy hair. Judy was yin; he was yang, and for many good years their marriage worked, precisely because Dan provided the rock-solid center of gravity that allowed Judy to circle joyously through her wide orbit of interests.

Eventually, the kids aged away from their claim to most of her time, creative energy, and emotion. Judy saw this as the opportunity to answer her inner directives pulling her toward the search for Something More. But at the same time, Dan, strands of gray beginning to fleck his hair, was coming home more and more tired every night, and was beginning to react with irritation to Judy's latest "Wouldn't this be fun?" schemes and self-improvement projects. It was impossible to ignore how out of sync they were becoming. Their intimate moments diminished; their regular and much-enjoyed lovemaking dwindled until it virtually disappeared, and their conversations rarely included any topic other than the family, finances, and the perfunctory "How was your day?"

Dan asked Judy to stop making plans for them on weekday nights and to try to keep more of their weekends free so that he could just stay home. But Judy had been home all week. Soon their vacations went from doing something active together, like biking through Napa Valley, to Dan's settling into a beach chair for a week with a good mystery. Judy's dissatisfaction began to settle into detachment, an attitude that Dan's behavior mirrored. One person's course of contentment became the other's source of conflict. In order to divert her restless energy into something positive, Judy signed up for adult education classes offered at the local high school. She learned how to reupholster her own furniture, grow orchids, and weave baskets. Then Thai cuisine called to her.

It was at the cooking class that she became reacquainted with Steve, who had been her son's first soccer coach. She'd never known him well, but she had heard that he'd lost his wife to breast cancer. As they struck up a conversation on their way to the parking lot after their first class, Steve explained to Judy that when he'd started cooking for his family, he'd found it a comforting outlet for all that had been weighing on him. With only one child still at home, he enjoyed indulging this and other new interests by taking the odd mid-week class. He liked to keep busy, he said, and enjoyed the stimulation of being exposed to new ideas and concepts. Judy and Steve were kindred spirits.

Before long, Steve and Judy found themselves conversing about a variety of subjects over what became their regular after-class cup of coffee at a diner. In addition to cooking, they discovered many shared interests over the next few months: bridge, a passion for used-bookstore browsing, cross-country skiing, bird-watching. Both, they discovered, had agreed to serve during the upcoming fall on a committee regarding a local school referendum. And so whenever Dan was either too tired or just not interested in going for a Sunday morning bike ride, Judy would call her new best friend Steve, just as he would call her if a fourth were needed for his weekly bridge game. Dan never seemed to mind; in fact, he didn't even seem to notice. It didn't take long for Steve's and Judy's friendship to deepen into sexual intimacy; their combined craving for companionship, coupled with their peas-in-a-pod temperamental blending, made becoming lovers as natural as it was inevitable.

But both Judy and Steve had the good judgment to stop their affair almost as soon as it started, before their commitment to it irretrievably overwhelmed their good sense and discretion. Steve was still grieving for the wife he had loved deeply; his heart wasn't ready to move on just yet. And Judy wasn't ready either — ready, that is, to throw in the towel on her marriage.

Even though she enjoyed her time with Steve, Judy had never stopped loving her husband. She cherished their shared history and their mutual love for their children. She'd never, ever expected to find herself in the arms of another man. Frequently to herself and in her prayers she would say, "If only Dan would meet me halfway, we could get back on track." One day she came to the realization that she'd transferred her craving for Something More in her marriage to another man. She realized that if she wanted to stay married, she'd have to share this quest for fulfillment with Dan, not just with Spirit and her best friend.

As Nadine Gordimer observes, "It is not the conscious changes in their lives by men and women — a new job, a new town, a divorce — which really shape them, like the chapter headings in a biography, but a long, slow mutation of emotion, hidden, all-penetrative; something by which they may be so taken up that the practical outward changes of their lives in the world . . . pass almost unnoticed by themselves. . . . This gives a shifting quality to the whole surface of life; decisions made with reason and the tongue may never be made valid by the heart."

Judy's heart still belonged to her marriage. She didn't want to walk away from it. She wanted it to expand and change and grow and *last*.

"We can't live with this loneliness anymore," she quietly told Dan as they closed their bedroom door one night. "I can't live this way." And then she proceeded to explain everything to him — well, not *everything*, but enough for him to know that she was at an emotional turning point and that their marriage was at a crossroads. "I can't save our marriage by myself," Judy told him. "We have to be in this together."

Dan was stunned by Judy's admissions. His exhaustion from years of work-induced stress had blinded him to his neglect of their relationship. To keep her and their marriage, he was going to have to start doing things again with Judy — beginning with a series of visits to a marriage counselor. The counselor recommended that Dan and Judy start by trying to reexperience each other — not as they once were, but as they were now. "People change and forget to tell each other," Lillian Hellman observed. Judy needed Dan to know the woman she had become; she wanted him to fall in love with her Authentic Self.

The Colombian writer Gabriel García Márquez once remarked about his thirty-year relationship with his wife, Mercedes, that at one point he realized he knew her so well, he didn't have the slightest idea who she really was. Most husbands don't. But García Márquez's bemused fascination with and appreciation for the mystery in the woman who shares his life, represent the other side of marital indifference; it's what keeps couples together. There is mystery in the mundane. We just have to be willing to look at it and show the men in our lives how to do it, too.

In order to get to know one another again, Judy and Dan began dating once a week. Their regular rendezvous became known as Imagine

You Don't Know Me night. Each week they would sit across the dinner table from one another, in a restaurant or location that was new to both of them, and begin to talk. They were forbidden to discuss their children, their parents, their work, or their finances. Instead, they talked about their dreams, their inner life, their wounds, their hopes and wishes — the shape and texture they wanted the remainder of their lives *together* to be. They learned a lot and found they enjoyed the learning process. Even more important, they found they truly loved the subject matter — each other. Slowly but surely, they saved their marriage and strengthened their bonds. They found their way not back, but toward each other and a future. They found themselves deeply in love with each other for a second time.

"It takes a long time to be really married. One marries many times at many levels within a marriage," the actress Ruby Dee observed. "If you have more marriages than you have divorces within the marriage, you're lucky and you stick it out."

My parents, who were married for forty-five years, had two little inside jokes, which, I now realize, weren't jokes at all but gems of connubial wisdom. Every wedding anniversary, they'd refer to "picking up each other's option" for another year. "Well, I'm going to pick up your father's option," my mother would say. Sometimes she would add, "Next year's bound to be better" or "It was a pretty good year."

And Dad had his January/July code. "Look, kid," he'd say to my mother, "if we can make it to January, we can make it to July." Growing up, I didn't have the slightest idea what either of them was talking about. But the kids in my family did know that the first hour after Daddy came home from work was "their" time together to sit, talk, and reconnect over a drink. Dad and Mom were not to be interrupted unless it was a matter of life or death. "Their" time together was inviolate and maybe, just maybe, they stayed together because it was.

In *To My Daughters, With Love*, Pearl Buck wrote, "Nothing in life is as good as the marriage of true minds between man and woman. As good? It is life itself." And even though her parents are divorced, I will tell my daughter the same thing.

There Are Only
Two Stories Worth Telling

*What is passion? Passion is surely the
becoming of a person.*

JOHN BOORMAN

*I have yet to meet a person who
has not felt betrayed.*

CAROLINE MYSS

The American novelist Willa Cather insisted that there are only two human stories, "and they go on repeating themselves as fiercely as if they had never happened before." Of course she was right, which is why every storyteller since the first campfire keeps telling them over and over again. From *Genesis* to *Pulp Fiction*, the two stories that keep our souls enthralled are passion and betrayal.

"In any triangle, who is the betrayer, who is the unseen rival, and who is the humiliated love?" asks Erica Jong. "Oneself, oneself, and

181

no one but oneself."

I cannot write of passion without bearing witness to the supporting role that betrayal plays in our search for authenticity. Binding betrayal's wounds has taught me as much, if not more, about my soul's inviolate duty to seek and seize happiness whenever and wherever it may be found, as has the profound peace I've known in passion's embrace.

Passion is embodied prayer.

Betrayal is embodied despair.

Passion is holy — a profound mystery that transforms through awakening and rapture.

Betrayal is human — a profane enigma that transforms through anger and rage.

Passion and betrayal are illumination and darkness.

Passion is driven by desire; the desire that your soul's longing for Something More is Spirit-directed.

Betrayal is fueled by fear, the fear that the emptiness that engulfs the world is all there is, all you deserve.

Passion and betrayal are the yin and yang of yearning. Inseparable. Undeniable. The divine paradox of their unseen presence hovers over every aspect of our daily round, colors every choice, embraces every challenge.

Passion is what might be. Betrayal is what might have been.

Passion is Paradise found. Betrayal is expulsion from Eden.

We cannot live without one. We cannot love without the other.

Usually we think of passion only as the explosive energy behind the sexual obsession between two people. White-hot. Combustible. A flash fire. A compulsion that cannot be resisted, controlled, or contained within the confines of convention (which is everyone else's opinion about your life). We think of passion as a synonym for the sinful, the clandestine, the forbidden.

But passion is not a sin. It's our saving grace. Dorothy L. Sayers, the deeply spiritual English writer, tells us, "The only sin passion can commit is to be joyless."

Who among us is finally ready to sin no more? As God is my witness, I am.

What is passion, then? How about a lighted match to the dry tinder of our hearts, meant to burn away the underbrush of self-deceit, the decaying deadwood of what's meant to become our immediate past when it's time for us to continue the search for Something More?

The medical-intuitive (a spiritual diagnostician) Caroline Myss, a pioneer in the field of energy medicine and human consciousness, tells us that when we know we are supposed to move on or out of a situation that is stunting our soul growth and we consciously refuse to do so because the uncharted terror of choice and change scares us, a celestial clock starts ticking. "If you're getting directions, 'Move on with your life, let go of something,' then do it. Have the courage to do it. This is the way it is. When you get guidance to let go of something, it's sort of like a time warning that says, 'You have ten days left. After that, your angel's going to do it.' So, the desire to hold on is not going to stop the process of change. . . . You know that that's true."

I'll never forget the moment I heard her tell me that while listening to her audiotape *Spiritual Madness: The Necessity of Meeting God in Darkness.*

Isn't that interesting? I thought . . . I wonder if she's right. Ten days later, my life was lying in smithereens around my ankles and I was shaking my head, terrified, stunned, and incredulous in the presence of passion and betrayal. When you hear, see, read, or intuit your authentic truth, pay attention. You can run, but you cannot hide.

A Lover Both Ancient and New

Experience teaches us in a millennium
what passion teaches us in an hour.

RALPH IRON

Tomorrow morning, give me one hour, and you will never be afraid of your passion again. Go to bed early. Set your subconscious for four o'clock in the darkness, the hour of the soul. Make yourself a pot of coffee or tea and take it to where you can sit alone — outside if you can, even if it's bundled up on your front stoop.

Now sit silently in the shadows as the Earth is seduced into being, coaxed into becoming, and slowly roused from her slumber by a lover at once ancient and new. Succumb to passion's embrace at a safe distance.

Watch the sun rise.

"Passion is what the sun feels for the earth," Ella Wheeler Wilcox, a nineteenth-century poet, tells us. "When harvests ripen into golden birth." Passion is what Spirit feels for you.

This probably isn't your first image of passion, is it? But it's much closer to the essence of passion than any clandestine bodice-ripping cliché. We must learn to recast passion's image to reflect our authenticity, not the world's lack of imagination.

The Soul's Duty

It is the soul's duty to be loyal to its own desires. It must abandon itself to its master passion.

REBECCA WEST

Most of us long to be swept away, to live passionate lives — but could we please do so at a safe distance and in small doses? That's why we're drawn to juicy novels, three-hanky movies, soap operas, celebrity love affairs and personality journalism that magnifies and glorifies lives larger than our own. Passion, after all — according to the tabloids — means the abandonment of reason in the reckless pursuit of pleasure: rushing off with an Argentine polo-playing paramour instead of picking up the afternoon car pool.

Passion is wild, chaotic, unpredictable. Permissive. Excessive. Over the top. Indulgent. Out of control. Women who get swept away by passion can't help but exult in their emotions, revel in their desires, run naked with wolves, make out in the mail room, howl at the moon, act out their X-rated fishnet-stocking fantasies, brandish knives, boil pet rabbits for revenge. Passionate women get burned at the stake, don't they? At the very least, they lose their children. Think of Anna Dunlap in *The Good Mother*.

Who wouldn't be afraid of this?

But passion's nature is most often cloaked in the deep, subtle, quiet, and committed: nursing a baby, planting a rose garden, preparing a special meal, caring for a loved one who is ill, remembering a friend's birthday, persevering in a dream. Passion is the muse of authenticity. She's the primordial, pulsating energy that infuses all of life, the numinous presence made known with every beat of our hearts.

If our moments of authentic passion have an indelible signature, it is this: they transcend all forgetting. The image, the gesture, the embrace, the exchange, the risk, the reach, the smile, the kiss, the power, the gift, the thoughtfulness — every passionate impulse lives with and resonates through us forever.

Think for a moment about romantic, passionate images from the movies. Some of my favorites are these: An elderly woman visiting her younger soul mate Christopher Reeve for a final good-bye in this life in *Somewhere in Time*. Kristin Scott-Thomas in *The*

English Patient admonishing Ralph Fiennes for behaving badly because he's in love with her and doesn't want to be. Daniel Day-Lewis burying his head in Michelle Pfeiffer's lap and caressing her leg through her silk gown until he's kissing her foot in *The Age of Innocence*. Kate Winslett hurling herself out of a lifeboat to sink or swim with Leonardo DiCaprio in *Titanic*. Bergman and Bogart in *Casablanca*. Your turn. What moments of passion were so romantic, exhilarating, and moving that you would have traded places with the heroine in a heartbeat?

How about Meryl Streep in *The Bridges of Madison County*?

Not me. And I hope not you. Self-sacrifice is not pretty and it is not noble. But self-sacrifice is one of a woman's seven deadly sins (along with self-abuse, self-loathing, self-deception, self-pity, self-serving, and self-immolation).

Ellen Glasgow explained why in 1911: "She had continued to sacrifice her inclinations in a manner which had rendered unendurable the lives of those around her. Her parents had succumbed to it; her husband had died of it; her children had resigned themselves to it or rebelled against it according to the quality of their moral fiber. All her life she had labored to make people happy, and the result of this exalted determination was a cowed and resentful family."

Self-Immolation

*The fiery moments of a passionate experience
are moments of wholeness and totality.*

ANAÏS NIN

Few contemporary stories have broken women's
hearts the way the movie *The Bridges of Madison
County*, based on Robert James Waller's novel,
did several years ago. And why? Because we saw
our own sorry selves in Francesca, the Iowa
farmwife whose destiny was a head-on collision
between desire and duty.

The story of the ill-fated love affair between
Francesca Johnson and Robert Kincaid is a
perfect example — not of passion, but of the
habitual betrayal of our authenticity that leaves
us lonely, vulnerable, and aching for anything
other than a self-imposed sentence of life im-
prisonment, even if it's the diversion of a
stranger driving a pickup truck.

After the death of their mother, the grown
children of Richard and Francesca Johnson return to the family farm in Madison County,
Iowa. She has left instructions for her burial

189

along with letters and journals that tell the story of a secret love affair she had while married to their father. As Francesca's children, Michael and Carolyn, sort through the memories of their mother's great love with a man named Robert Kincaid who had come to photograph the area's lovely covered bridges for *National Geographic* a quarter of a century before, the children come face-to-face with a woman they never knew. There are smiling pictures of her taken at the bridge; there are cameras and photographic equipment; there is her will that asks that she be cremated and her ashes thrown over Roseman Bridge — the bridge that Robert was trying to find on that hot late afternoon when he stopped at the family farmhouse to ask directions, and their mother's life changed.

How many of us know or knew the women our mothers are or were? How many of our children know who we are? How many of our children will find shards of our passionate remorse in the same way that Francesca's children did? Wouldn't a more loving legacy be for them to find shards of our passionate rejoicing in the life we cherished so much that we lived it and they knew it?

In the story, Francesca, the Italian-born war bride of the decent, steady, and "good" Richard, is given what every woman with a family dreams of — four days on her own while her husband and kids attend a state fair. While they are gone, a chance meeting with the handsome Robert awakens long-dormant desires, and she falls in love. But with whom? Is it only with Robert Kincaid? I don't think so. "I was acting like another woman, yet I was more myself than ever before," she explains to her children. Francesca Johnson falls in love with her Authentic Self.

Four idyllic days pass, and Robert and Francesca realize that they are soul mates. He asks her to come away with him. She wants to, and even attempts to pack to leave. But she has her duty, her obligation to her husband and family. She can't.

More important, she tells Robert, "The moment we leave, everything will change. . . . We are the choices we have made. . . . When a woman makes a choice to marry and have children, in a way her life begins and in another way it stops. . . .

You just stop and stay steady so that your children can move on. Even as they grow up and leave, taking your life of details with them."

With this bittersweet stoicism, Francesca gives up Robert and spends the rest of her life mourning him and her lost Self. For me, one of the movie's most heart-wrenching scenes happens after she's seen Robert for the last time. She comes back into her kitchen loaded with groceries and rushes into a little pantry, where she begins to sob. Is she crying because she has thrown happiness away with both hands? Is

191

she crying because, having really lived for four days, she knows she's going to be reentombed? Or is she crying out of rage, because she's denying her truth? I think she's crying for all these reasons. And so was every woman watching. We watched in horror as Francesca betrayed herself; we were grief-stricken because we know we would do the same. Hell, we've done it. In the end, Francesca's last wish for her children is that they do for themselves what she could not: find the courage to "do what you have to do to be happy in this life."

Almost every woman I know is secretly terrified that this will be the truth she needs to convey to her own children before she dies. Not because she's done it herself, but because if there is reincarnation she knows she's going to have to come back and learn this truth all over again. Repeat and return.

Passion is part of Real Life's package — we were created by Love, for love, to love. If we're unsure of our passions we must continue excavating until we rediscover them, for if we don't give outward expression to our passions in little ways every day, we will eventually experience self-immolation — the spontaneous combustion of our souls.

This is hard to remember when we get caught up in what Francesca calls our life of details — runny noses to wipe, dogs to walk, FedEx pickup deadlines to meet, Brownie snacks to prepare, sales conferences to attend, orthodontist appointments to make, summer-camp forms to fill out, trains to catch, bills to pay, supper to put on the table. Where is there room for passion? Take another look. Everywhere.

If we are to lead deep, rich, fulfilling lives that are anchored in what's important, what's precious, what's real, so that our souls can soar, passion must fuel our flight. You may not believe me, but we are meant to wake up every morning exhilarated, with a smile on our face. We're supposed to go to bed at night looking up and saying, "Thank you, thank you, thank you for the gift of this incredible day," whether we are alone or not.

What I have only come to realize is that asking to be delivered to my passion is the only thing worth praying for. It is so important for me that I have created a wonderful prompt to remind me every day of my need for Something More. At the top of my white bedroom walls I have stenciled in gold letters what passion means to me: *True passion is intoxicating and invigorating, soothing and sensuous, magical and mystical. I just thought you should know what you're in for.*

[I wish I could claim to be the cleverest woman in the world, but I discovered and adapted this fabulous definition of passion found on the back of a Tazo tea bag called "Passion." Just goes to show you that inspiration's everywhere we look if we just keep awake!]

Whether we are comfortable with this truth or not, we were conceived in passion, born in passion, and will die in passion. The search for Something More is simply the soul's plea to live passionately. "Only connect!" E. M. Forster implores us. "Only connect the prose and the passion, and both will be exalted, and human love will be seen at its heights. . . . Live in fragments no longer."

Time Out

When action grows unprofitable, gather information;
when information grows unprofitable, sleep.

URSULA K. LE GUIN

During the 1800s the expression *settling down* took on a new association — setting time apart for the quieting of one's nerves, centering, and becoming calm. Usually this instruction was given by mothers to their children. *All right, children, it's time to settle down now.*

Woman, listen to thyself.

Writers like to believe that the sage advice

Ernest Hemingway left to all of us was, "Write the truest sentence you can," which is difficult enough, words being the feral beasts they are. But he didn't. Hemingway said that if you're going to bother writing at all, then by God, "Write the truest sentence you know." There's a significant difference between writing what you *can* and writing what you *know*. Just as there's a significant difference between doing what you can to make it through the day and doing what you *know* you've got to do to be able to wake up the next morning and not feel the way you did yesterday.

It's called sleep. Before we go any further, you need time out for a little R&R&R — *Rest, Regrouping, and a Reality check*. You need a little self-nurturing, a little authorized settling down. I'm serious. Every woman I know, without exception, is exhausted to the point of no return (as in "no return" to the marriage, to the job, to the kids). We're worn to a raveling. We're unsteady in our gait, asleep at the switch, shouldn't be driving cars, sending E-mails, or having telephone conversations. There's no doubt in my mind that sleep deprivation is the hidden number one cause of arguments and cybersex. I'm convinced that countless good relationships end and bad ones begin because of chronic fatigue. Never make a major decision until after you've taken a nap.

When I excavated my pattern of choice making, I was dumbfounded to discover that the one constant in the wrong ones I made was that I made them when I was physically and emotionally exhausted and couldn't think clearly. Good choices were made when I was fully awake and engaged and the synapses were connecting. And the bad choices? I was in a coma, worn down by crisis, commotion, confusion, and chaos.

How do you feel right now? Tired? Overwhelmed? Then close this book and close your eyes. Even fifteen minutes in a chair, or with your head down at your desk or table (the way we did when we were little, remember?). Try to go to bed early tonight. Take a nap on Sunday (maybe it will be raining). Don't worry. I'll be waiting for you. So will the rest of your life. So settle down!

Settling For

It's a funny thing about life. If you refuse to settle for anything less than the best, that's what it will give you.

W. SOMERSET MAUGHAM

We do not lose ourselves all at once, the novelist

Amy Tan reminds us. We lose ourselves day by day, washing away our pain "the same way carvings on stone are worn down by water," until one day, settling down "stealthily and loosely lying" becomes resignation — settling for something else instead of pursuing Something More. We settle for a loveless marriage, a dead-end job, a diagnosis that predicts we won't get well, or someone else's opinion of our gifts, dreams, and what should make us happy. We settle for a passive, rather than a passionate, life.

If there's one woman one could never describe as passive, it's Gloria Steinem. She has written movingly of the search for Something More in her book *Revolution from Within: A Book of Self-Esteem*, a guerrilla guide to personal redemption. Because her parents divorced when she was ten and her mother suffered from a debilitating depression, the legendary editor of *MS* magazine assumed the role of family caregiver at an early age. Decades later, as a leader of the feminist movement, she organized, traveled, lectured, campaigned, and successfully raised money for causes, but she didn't know how to take care of herself — emotionally, psychologically, physically — even though she had spent her life taking care of others. A woman does not have to be married and/or a mother to be a martyr.

There are so many insidious ways that we betray ourselves. Self-sacrifice is one of the more popular ones for women because it's condoned by society. What a good woman you are, offering yourself up on the altar of self-abuse. Do we get extra points for suffering gratuitously? How about with a smile? I don't think so. Did you know that the Koran, the sacred book of Islam, and the Jewish Talmud teach that we will be called to account for every permissible pleasure life has offered us and that we have refused to enjoy while on Earth? I don't know about you, but I shudder to *think* about that reckoning.

Here's another frightening thought. What if, for every pleasure we pass up, we're assigned a miserable moment to endure? (And in this life, sweetheart.) That should make us think twice before just saying "no"!

"Is devotion to others a cover for the hungers and the needs of the self, of which one is ashamed?" Anaïs Nin asks. "I was always ashamed to take. So I gave. It was not a virtue. It was a disguise."

Gloria Steinem's cautionary tale is a universal, archetypal story of the savvy woman's subterfuge — a desperate attempt to hide from self-loathing through reinvention. Like many of us, little Gloria hoped and expected that marriage would complete her, finish her, make her "a whole person." Steinem describes her romantic fantasies as a kind of dressing-room exchange, in which she would "try on the name and life of each person [she] thought she might marry." I know what she means — I began writing the prefix *Mrs.* in front of my name from the time I was ten. She reminds us that in our society "shopping and romance are two of women's few paths to a sense of power and well-being," and that when Mr. Possible asks for our telephone number, we instinctively tap into the mother lode of feminine wiles, traits, or tricks in order to "make [a man] fall in love with us." One of them is the chameleon conquest — becoming whomever we think the man in question wants us to be this week.

It's fascinating how, after years of thinking deeply about the meaning, role, and implications of marriage in our culture, after years of activism and advocacy, and despite the vigor with which she helped to shape, guide, and raise the expectations of millions of women so that they might achieve happier and more complete lives, Gloria Steinem felt so acutely the incompleteness of her own life.

This is very important to process. The search for Something More doesn't ask how much we actually have or haven't. It asks us how much we *feel* we're missing. Money, marital status, fame, admiration, and accomplishment mean nothing if the soul is starving.

To make Steinem's longing even more acute, she was exhausted. Physically, psychically, and emotionally. A tired woman is a sitting target. So when Steinem met a man who had traits she "found magnetic," such as not minding her traveling and crazy schedule (because his was the same), acting like a grown-up (very appealing to a woman over forty), and able to make social arrangements easily (via his staff), she was hooked. "All I had to do was show up, look appropriate, listen, relax at dinners, [and] laugh at his wonderfully told stories. . . . Since I had been helplessly recreating my caretaking patterns left over from childhood [in other relationships], he seemed the perfect answer: someone I *couldn't* take care of."

In hindsight, what big Gloria needed was a personal assistant and regular naps.

Eventually, Steinem succeeded in making the object of her desire fall in love with her phantom self, but as she recalls, "the only problem was that, having got this man to fall in love with an inauthentic me, I had to keep on not being myself."

Her self-loathing intensified, but like all of us when we get deeply invested in a romantic attachment that isn't healthy and wise, she had a "huge stake in justifying what she had done" — that is, in making it work. This required her to overlook the obvious: that her lover appeared indifferent or insensitive to ideas and causes of deep importance to her, that her chosen family of friends wasn't comfortable in his company, and that he really did nothing to extend himself to them, even though he must have known how it would please her. But she continued to hope — as we all do — that somehow he would change. After all, hadn't *she?*

The answer of course is that no, of course he wouldn't change. But more important, thank God, was that neither could she, completely. Steinem could temporarily disguise her Authentic Self and her disgust at denying her true identity, but she couldn't keep up the masquerade forever. Finally she realized that she had betrayed herself by "loving someone for what [she] needed instead of for what he was," and the curse was broken.

She started over from scratch, recovering her real and immutable Authentic Self by beginning to take care of herself. All her adult life she'd lived in an apartment that was little more than "a closet where I changed clothes and dumped papers into cardboard boxes." Gradually she came to the belated awareness that one's home was "a symbol of the self" and in her fifties created and began to enjoy her first real home, alone or not.

Settling for anything less than we desire or know we deserve is how we begin to betray ourselves, moment by moment, day by day. When we disown and discount ourselves, so does the world, including the men we want to share our lives with. "Self-esteem isn't everything," Gloria Steinem tells us, "It's just that there's nothing without it."

Settling for the Sizzle

Some of my best friends are illusions.
Been sustaining me for years.

SHEILA BALLANTYNE

There's a great con artist expression that goes, "Give 'em the sizzle, not the steak." Since most women consume hearty portions of illusion as their daily fare, you'd think we'd all be as thin as rails. Perhaps illusions have hidden calories, like a chef salad with blue cheese dressing.

One of the biggest illusions we swallow every day is that because our job *sounds* great, it *is* great. However, just because another woman would *love* to have your job, doesn't mean you have to keep on pretending *you* love it, if you don't.

I know a woman who's the creative director of a large fashion design house. Well, that's her official title. What she actually does is a kind of lace-trimmed industrial espionage. She goes to the fashion collections in Paris twice a year, then on to Rome, Milan, and London, scooping up whatever is bringing oohs and

202

ahhs down the runways this season. Once home, she gives her harvest of purloined sketches, photographs, and a few glamorous sample outfits to her staff and they begin to "rip them off." (If you've wondered why everything that's *fashionable* looks alike, wonder no more.)

While she's doing this, she's eating at great restaurants, flying business class, and racking up frequent-flyer miles that allow her children to enjoy Western ski vacations every February. But the gloss is off, and if she could think of something else to do with her life, she'd be doing it. She hates the travel, misses her kids terribly when she's away, and finds her work anything but inspiring.

Ask her why she stays, and she says she's too beat to think about doing something else. She's too physically exhausted even to discreetly "put herself out there in the job market," because that would mean extra lunches and attending more social events, and if she has to look at one more stuffed mushroom she thinks she'll gag.

Mentally she's too tired even to fantasize about what else she might be doing. She's afraid that at her age — forty-seven — and as heavily invested as she is in fashion, it would take her too long to start over in some other field, even if she could think of one. She'd also probably not be able to bring home the six-figure salary she's come to rely on. She and her husband are carrying a large mortgage, the kids are in private schools, and appearing to be successful requires a certain amount of upkeep. Besides, she holds a very prestigious position, what would everyone think? How could she explain so that people would understand? She's stuck and scared and hates herself for settling for something less by selling out.

"Disillusion comes only to the illusioned," Dorothy Thompson reminds us in *The Courage to Be Happy*, written in 1957. "One cannot be disillusioned of what one never put faith in," especially ourselves.

No One to Fear but Yourself

It's a sad day when you find out that it's not accident or time or fortune but just yourself that kept things from you.

LILLIAN HELLMAN

Maggie is outwardly one of those take-charge types: president of the neighborhood association, soccer coach, someone who, seconds after the latest political scandal breaks, can tell the funniest joke off the Internet. (Needless to say, Maggie was the first of our group cruising the Internet before the rest of us even knew what it was.)

Maggie is also a fabulous cook, a gifted gardener, and an articulate and impassioned contributor to her book group. But perhaps what redeems her from one's terminal envy is that she's so palpably restless — and, beneath her cheery smile, so unhappy, despite the devotion of a great guy and two healthy kids. Over the years that I've known her, she has come up with more career schemes than a college guidance counselor, but somehow there's never been much follow-through. First it was returning to the interior design business (before her kids were born, she used to run a fabric showroom); then (before Starbucks) it was opening a gourmet coffee bar; then (before *This Old House*) it was buying an old house in the country and turning it into a restaurant. Then it was living in the old house in the country, renovating and reselling it.

That one got her going — for two weeks. But soon she'd jettisoned the idea of moving away for moving up. She'd sell her house and buy an older, grander one that she could fix up while living there and then sell, renovate and trade up until . . . until . . . she could afford a house near the water, her community's equivalent of the right side of the tracks.

But somehow that plan got derailed, too.

Although Maggie is the epitome of a woman in desperate need of Something More, something is holding her back. "Maybe someday," she says with a sigh, as each new scheme dies a quiet death.

I'd always figured she was just chasing the wrong dream and wisely had decided to "scheme" some more. But this has been going on for years. Now I think it's that she's suffering from another variation of settling for less than we deserve: she's scared. I think she's scared of investing more than her imagination in herself. She's afraid of failing. And failure doesn't happen in a fantasy job or relationship. It's one thing to enliven a gathering with fascinating dinner party chatter (*I'm thinking of opening a coffee bar . . . What do you think?*). It's quite another to act on it.

"Maybe someday" thinking is great for quieting down your wants — the dream vacation, kitchen renovations, winning big on *Jeopardy!* But when it denies your needs, "someday" haunts and taunts. As Helen Waddell put it in 1933, "[Is there anyone] over thirty-five who [has] not some secret agony, some white-faced fear? . . . Half one's life one [walks] carelessly, certain that someday one [will] have one's heart's desire: [then] for the rest of it, one either goes empty, or walks carrying a full cup, afraid of every step."

"I realize that if I wait until I am no longer afraid to act, write, speak, be, I'll be sending messages on a ouija board, cryptic complaints from the other side," the poet Audre Lorde confessed. So Maggie talks and talks, and there's no one more fun to listen to. But I wonder if her Authentic Self and her therapist feel the same way.

There's the would-be-if-I-could-be, could-be-if-I-would-be syndrome in all of us, but it gets more anxiety-provoking the more you think you have to lose — especially when you're a woman who seems to have everything.

Joanne was a gifted pediatric surgical nurse when she married her high school sweetheart, Stan, right after he finished college. Like his father before him, Stan considered being a good provider for his family his highest priority. After Joanne gave birth to the first of their five children, Stan took pride in being able to give his wife an opportunity so many other women don't get: the chance to stay home and be a full-time mom and homemaker. And Joanne could teach Martha Stewart a thing or two. From handmade Halloween costumes to jars of her own marmalade, she's raised domestic bliss to an art form. But somehow her husband's success has become her curse instead of her blessing. Now that her youngest child has entered middle school, Joanne longs for something more challenging than experimenting with the newest recipe for low-fat risotto; she wants to go back to nursing. But Stan won't even let her bring up the subject for discussion. He says if she wants to take care of kids, she should concentrate on her own. For the last twenty years they've had what Joanne feels is a wonderful marriage, except for this one issue.

Lately Joanne has been wondering if Stan's insistence that she continue staying at home isn't more about his need for control than it is about maintaining a happy family. Stan's generous, but Joanne relies on him for all her financial needs. She misses having her own money to spend and having her own pride of accomplishment outside their home, especially now that their children are older and more self-sufficient. On the other hand, Joanne also knows that reentry into the nursing profession after all these years means that she'll be low woman on the totem pole, and seniority counts in scheduling working shifts. She believes the real reason for Stan's reluctance about her going back to work is the unpredictable effect it would have on their daily lives, from dinner at six to choir practice on Thursday evenings to Saturday golf games with his buddies. It can be a very delicate situation when our authentic dreams interfere with other people's plans and lifestyles. Joanne adores her husband, and she's scared that the changes in their life that would be caused by her going back to work wouldn't be worth the attendant risks to her marriage. She can't see that her biggest risk is settling for playing it safe. And so, whenever that panicky

"I've got to do something with my life" feeling comes back — as the spiritual directives to search for Something More inevitably do — Joanne simply plans another trip, another party, another new project. "It's like the smarter you are, the more things can scare you. . . ." Katherine Paterson muses, "[but] to fear is one thing. To let fear grab you around the tail and swing you around is another."

The Other Side of Scared

"What difference [does] it make if the thing [you're] scared of is real or not?"

TONI MORRISON

While our fears are always particular, they are also, thank God, universal. I'm thankful for that because it means you're not crazy, nor am I, and we're not alone when fear paralyzes us. And what are we afraid of? You name it. Not being successful? Not being as successful as our sister? Not living up to the expectations of others? Not living up to our own expectations? Not being good enough? Not being pretty enough? Not being smart enough? And we have to be all these things, because if we are, we'll be truly loved at last, won't we?

Won't we? Not necessarily.

It's taken me years of struggle to get over most of my fears, except the Big One. Not being loved. Not being loved by a man in the way I want and need to be loved — passionately, exclusively, commitedly, and unconditionally. I have always overwhelmed men. I used to think it was because I was lacking. Now I realize I'm the living embodiment of abundance — too much woman, too much love, too much passion. A woman fully formed is a wondrous but fearsome creature. It has taken me a very long time to get to the point of accepting my authenticity; no longer am I embarrassed by who I have always been. Instead, I'm finally grateful to be who I am, a woman who feels so deeply, generously, and spontaneously that those who know me frequently describe my style as "over the top." Of course, what they're gently suggesting is that tangos with tornados have a tendency to overpower most of the human race, and could I possibly tone it down?

Believe me, I've tried. Perhaps you have as well. But every time I've pretended to be a woman I'm not — perhaps holding back for fear of looking foolish, being rejected, not being loved — a sacred fire smolders within me until I suffer from the searing eruptions of first-degree heartburn. Your mind might be able to pretend you're someone you're not, but your body can't. So now instead of being polite and reserved because it makes others feel more comfortable, I just have to warn newcomers to my life about what they're in for. There is a Shaker axiom that says, *Be what you seem to be, and seem to be what you really are* — and in that loving advice is a clue to what Something More can be for all of us. This is what it means for us to live authentically. This is what you must do in order to find the happiness that is your constant craving.

But time and again, fear stands in our way.

However, the other side of being scared is the *sacred*. Just move the c — which could stand for courage, confidence, criticism, confusion, conflict, children, circumstances, challenge, caution — and one word can be transformed into the other. Over the last three decades I've derailed and detoured my dreams for every one of those reasons. *Reality*, I called it. Isadora Duncan observed that most women waste some twenty-five to thirty years of their lives before they break through the actual and conventional lies they tell themselves — especially when it comes to what they need to make themselves happy.

Just as we can learn to trade in being scared for embracing the sacredness of our dreams, we can acknowledge and diffuse the lies we tell ourselves that keep us from living authentically. At some point we will have to, whether

211

we like it or not. Our only choice seems to be to do it willingly, on our own timetable, which at least gives us advance warning, or do it on destiny's schedule, which is never convenient. For, as Gail Sheehy points out, "No sooner do we think we have assembled a comfortable life than we find a piece of ourselves that has no place to fit it." Something More is that mysterious, missing, odd-fitting piece of ourselves, and Spirit is determined we're going to find it one way or another.

FIELD WORK

 ### *The Return to Self*

"You certainly are not yourself today."
"I so seldom am," said Cecelia.

ELIZABETH BOWEN

Sarah was not my baptismal name; it was Cecelia. But I was so dramatic as a child that I was constantly called Sarah Bernhardt. "Don't be a Sarah Bernhardt," I was admonished during my wonder years. And why not? Since Sarah Bernhardt was so much more fun to be with than meek-as-a-mouse Cecelia, I decided when I was about ten to call myself "Sarah." Eventually everyone else started to as well, especially if they wanted to get my attention, and Sarah I became. During my twenties I lived in Paris and wrote a one-woman show about her.

Have you ever used another name for yourself? Why did you choose it? What facets of you was it expressing?

As we think about returning to your Authentic Self, let's put a romantic spin on our fantasy. Like a movie star, you're *making a comeback*. When you make a comeback you get to come back as whoever you want to be. You get to pick the attributes or qualities you like and discard the others.

Consider Madonna. A *USA Today* article points out that, since the birth of her daughter, Lourdes, Madonna is seeking serenity. She is "newly immersed in spirituality and self-discovery."

Her past incarnations, as "the avaricious *Material Girl* or the slutty bride in *Like a Virgin*," were just "mileposts of her evolution," notes the article.

" 'I am not reinventing myself,' " Madonna says. " 'I am going through the layers and revealing myself. I am on a journey, an adventure that's constantly changing shape.' "

I'd call her metamorphosis excavating her Authentic Self.

" 'I was trying to fill myself up with the wrong things,' " she declares. " 'For years, I've been imploring people to express themselves freely and to not be ashamed of who they are. But I was really saying it to myself, because I was raised with so much repression.

" 'I used to be extremely goal-oriented. This time, I was living in the moment and enjoying the journey and not thinking, What am I going to get out of this? I was in free fall for the first time.' "

Madonna says she's just "growing." What's the distinction between "growing" and "reinventing"? To me, *reinventing* sounds artificial, external; *growing* sounds organic. I like to think of it as "being repotted."

In the June 28 entry in *Simple Abundance*, I described how my little plant was drooping; when I picked it up and looked at its underbelly I saw that its tiny white roots were frantically pushing in a futile attempt to find more breathing space. I realized it was pot-bound. Plants need to be repotted at least every two years, I've learned. Even if the roots don't need more room to grow, the old soil should be replaced because all the nutrients have been consumed.

We, too, need to consider repotting for growth. When we wilt before the day begins. When we can't seem to visualize, or dream. When we can't remember the last time we laughed. When there is nothing in the next twenty-four hours we have to look forward to. When this happens week in and week out, we need to loosen the soil around our souls gently and find something that sparks our imagination, quickens our pulse, brings a smile.

We don't have to quit the job or leave the marriage. It just means we need something *new*.

There's a little book I love, *The Wish List* by Barbara Ann Kipfer, that lists some 6,000 wishes, large and small, to jog your memory about things you may always have wanted to do. Here are some of her examples:

Create a best-selling detective character.

Be asked to submit a weekly opinion column for the local newspaper.

Attend [your] elementary school reunion.

Serve regularly at the local soup kitchen.

Study cooking at Le Cordon Bleu in Paris.

Take [your] family on a backpacking trip through the Grand Tetons.

Tour the great sites of ancient Greece.

Learn carpentry.

Gather the neighbors and plant a community garden.

Learn to speak French.

Join a string quartet.

Paint the sets for a show.

Act the title role in *Hedda Gabler*.

Swing on a trapeze.

Run the Boston Marathon.

Read the complete works of Shakespeare.

Volunteer time at an animal shelter.

Deliver fresh flowers regularly to the local nursing home.

Take up yoga.

Become a middle school teacher — getting kids at their most curious.

Deliver a sermon in church.

Become an anthropologist.

Site Report

Jot down some of your own buried dreams. Make sure to include some that you can actually accomplish today if you set your mind to it. It's not too late to act on them!

Write in your discovery journal. Your local newspaper is doing a feature on *Ten Women Who Have Made a Difference* in your area. They have chosen you. Why?

Now pretend a decade has passed and you're still one of the top ten women. What's different about the story now?

FIELD WORK

 *Mystery*

Even the most ordinary life is a mystery if you look close enough.

KENNEDY FRASER

"Imagination has always had powers of resurrection that no science can match," writer Ingrid Bengis observes. That's because imagination is a spiritual grace. One way to feed your imagination is with children's fairy tales. Here at your excavation site is an old copy of *Hans Christian Andersen's Fairy Tales*. As with my re-reading of *National Velvet*, you can find hidden parts of yourself buried between the lines of your favorite fairy tales: "The Emperor's New

Clothes," "The Princess and the Pea," and by all means "The Ugly Duckling," which especially speaks to our theme of finding one's true and Authentic Self. Reread your favorite books from childhood: *The Five Little Peppers*; *Heidi*; *Little Women*; *The Wizard of Oz*; *A Thousand and One Nights*; *Black Beauty*; *Anne of Green Gables*; *The Bobbsey Twins*; *The Little House* books by Laura Ingalls Wilder. Don't forget the vintage adventures of the ace girl detective Nancy Drew. (Remember Nancy's little red roadster, twinsets, Bess, George, and Ned, and such baffling cases as *Secrets in the Old Attic* and *The Mystery at the Moss-Covered Mansion*? Solve them once more with feeling.) If you don't have these on hand, you can always go to your public library and prowl around. Or buy them for your children if you haven't already, or for a young friend. They're easy to find in secondhand bookstores. It would be interesting to read and recast the story of Cinderella now, with fresh eyes, from your vantage point as a wisewoman, reflecting on all the layers of meaning in the story.

Gloria Steinem tells us it's never too late to have a happy childhood, and I believe her. The childhood I would have chosen is captured in Maud Hart Lovelace's wonderful *Betsy-Tacy* series. If you want pure and simple escapism, run away to Deep Valley, Minnesota, at the turn of the century to enjoy escapades with Betsy Ray and her friends Tacy Kelly and

Tib Miller. There are ten books in the series, beginning when Betsy and Tacy are five, in 1892, and ending with Betsy's wedding after World War I. What I like most about reading children's books from the past (now that I'm old enough to appreciate their subtle nuances) are the charming domestic details of these cozy worlds — the kind of cooking, decorating, entertainment, and pastimes that filled their perfectly contented (albeit fictional!) daily rounds.

How can we explain our love for certain things — our "favorite things," as the song goes? Why have you kept this old record of bagpipe music? This length of Victorian lace? This picture of a rosebush? Why do you sigh when you see this photo of a golden retriever? Let's not try to explain these things; let's just attribute them to Mystery. Let's celebrate them.

Site Report

"Keep the channel open," dancer and choreographer Martha Graham urged. "There is a vitality, an energy, a quickening that is translated through you into action."

We cannot understand the mystery of life, of energy. All we can do is remain open to it, to clear the way for it, and then let it move through us.

How can you make room in your home and in your heart and mind for new thoughts, new ideas, new people, new appreciation for those already in your life? Let your Authentic Self count the ways.

Stumbling

*One cannot divine nor forecast the conditions
that will make happiness; one only stumbles
Upon them by chance, in a lucky hour, at the
world's end somewhere, and holds fast
to the days, as to fortune or fame.*

WILLA CATHER

The Wilderness

*The Promised Land always lies on the
other side of the wilderness.*

HAVELOCK ELLIS

The Israelites of the Old Testament were lucky.
They wandered in the Wilderness for only forty
years. Most of us stumble through the trial,
terror, and triumphs of life's terrain a lot longer,
usually until we're ready, willing, and able to
come face-to-face with the truth about ourselves: what magnificent, extraordinary, glorious,
powerful, courageous, and lovable beings we
are. That's right, *lovable*. We know we're
loving; to love is a woman's reason for being.
But we don't know we're worthy of *being* loved
until we set out in search of the Promised Land
or stumble toward Something More.

Which is where the Wilderness comes in. It's
a very necessary, crucial, and Divine detour
to bring us home to ourselves after a lifetime
of running away.

Wilderness — a bleak, numbing word that
instantly calls to mind a feeling of hopeless-

223

ness, nothingness, barrenness, and most of all, a sense of powerlessness. There's a reason that the biblical expression "the voice of one crying in the wilderness" has come to mean abject abandonment. You can wail and gnash your teeth all you want, but in the Wilderness no one hears your heart tearing asunder except God, who presumably sent you there. Ironically, according to ancient legend, the word *Wilderness* didn't conjure up a place of punishment, but rather a place of learning, spiritual growth, understanding, healing, and accomplishment. It referred to a wellspring of Divine energy in the guise of despair, hardship, and pain; your experience in the Wilderness was designed to prepare or propel you toward your destiny. Or pry you loose from whatever was keeping you from it.

Still, one does not enthusiastically sign up for the Wilderness cure the way we might for a restorative spell at Canyon Ranch or a confidence-building week at Outward Bound. Instead, we are usually thrust into the Wilderness by horrific circumstances that not only try our souls but seriously call into question our belief in God. And if there is a God, is He or She a compassionate God? A Divinity you might be interested in pursuing or continuing an intimate relationship with? In the Wilderness, you don't think so. Not today, anyway.

The Wilderness is tough-love. A love so ferocious it's meant to alienate us from others, estrange us from the world, and cut us off from ourselves, if that's what it takes to fully regain our focus. A lot of us suffer from undiagnosed chronic adult attention deficit disorder. Although it frequently doesn't fit into our plans, care of the soul requires more than a thirty-second "How ya doing?" check-in. In the Wilderness, the soul gets all the time and attention it needs.

Think of the Wilderness as a radical spiritual amputation of the weaker and toxic parts of our personalities — our neediness, our hubris, our willfulness, our self-loathing — that are holding us back from manifesting the Divine Plan of our lives. "To be born is to be chosen. No one is here by accident. Each one of us was sent here for a special destiny," Irish poet and Catholic scholar John O'Donohue reassures us in his exquisite book *Anam Cara: A Book of Celtic Wisdom*. "For millions of years, before you arrived here, the dream of your individuality was carefully prepared. You were sent to a shape of destiny in which you would be able to express the special gift you bring to the world. . . . Sometimes this gift may involve suffering and pain that can neither be accounted for nor explained. . . . It is in the depths of your life that you will discover the invisible necessity that has brought you here."

You are sent into the Wilderness for one reason, and one reason only: Woman, find thyself.

Braveheart

Courage is as often the outcome of despair as hope;
in the one case we have nothing to lose,
in the other, all to gain.

DIANE DE POITIERS

Once there was a beautiful actress — a habitué of the pages of the glamour press — who was the secret love of a professional athlete. Unfortunately, he was a very married man.

She was the love of this man's life, as he was hers. They were soul mates. But circumstances conspired against them. In an especially ironic and sad twist for someone whose lifework was centered around his own physical prowess, one of the man's children, a son, had been born with severe handicaps. As a result, much of his nonplaying time was spent championing the physically challenged and raising money for their causes. He was a man much admired for his compassion and lauded for his goodness, which meant, in both his mind and the public's, that he couldn't admit to being human. "When we are happy we are always good," Oscar Wilde reminds us, "but when we are good we are not always happy."

And the athlete wasn't a happy man except when he was with his lover. Even though his marriage had been for many years a luxurious shell — a legally partnered caretaker agreement — he didn't know how to end it. How would it look leaving the devoted mother of his children, especially the little boy? "I don't think the world will understand," he would explain, and while this was an excuse, he believed it. But the actress did understand. She hoped, she wished, she prayed that someday he would find the courage to walk to her or that she would find the courage to walk away from him. Until then, she would understand.

Like any karmic relationship, their passion was so intense that it felt as if they were chemically addicted to one another. But the actress knew in her heart, especially when they were in silence and apart on holidays and during family vacations, that even if they were soul mates, this part-time, hidden relationship was not for her highest good. Over the years she tried, really she did, to sever their bond, but she could never sustain the parting. His need for her was overwhelming; no one had ever needed her as deeply as he did, and she found his love very moving. For six years they attempted as best they could to create a world of their own that had rhythm, resonance, and reverence, a life apart from his wife and children. "Our relationship has a sacred destiny apart from your marriage," she would tell him. "Loving you was what I was born to do."

"I don't feel a shred of guilt about us because we sustain and nurture each other," he would tell her. "Someday we'll be together." Both of them believed they were telling each other the truth, and half the time, they were. But half-truths are the devil's IOUs.

For years, the athlete had played on teams that were hardworking, but never top-rung competitive. Finally, though, his team had beaten all the odds and made it to the ultimate test in its sport. The team's effort was admirable, but the real standout — many even said the key to their eventually winning the championship — was the depth and quality of the athlete's personal performance. He was lauded in the press and by his peers, and nobody was more proud of him than the actress.

It was then that the actress had a brainstorm. She was associated with a charitable organization for handicapped children; in fact, the lovers had first met at one of their functions. What if the athlete were to create and present a Most Valuable Player award for the disabled child who was chosen the most courageous in the face of personal adversity during that year? The athlete thought that this was a brilliant idea, and the actress called on her own celebrity contacts and press people to ensure that this would become an annual event that drew big names and lots of publicity to the charity.

Then came the Test. The spiritual crucible. The Wilderness wake-up call. The athlete told the actress that under no circumstances could she be at this event because, if she was, he could not in good conscience present the award. Having his mistress in the room made him feel unworthy of handing the award to the exemplary kid to whom it was being given. Plus, his wife and children would be there too. That the world would see him as a "noble" man as his mistress looked on would seem a sick joke. No, he wouldn't be such a hypocrite. He was aghast that she would even consider being there.

"This is a significant milestone for both of us and it's an important cause," she pleaded. "I can handle being in the same room with your wife. It won't be easy, but I can do it."

He couldn't.

Men treat you badly when they don't love you, *but they treat you even worse when they do love you but don't want to.* "Can't you take some work and go on location?" he asked her, as if this canard would make him feel any less torn between duty and desire. Because she loved him, she acquiesced to his wishes. Again. But she was very disturbed and deeply wounded and it was hard to pretend she wasn't.

"I'm being *banished* because of love?"

"Be brave for both of us," he entreated.

Because she needed to get out of town

quickly, she accepted a small role in the first movie her agent could find, an independent adventure film being shot on location in the mountains of South America. The part was an "are you completely crazy?" career choice but she was brokenhearted; she didn't care how small or ludicrous the part was, what she looked like, or how much money she wasn't making. And because the whole thing was a reckless, impetuous endeavor anyway, she agreed to do her own stunts. Since the film was being shot on a tight budget, the producer thought this was great.

On the night that her lover presented the award in front of his family, friends, and teammates, as well as the luminaries and press the actress had convinced to attend, she herself was thrust into the Wilderness. While filming an action scene in the waning hours of the afternoon, she lost her footing, stumbled, and slid two hundred feet down the mountainside until her safety line became entangled in a sharp crevice. This broke her fall but catapulted her, like a stone from a slingshot, off the mountain. When she finally came to rest, she found herself swaying over a rocky ravine with a perilous drop. It seemed like an eternity before a rescue crew could make its way through the forest to reach her.

Any day that ends up with you dangling off the side of a mountain (or hanging by a slender psychic thread) should prompt the very valid question *How the bloody hell did I get here?* You can do a lot of thinking between wondering whether or not you're going to live. A lot of reckoning. A lot of regrets. A lot of reconciling. Unlike the movies, the actress's life didn't flash in front of her. Instead, her replay was a nightmare in slow motion. She relived virtually every nuance of her love affair with the athlete, starting with her question, "You're married, aren't you?" through the chain of choice that got her where she was at that moment. She knew that if she lived through this ordeal, nothing would ever be the same again. But she was so exhausted. So tired. Too tired to change, she was sure. Courage is a well-rested reflex and hers had been in cold storage for a long time — so long, she wasn't even sure she'd be able to find it again.

When darkness fell, she decided to let go. Just let go and it would all be over. No one would see her loosen her safety harness, only God. She prayed she wouldn't feel too much pain for too long.

Suddenly a strong arm was within reach. "Grab on to me," she was told.

"I can't." *She'd be walking away from the love of her life. She'd be alone.*

"Grab on to me." *She'd never been able to say "no" to him or "yes" for herself.*

"I can't do this."

"Work with me, honey. You haven't held on

this long to give up now. It takes more courage to live than it does to die. On the count of three." And she was pulled by Spirit to safety and her Self.

In all honesty, I don't know exactly what happened after the actress returned to Hollywood, except that her love affair with the athlete ended. I don't know what she said to him when he begged her to forgive him. I don't know how many times she let the telephone ring without answering it until finally he stopped calling. I don't know how many letters she burned without opening them. I don't know how many nights she got drunk or cried herself to sleep.

I don't know if someday she'll win an Academy Award. I don't know if someday the athlete will show up on her doorstep with a white mark on his ring finger. I don't know if the actress will ever have the courage to fall in love again. But then, she never did describe herself as brave.

All I *do* know is that most days it does take more courage to live than it does to die, and that, as Mignon McLaughlin tells us, "The only courage that matters is the kind that gets you from one moment to the next."

Destiny's Darlings

Luck is not chance
It's Toil
Fortune's expensive smile
Is earned.

EMILY DICKINSON

Sometimes it seems there are just two types of women. There are destiny's darlings, those lucky ones sent into the world prepared and primed for this lifetime — born knowing their destiny. You hear about such women; they always knew they were meant to create, to lead, to mend broken lives or broken bones; to perform, to teach, to guide a thoroughbred to a first-place finish.

And then there's you and me, doomed from our kindergarten report cards to go stumbling toward our destiny. *Often unfocused and fidgety. Tendency to stare dreamily into space. Sidetracked and scattered. Stubborn! Too sensitive for her own good; feelings easily hurt. However, plays nicely with others.*

I used to think that the "born to's" were the

lucky ones — born knowing what their life roles were meant to be, or born simply knowing how to be happy. I love what confirmed Hollywood bachelor Warren Beatty said about what drew him to ask Annette Bening to be his wife: "She has a great capacity for happiness." Those of us lacking this capacity are drawn instinctively to those whose energy is radiant and composed. We marvel at their clear paths, seemingly marked from the start by bread crumbs or bright lights. The rest of us end up with skinned knees but not a clue as to how we got to where we find ourselves today.

I know a woman who got tired of stumbling her way to happiness and decided to short-circuit the trial-and-error method by sending out a personal survey to all her friends seeking their help in designing the rest of her life. "I'm spinning my wheels, and I'm out of ideas," she wrote. "You know me. Should I: Start a new business? Open a restaurant? Sell everything and relocate across country? Return to school? Marry my boyfriend?" Alongside was another check-off column, this time with a list asking which ones best described her most pertinent personal qualities. Mail everything back, she instructed, and the results, like a personal spreadsheet, would be tabulated by a professional. (Professional *what?* Therapist? Career counselor? Price Waterhouse?) Within weeks the woman expected to be presented with documents that would add up to something like a business plan. The envelope, please.

Unfortunately, no documents prepared by outsiders can reveal the truth locked within your heart, which is why this woman's friends thought she was nuts and told her so. Now she's back to figuring out her own life like the rest of us.

We'd love to think that our life's journey is linear, but we stumble in fits and starts on our way to authenticity. The writer Franz Kafka, whose lonely and tormented characters came to represent twentieth-century angst, believed that destiny's true path "seems more designed to make people stumble than to be walked upon."

Certainly most of the stumbling stories I've heard have a kafkaesque quality to them — a bizarre inevitability. A long-distance runner discovers that the tingling in her legs is multiple sclerosis. She has to give up the career she's trained half her life for; she pours her pain onto the page and becomes a poet. A ballet dancer twists her ankle and seriously injures herself. She must stop dancing. She's always dabbled in photography, so when her former troupe needs some pictures for a fund-raising brochure, she's enlisted; she "knows" dance, and can convey a dancer's energy, passion, and persistence. The pictures turn out so brilliantly she now photographs performers professionally. This woman literally stumbled upon her authentic path.

Sometimes stumbling is more subtle. A successful stockbroker's husband was diagnosed with late-stage cancer and spent his last few weeks in a hospice. The woman was so moved by the care, compassion, and calling of the people who tended both of them that she became a hospice volunteer just to show her thanks. Now she runs a hospice for women dying of AIDS and their children.

All Rosa Parks was doing was "trying to get home from work" when she stumbled into becoming the symbol of the Civil Rights movement by refusing to go to the back of a bus. Did she feel "that small shiver . . . when events hinted at a destiny being played out, of unseen forces intervening," as writer Dorothy Gilman describes the inescapable? Perhaps not, but the powerful impact of her soul-directed, though unplanned action has resonated for her, and for us all, ever since. That is authenticity.

Two Ways to Live

Occasionally the impossible happens; this is a truism that accounts for much of what we call good luck; and also, bad.

FAITH BALDWIN

Albert Einstein insisted there were only two ways to live: as if everything were a miracle or as if nothing were. I dare you to spend one day consciously trying to prove him wrong. I can't last ten minutes. But often, especially when life inexplicably shatters us and sends us tumbling in terror toward the unknown, we're more comforted by what he wrote to friends after the sudden death of their child. "When the expected course of everyday life is interrupted, we realize we are like shipwrecked people trying to keep their balance on a miserable plank in the open sea, having forgotten where they came from and not knowing whither they are drifting."

With her verve, her dark, vibrant eyes, and her enormous self-confidence, Janet had always been the kind of woman who made you believe she could do anything — this was her authentic gift. She could also make others believe they could do anything, too. People were drawn to her uplifting, positive, enthusiastic aura like magnets; her radiant energy was palpable.

Five years ago Janet was a counselor at a residential treatment center near Boston specializing in substance abuse. Like a lot of us, she had stumbled her way through one disastrous romantic relationship after another. She decided she'd give up men entirely for six months as a respite from the rigors of unrealistic expectations. Shortly after this hiatus, she met Kevin, a telecommunications business consultant. They hit it off immediately. After their second date, Kevin invited her to Utah, where friends had taken a large house on a mountain for a last weekend of spring skiing. An accomplished, aggressive skier, Janet had just taken a small jump in the fading afternoon light, a dangerous time of day because the terrain begins to appear deceptively flat. Out of nowhere a snowboarder came pounding over the same jump — and smashed right into her, literally hurling her ten feet down the steep slope until she landed with the velocity of a human missile and with a deafening, terrifying crack. But it wasn't thunder. It was her back.

With a concussion, compound fractures of both legs, and a broken back, Janet was a mess and lucky to escape with her life. There were multiple reconstructive surgeries, in which fragments from her ribs were used to fuse her fractures, and a lengthy hospital stay followed by three more months in a rehabilitation center, where Janet literally had to be taught to walk again. Kevin, who had been a virtual stranger to her when the accident occurred, became her constant companion, flying back and forth between Boston and Salt Lake City, where she was recovering, in order to be with her. "Have laptop, will travel," he said with a smile, often conducting business on a mobile phone outside her room while she worked with her physical therapists. His wave and wink through the glass partition kept her going.

These last years — her Wilderness time — have been a long ordeal. Her body is scarred and the pain unending. But throughout it all Janet and Kevin have discovered each other. They have come to know and admire each other's strength and have fallen in love with each other's character and courage. Three years ago they married, and have recently welcomed into their lives a tiny miracle — a beautiful baby boy.

That plunge down the mountain threw Janet into a new professional life as well. Sometimes adversity helps us identify in new and profound ways with the personal challenges of others. In Janet's case, the trajectory of her life went in the opposite direction — from outside herself to within. She'd been a wonderful rehab counselor because she'd drawn on what seemed to be unlimited reserves of compassion and determination to help others. But her accident forced her to redirect her energies inward; she needed to become extremely focused on her journey back to health and wholeness. Whatever the reason, her once-fervent desire to put the well-being of others ahead of her own was gone. She discovered that she no longer had the patience or even the empathy for her old clients, many of whom would not, rather than could not, take the necessary steps to repair their lives and get back on track. Instead, Janet put herself first, and that meant discovering meaningful work that engaged her *as she was now*. As George Eliot remarked, "It so often happens that others are measuring us by our past self while we are looking back on that self with a mixture of disgust and sorrow." Janet began to think that maybe she focused on the needs of other people because she didn't believe her own needs counted for much.

She thought a lot about what had been her personal passions before the accident and the lessons she had learned from it. She had always had a deep appreciation of art; she had been an art history major in college before switching to social work because she thought it was a more practical choice for her life's work. After she moved back to Boston, one of her great pleasures was visiting the city's many fine museums and galleries. She recognized that, after experiencing so much pain, she wanted to fill her life with as much beauty as she could. She also realized that when we make choices, the soul doesn't think much about the practical eclipsing the passionate. Janet apprenticed herself at thirty-something to an art restorer, learning how to bring back to life the cracked and broken pieces and half-ruined treasures of the ages. It became a powerful personal metaphor for her. Now she has her own consultancy business that allows her to balance traveling with being a new mom; gradually she's building an impressive client portfolio of museums and dealers here and abroad. She's having a marvelous time and every day feels as if she's discovered the secret of the ages: how to be happy. She's grateful she has finally excavated her Authentic Self — fragile, fallible, wounded, but whole and wholly wonderful. Janet has become the living embodiment of Something More. As writer Agnes Repplier astutely observed: "It is not easy to find happiness in ourselves, but it is not possible to find it elsewhere." And if that isn't a miracle worth believing in, I don't know what is.

The Divine Collaboration

The universe works with you and for you.
It is not your enemy.

DAVID SPANGLER

A woman named Marie was on the fast track as a Chicago-based advertising copywriter when she met a journalist who was about to be transferred to London as his news magazine's assistant bureau chief. Why single men who know they are moving in a month are allowed even to nod in a woman's direction is an unsolved mystery waiting to be cracked. Perhaps the Universe likes to surprise us with the rather novel notion that stumbling does not always mean suffering, unless we insist on making ourselves miserable. Which is exactly what Marie almost did.

"But he's asking you to come to London with him," her best friend practically screamed. "Are you nuts? Be happy! You're putting your life in turmoil for all the *right* reasons."

Still, quitting a job, leaving friends and family, not to mention giving up a fabulous sublet with views of Lake Michigan, was a risk. Suppose her "perfect" romance "went south" — a nice euphemism for checking into the Heartbreak Hotel? She didn't know a soul in London. How would she get a job there? Or make friends?

After much soul-searching, she decided to make the move. At first, she just wandered around the streets of one of the world's most stimulating cities, wondering if it were all a dream. One day she came across an old, out-of-print book at a curio shop in Camden Passage. It was the memoir of a woman who had been a member of a close-knit coterie within the English elite around the turn of the century. Known as "The Souls," this glamorous circle of Victorian friends provided a fascinating window on late-nineteenth-century society, and especially on the institution of country house parties. Marie was entranced by the obscure writer's adroit and charming observations about some of Britain's most famous politicians and artists — not to mention her own surprisingly erotic confessions. Marie's fascination grew and took her to the British Library's Reading Room, where she steeped herself in everything she could find about the mysterious figure. She began to play with the idea that here was a fascinating bit of social history that had fallen through the cracks of academic study. The reams of notes she took began to take shape, and soon she found herself writing a biography, something she never would have done had she not been living in London. Having never considered herself a scholar or a literary writer (she had, after all, made her living writing ad copy), she found the next few years exhausting but exciting as she labored to learn the mechanics of research and find her voice as a biographer. By this time her work had become a labor of love, as only great, satisfying, and authentic challenges are. When her book was published abroad, it was praised and admired for its freshness, perceptiveness, and graceful writing. Around the same time, her boyfriend, now her husband, was again promoted and transferred — this time to the Far East. Marie is now at work on another group biography, about the lives of female concubines in the court of the King of Siam.

"A biography is considered complete if it merely accounts for six or seven selves," Virginia Woolf observed, "whereas a person may well have as many as a thousand lives." Don't you think that, out of a thousand lives, a few of our destinies could be driven by joy, not by adversity — the challenge of illness or job loss or romantic heartache that we've all come to associate with life changes? It's a crazy thought I know, but one worth considering.

"You pray in your distress and in your need," Kahlil Gibran admonishes us. "Would that you might pray also in the fullness of your joy and in your days of abundance."

If we did, we might experience more of them.

Taking Liberties

It is never too late to be what you might have been.

GEORGE ELIOT

I've always wondered what it would be like to live as a *libertine*. Isn't that a delicious word? Sarah Bernhardt, Isadora Duncan, Josephine Baker, George Sand, George Eliot, Victoria Woodhull, and Isak Dinesen were libertines.

"Yes, of course, she's accomplished, but you do know she's a libertine." Please God, before I die, let someone say that about me.

How to know if you are at least moving in the direction of being a libertine? A libertine never gives up a room with a view and can't remember the last time she was patted on the back and thanked for "being a doll." Instead, she's accused of being a "gutsy broad." A libertine is invited everywhere but rarely goes out (which always makes her presence an event) and believes in a body-mind-spirit approach to nutrition, consisting mainly of grapes (red seedless), chocolate truffles, and champagne. She gives great gifts, follows boxing as a spiritual path, considers that she has been sexually harassed when she is *not* told she looks beautiful, and worries when they *aren't* whispering behind her back: "Isn't she a piece of work."

All of history's really interesting women were libertines — freethinkers, women who lived by their own conventions, their own sense of what was right and wrong for *them,* what they could live with, what they couldn't live without. Come to think of it, living by your own lights and not by the opinions of others is one way of defining authenticity, so maybe I'm halfway there. But there is still too much of the residual good girl in me for my own highest good — unalloyed happiness — if you know what I mean.

And you probably do, because I'll bet you were born a good girl, too. However, Kate White, a charter member of the good girl club until she was passed over for the job of editor-in-chief for a magazine she had been running for months, believes that good girls are made, not born. The "seeds of the good girl are planted very early, as a daughter observes the way the individuals in her home interact with each other and absorbs the messages her parents send," she writes in her wonderful primer on how to stop stumbling sooner rather than later, *Why Good Girls Don't Get Ahead But Gutsy Girls Do*.

"The mother, even if she has a job, makes the arrangements for school, for play-dates, meals, holidays, celebrations, dentist and doctor appointments, vacations, and trips to relatives. She buys the clothes, the underwear, the shoes, the toothbrushes, the birthday gifts (for her own kids as well as her kids' friends), the books, the Play-Doh and paint sets. She drives for the car pool, makes the snacks, applies the Band-Aids, wipes the noses, cleans up the spills and messes, supervises the homework, calls the teacher, gets the camp applications, writes the thank-you notes . . . it never stops."

Whose week does that sound like? "The message a daughter hears through all this is that one of the most important jobs a female has is considering and taking care of others' needs, and in the process that often involves putting her own needs aside."

This goes a long way toward explaining the late-onset pull of the libertine lifestyle, at least for me. Becoming a libertine — she who puts her own needs first — is Darwinian in nature. It's an evolutionary process — slow and steady growth over many lives — which is why the reembodiment theory gives one hope, if not a game plan. Get through your major soul lessons and you'll get a few free periods for extracurricular activities. Keep in mind we're really not going to *remember* much of this life in the next go round, so why don't we become girls who would like to have *some* fun? The authentic spiritual path is not meant to be sackcloth and ashes. Ecstasy is the hallmark of the mystical experience. Joy awakens the soul and convinces the mind beyond a shadow of a doubt that there *is* Something More — the existence of another way of living.

"Ecstasy is what everyone craves — not love or sex, but a hot-blooded, soaring intensity, in which being alive is a joy and a thrill," Diane Ackerman tells us. "That enravishment doesn't give meaning to life, and yet without it life seems meaningless."

Crossing the Threshold

Age doesn't protect you from love.
But love, to some extent, protects you from age.

JEANNE MOREAU

Life begins at forty," the original red-hot mama Sophie Tucker tells us — although, if you're just turning 30, you won't believe her.

Forty is a very mystical, transformative threshold. It's as if you wake up one morning fully grown, speaking the language of the natives and knowing how to ride a bicycle — as Annie Dillard describes turning ten. Today a young girl turning ten is in her dotage; thank God that at forty, the growth process reverses.

During our first forty years we wander a circuitous path toward vaguely or distinctly delineated destinies, even if they remain unarticulated. We pass predictable milestones, reject our family's choices (or try our best to), and struggle to define ourselves in the eyes of the world. When we can't live up to anyone's expectations, especially our own, we burn with what Mary Lee Settle calls "the terrible unfairness of disappointment."

Life becomes a series of losses, and if you believe in chance, accident, or statistical probability (I don't), you're bound to lose something from *Column A* or *Column B:* your looks, your figure, your husband, your job, your identity. I believe we choose — consciously or unconsciously — to shed these things.

At some point we have to come to peace with this, or we'll never reach the Promised Land. Moses didn't. It was the next generation of Israelites that did.

Sometimes we must go on living longer than we'd like with the choices we made before we knew better. But we can learn to *benefit* from the delay or the detour rather than die in the Wilderness. Sometimes we choose tracks left by others that plant us right back where we started from; sometimes they are our own tracks. But invariably, if we keep on going, picking ourselves up each time we stumble, we learn the joy of delayed gratification. We look back and see, like an oasis, the Wilderness as a fertile place after all. Think of how many took the forty-year journey before they began really *living* their lives. Edith Wharton only felt she had come into "a real personality of her own" at the age of thirty-seven, and she was forty-five before she fell madly and passionately in love for the first time. "I had to fight my way to expression through a thick fog of indifference," she wrote.

The poet Elizabeth Barrett Browning acknowledged that her husband, the poet Robert Browning, whom she married when she was forty, had "loved her into full being." But then again, she was, for better or worse, an inhabitant of her time — cloistered, reserved, a semi-invalid, not in the world. It was a man and not experience itself that coaxed her into authenticity. A century later, what's our excuse? We can claim more. But do we? We can point proudly to a more authentic courtship with Wholeness. Our paths have been infinitely variable, rife with false starts and circlings back. But they are of our own making, and they are lavish in their brilliance, mystery, and mistakes. We might cringe occasionally when we have total recall, but when we *disown* our experience — when we look away from what makes us human, what has made us the women we are, and what has made us authentic — we become like the incredible shrinking woman, and our self-worth evaporates.

True, we may be disappointed by what we haven't done yet — learn to speak another language, compose symphonies, write poetry, or paint. We might not have run a marathon, won the Pillsbury bake-off, or spent enough time with our children/partner/aging parents as we would like. But the search for Something More, the process of excavation and reembodiment, tells us that *we might just do those things yet*. And much better, I think, because of the struggles of the Wilderness behind us.

Isak Dinesen did not begin to write in a serious and sustained way until her life, as she had loved and expected to live it, was over. She was past forty. Her marriage to Swedish Baron Bror Blixen had ended in divorce; her love affair with the romantic adventurer Denys Finch Hatton had ended with his death in a plane crash. She had lost her beloved coffee farm in Africa where she had spent close to twenty years, and she had been forced to return to her native Denmark, a country she found inimical to her spirit. Syphilis, contracted from her husband, was beginning to make its slow and deadly progress through her body. But, as her biographer Judith Thurman shows, the end of Dinesen's erotic life and physical world was the price she had to pay for her gifts as a writer, for she turned to writing only when she had nowhere else to go. Her voice came to her, Thurman says, "only when she had lived enough to make a 'reckoning' with her losses." Sometimes it takes more than four decades of stumbling, not to mention a bad case of syphilis, to recover fully from the notion that you have to live your life through a man. But there's an easier way, I assure you. "One may take many liberties with God which one cannot take with men," Isak reflected at the end of her life.

As every Wilderness woman soon discovers, the beginning of wisdom is learning to light your own fire. (And this could be crucial knowledge if you get a midnight craving for "S'mores." Take two graham crackers and sandwich between them a thin chocolate bar with a toasted marshmallow. Eat one. Eat some more!)

Can you think of three liberties you'd like to take? Now go ahead — take them.

A Woman of a Certain Age

After fifty most of the bullshit is gone.

ISABEL ALLENDE

Turning fifty is an entirely different matter altogether.

"At fifty, the madwoman in the attic breaks loose, stomps down the stairs, and sets fire to the house. She won't be imprisoned anymore," Erica Jong confesses in *Fear of Fifty*. A woman at fifty wastes no more time waiting for that second, third, or fourth chance at ravishing life. Why? Because you've no longer got time for the pain, angst, unfocused anger, jealousy, or envy. "I have enjoyed greatly the second blooming that comes when you finish the life of the emotions and of personal relations; and suddenly find — at the age of fifty, say — that a whole new life has opened before you, filled with things you can think about, study, or read about," Agatha Christie confided in her autobiography. "It is as if a fresh sap of ideas and thoughts was rising in you."

However, you probably won't feel that way

until you turn fifty-one. For many women, turning fifty is a watershed, a wasteland of self-loathing. I'd hazard a guess that it's that way secretly for *all* women, but I know that some of my more evolved and enlightened readers will take me to task for such a sweeping assumption, so I'll take cover behind quasi-qualifying. At fifty-one you know how to pick your battles.

Turning fifty was such a trauma for me, I refused to do it. I flat-out said to Sister Age, "Forget it." Turned off the phone, didn't answer the door — even for floral tributes. Wouldn't celebrate my birthday, wouldn't allow it to be observed, or even acknowledge it. (This did mean forgoing gifts, but that shows you how serious I was.) "How old are you?" I'd be asked, as if it were anyone's damn business — especially the American Association of Retired Persons. *You know I really can't remember. I was very young when I was born.*

What I did do: Refused to engage in social conversation with men over the age of thirty-eight. *Threw out* all my cotton underwear, invested in enough Italian silk lingerie to last several lifetimes. Learned to walk again in high heels and practiced the art of regular waxing. Started wearing stockings and garters, capri pants, mules, and twin sets. Cut my hair. Began to work out in a gym. Excavated my authentic passion for red nail polish, fabulous earrings, sleeping in the nude. Would not go quietly, would not go at all.

Call me shallow. I'll deny it.

It worked. Just go straight from forty-nine to fifty-one. Or perhaps your freaky threshold is forty-five; the principle is the same. Skip it. (But as I remember it, forty-five was a really good year.)

What do you mean, can you just *do* that?

Yes, of course you can. They can strap you down, but they cannot make you swallow birthday cake. If it's your party, you don't have to show up. This way, when the extremely rude and crude inquire about your chronology, you can honestly say, "Well, I've not cele-brated my *whatever* yet."

Granted, a month before the half-century mark, my marriage had just ended, I moved, and found myself roommates with my gor-geous fourteen-year-old daughter. I'm open to the suggestion that these circumstances could have contributed to my agitation, but I really think it's the word *crone* that throws me for a loop.

What an ugly word to describe such a cre-ative chapter in a woman's story! You can be a wisewoman without being a hag. Personally, I think invoking the image of a crone as a figure to emulate diminishes a woman's sense of well-being. The French call feminine act-two players "women of a certain age," and that de-scribes a lot of us very succinctly; we become more certain of ourselves as our authenticity emerges. When it comes to a choice between the sexy chuckle of songstress Lena Horne and the gleeful cackle of sorceress Madam Mim, I'm much more inspired by the lady and her music than I am by the lady with the magic spells.

The fiftysomething decade sizzles. "Women at this stage of life find themselves blazing with energy and accomplishment as never before in history," Gail Sheehy reports. "The struggles that sapped so much of their emotional energy have subsided by now." Sheehy studied women for five years while she was writing *New Passages: Mapping Your Life Across Time*. The results of her research "strongly suggest that the dominant influence on a woman's well-being is not income level or marital status; the most decisive factor is age. Older is happier."

Coco Chanel reminds us that "nature gives you the face you have when you are twenty. Life shapes the face you have at thirty. But it is up to you to earn the face you have at fifty." As long as the face staring back at you is authentic, you can call yourself anything you want to. But you'll find me hanging out backstage with red-hot chanteuses, *not* my "crone-ies."

Women's Work

One sad thing about this world is that the acts that take the most out of you are usually the ones that people will never know about.

ANNE TYLER

It shouldn't come as much of a surprise that many women stumble upon their authentic calling later rather than sooner — after their children are older. Men (with some exceptions) rarely work around the needs of their children; women rarely work any other way. The novelist Fay Weldon was once asked why she wrote longer sentences in her later novels. Why? Can't you guess? As her children grew older, she had fewer interruptions.

My daughter casually informed me last night that tomorrow is her softball team play-off game. But I have just seven days to finish the biggest deadline of my career. "Honey, I can't . . ."

"I understand . . ."

"Seven more days, I promise . . ."

"How does it *feel* not to have seen *one* of

my games this season?"

Lousy. And not very successful. It feels out of kilter. Insane. I'm back at survival level. But my priorities are not out of whack. I'm a single mother now, responsible for this child's well-being. Which is why I'm writing this at three a.m. I *will* be at that game; I *will* make this deadline. Not even my regret reminder helps much this morning. I write what I know is my truth; that doesn't mean living your truth is easy. "At work, you think of the children you have left at home. At home, you think of the work you've left unfinished," Golda Meir, the only woman to be prime minister of Israel, once confessed candidly. "Such a struggle is unleashed within yourself. Your heart is rent."

In a collection of essays called *The Writer on Her Work*, Anne Tyler reveals how difficult it is to create around family life. Writing is her frame of reference, as it is mine, but the same principle applies to any work we do. One March a character arrived in her consciousness as she was painting the downstairs hall. She knew that if she "sat down and organized this character on paper, a novel would grow around him. But it was March and the children's spring vacation began the next day, so I waited." By July she was finally able to start. But even with the inevitable tug-of-war that daily life brings, the struggle and the stumbling toward Something More with children

258

growing up around you brings hidden gifts. "It seems to me that since I've had children, I've grown richer and deeper," Anne Tyler confesses. "They may have slowed down my writing for a while, but when I did write, I had more of a self to speak from."

Dorothy Reed Mendelhall was a graduate of Johns Hopkins Medical School and a laboratory scientist. Following her marriage, she remained for nearly a decade at home as the mother of young children. Her authentic path was reshaped by what at times must have seemed like an enormous stumbling block, as she struggled to rechannel her intellectual energy. With small ones all around her she became interested in maternal and child health. This led her to author an influential study in 1929 that argued in an eerily prophetic way against America's increased inclination toward technological intervention in the natural birth process.

Still, she remained haunted, heartbroken, and angered by the fact that, despite her enormous accomplishments, her efforts were belittled by the professional medical community as "woman's work." At no time was this more hurtful than the day she learned that, during a heated debate at Harvard Medical School over the subject of admitting women, she had been cited as a perfect example of an able woman who had married, had children, and *failed to use her expensive education.*

Imagine for a moment how devastated she must have felt when she heard that? Chaos was probably swirling around her, but she needed to carry on, rise to the occasion, and answer a higher call that probably sounded like "Mom . . ."

Yet Dorothy continued to follow her authentic path. Eventually her work had a greater impact on our *actual* lives than that of many of her male colleagues. "At first people refuse to believe that a strange new thing can be done, then they begin to hope it can be done, then they see it can be done," Frances Hodgson Burnett wryly observed. "Then it is done and all the world wonders why it was not done centuries ago."

Work with Me

All the great blessings of my life
Are present in my thoughts today.

PHOEBE CARY

One, two, three, infinity. How many times does Spirit whisper *One, two, three. Work with Me?* Every day, every hour, probably every minute.

But do we hear? Are we listening? Sometimes it's the very frustrations of our stumbling that provide us with the detour we need to get back on track toward our authenticity. Stop limiting Spirit. Work with Divine Intelligence and be grateful that God doesn't think like us.

Margaret Morse Nice was trained as a research fellow in biology, but her work thereafter was directed by the trajectory of her husband's medical career — in Boston, Oklahoma, Ohio, and at last Chicago — and by the care of four daughters. Of her life at that time she wrote: "I was truly frustrated. I resented the implication that my husband and the children had brains and I had none. He taught; they studied; I did housework. . . . My life became so cluttered with mere *things* that my free spirit was smothered. My desires were modest enough . . . an occasional walk to the river."

One day she finally got to the river and just sat there. Looking up, she saw a mother bird tending her babies in a nest. "I decided it would be better to be a bird. Birds are very busy at one period each year caring for babies, but this lasts only a few weeks with many of them, and then their babies are grown and gone. Best of all they leave their houses forever and take to camping the rest of the year. No wonder they are happy."

From this simple observation and personal

connection, she developed a keen interest in birds that flamed into an authentic passion and a career as a noted ornithologist. Eventually she became a pioneer environmentalist.

Whatever you're doing today, whatever's frustrating you, stop for a few minutes and think about your situation. There's a clue embedded in the heart of your frustration that can lead you to the next step. In our role as archaeologists of ourselves, every clue counts, and in the spiritual world, nothing is for drill and no experience is wasted. There's one clue given to each of us every day that will lead us to Something More.

Little Miss Perfect

Perfectionism is the voice of the oppressor, the enemy of the people. It will keep you insane your whole life.

ANNE LAMOTT

Irene Mayer Selznick was the daughter and wife to two of Hollywood's most powerful men, MGM boss Louis B. Mayer and producer David O. Selznick. To one she was a classic Daddy's Girl; to the other, the perfect Hollywood Wife;

to both she was dutiful, subservient, and nearly neurotic in her need to serve, stroke, and protect. Of her Old World father, who didn't want the outside world to "corrupt" his daughters and so outlawed boys, camp, college, and independent thought, she wrote in her 1983 memoir *A Private View*, "Togetherness hadn't been invented yet, but rarely has it been practiced more intensively." Instead, she adapted as best she could and became an appeaser: "My family gave me everything except privacy and a sense of my own worth." She also developed a lifelong stutter.

Enter, stage right: David O. Selznick. He was Hollywood's wunderkind, her first boyfriend (approved by her dad), and the only man she ever loved. Everything about him was over the top: his enormous successes (*Gone With the Wind*, *Rebecca*, *Dinner at Eight*) but also his failings: gambling losses ($1 million a year), his addiction to Benzedrine, his affairs with his movie star protégées, his breakdowns, his legendary Type-A work habits, his missed appointments with his psychiatrist. One day Irene began to take his place on the couch. In order to save what shreds of sanity and self-esteem she had left, she stayed there until she could finally call it quits after fifteen years of marriage. She was thirty-eight.

It wasn't until she left both Selznick and Hollywood that Irene at last grew up. She moved to New York and stumbled into a life of her own. She turned her back on filmmaking but recast her experience and talent for organization, facilitation, and handholding by becoming a successful Broadway producer.

"I didn't turn out to be what I or anyone expected, not in any possible way," she admitted, when she took a long look backward. The loving family, the happy marriage were scriptwriters' fantasies; but what Irene did achieve was the one thing she never started out thinking she'd want: a career and a contentment no one could have scripted for her. "Actually, I see now that I've had three lives — one as the daughter of my father, another as the wife of my husband. The theater furnished me with a third act."

It's fascinating, when we begin the excavation process, to discover how each of our different lives are buried in their distinctive shrouds. For several years after my first book was published, I gave workshops and lectures. Because I was the author of a book on Victorian family traditions, people expected me to look the part, and I didn't want to disappoint. When I wasn't wearing authentic reproductions of Victorian gowns, I was wearing flowery, romantic, fussy clothing, and my hair was long and curly. But after I embarked on the *Simple Abundance* journey, I began evolving into my next incarnation, although it wasn't apparent on the outside. As the inner changes increased in strength, I began to feel physically uncomfortable in my own body a great deal of the time, as if I were a ghost unable to move on. Remember Divine Discontent? Eventually I did change my appearance and move toward who I was becoming. But this becoming is a continuous process. "One is not born, but rather becomes, a woman," Simone de Beauvoir tells us. Now when I look back on those old photographs, I don't even know who that woman was. It was another lifetime.

Constant Craving

To crave happiness in this world is simply to be possessed by a spirit of revolt. What right have we to happiness?

HENRICK IBSEN

In 1879 the Norwegian dramatist Henrik Ibsen caused a sensation when his play about a woman's suffocation in a loveless marriage, *A Doll's House*, debuted. What was so shocking about the play was that Ibsen's characters were instantly recognizable; everyone in the audience knew the couple, knew the marriage depicted, even if it was not their own.

It is just before Christmas when the play opens, and Nora Helmer is getting ready to make everyone's holiday dreams come true. The season is full of expectation and promise: Nora's bank manager husband, Torvald, is to begin a new job after the New Year at a salary that will finally secure their comfort and happiness.

As Nora twirls and trills among the holiday preparations, her stolid husband smiles indulgently. His wife is a child in his eyes, a child whom he has shielded, protected, and instructed — much as her father did before Torvald carried her away and made her his dollhouse bride. It is clear that he sought a playful "squirrel" who could perform tricks when he required amusement; a "skylark" who could banish his melancholy moods through song; a "nibbly cat" to be rewarded with the occasional bit of candy. "I do not want you to be anything but what you are," he tells his wife, "my lovely, dear little skylark."

So Nora has been just that — and a clever young fox as well. Their life together, we learn, is a paper-thin construct of deceptions and differing expectations — and a secret. Confiding in a friend, Nora reveals that years before, when her husband was seriously ill and the doctors advised her that his best hope was to spend many months recuperating in a warmer climate, Nora frantically sought money to finance a trip to Italy. Because her father was on his own deathbed and could not be approached, she took the naïve and foolish step of borrowing money from an unsavory businessman, securing the loan by forging her father's name to the note. Torvald, believing the money was his father-in-law's gift and that he was taking the trip for the sake of Nora's pleasure-seeking whims, remained none the wiser. After he became well again and returned to work, Nora deceptively managed to divert small amounts from the household funds he gave her to make regular payments to pay off the secret debt. With Torvald's prospects rising, she will soon be freed of her obligation.

But then we learn that Krogstad, her shady benefactor, is none other than one of her husband's new employees, and a man who has worked hard to reverse his ill fortune and disreputable past. Torvald, however, plans to let him go, and Krogstad, a widower with children to care for, threatens Nora that unless she intercedes, he'll reveal the truth to her husband. She will be arrested and jailed; what's more, the revelation of the lies and secrets Nora has kept from her husband these last eight years will destroy everything between them.

As Nora slowly recognizes that her position in the eyes of the law is perilous despite the selflessness of the gesture made to save her husband, she panics. She goes to Torvald to persuade him to keep the reformed Krogstad, but even her flattery and coquetry do not move her inflexible and moralistic husband, who is insistent that he will not have his colleagues think the new bank director's business decisions can be influenced by his wife.

His position astonishes Nora, piercing for the first time her idealized vision of his character and her understanding of their marriage. But time is also running out: Krogstad's letter revealing everything sits in their mailbox, and once Torvald knows, she will be lost. The only thing that sustains her is her belief that his love for her will prevail; that her husband will see her not as the child-wife she has been, but as the woman who has sacrificed herself for him. She believes that, when he understands the truth, he will willingly sacrifice his pride for her.

But it is not to be. Instead, Torvald's response to the news is completely selfish and self-centered; he is seized by an overwhelming fear of the consequences of Nora's past actions on *his* reputation. He lashes out at her for deceiving him, for her worthless character, for the weaknesses that now render her unfit to be his wife and his children's mother. He tells her he will cast her out of his heart but, for the sake of appearances, not out of his house. Everything will appear to the outside world as it was before — the perfect couple and loving family — as if nothing has changed.

But everything *has* changed. At first shocked

and stunned by her husband's cruelty, Nora suddenly begins to see her life as it really is — as she has unconsciously co-conspired to let it be. She realizes that by living through and for another person, she has betrayed herself, and has sold herself short. The irony, of course, is that Nora had feared that once her husband learned her secret she would lose him, never imagining that the truth was even more painful — that years before she had lost herself. In the midst of this epiphany, a second letter arrives from Krogstad. He has fallen in love with a friend of Nora's and the strength of this woman's belief in him has caused him to look more confidently to the future. He releases Nora from her obligation and encloses the forged bond.

"Nora, I am saved," a relieved Torvald exults.

"And I?" she quietly asks.

Torvald is now suddenly willing to forgive all, touched by his wife's efforts on his behalf, and even sympathetic to what she has been through. Her inexperience and helplessness endear her to him all the more, for she is really just a child who needs to be guided and protected by this benevolence.

But Nora will have none of it. She seizes her life back with her own strength and determination. Nora tells Torvald that she is leaving him — to find her inner life, her soul, and her own direction. She has another duty, equally sacred to being her children's mother and a wife: "My duty to myself."

"I have the strength to become someone else," her husband cries as she walks out the door. But Nora is firm. Whether or not he can change is not the issue. What matters is that *she* has. She has heard Spirit call her name, she is ready to walk out of the darkness of self-denial and live by her own Light. She senses that there is Something More.

FIELD WORK

 *Your Spiritual Journey*

The spiritual journey is one of continually falling on your face, getting up, brushing yourself off, looking sheepishly at God, and taking another step.

AUROBINDO

Why indeed must "God" be a noun? Why not a verb — the most active and dynamic of all?

MARY DALY

"Faith is the centerpiece of a connected life," Terry Tempest Williams tells us. "It allows us to live by the grace of invisible strands. It is a belief in a wisdom superior to our own. Faith becomes a teacher in the absence of fact."

Let's go in search of your talismans of faith. What's this interesting medal in the small tattered leather box? A Star of David? A St. Christopher's medal? Is this a photo of you, in your First Communion dress?

Jot down a few memories of Sunday school or other religious instruction. What was your spiritual grounding? Have you stayed with the religion you were born into? If you were raised in a family without spiritual moorings, that's your grounding too.

What are the meaningful events of your own spiritual journey? Being confirmed? Having a bas mitzvah? Joining a congregation? What did you like or love about your religious training? How do you define the role of the sacred in your life?

Remember, though: if you switch the *a* and the *c* in *sacred*, you get *scared*. How do you define your relationship to the scared, as well?

There is nothing except fear holding you back from awakening to discover the woman you really are deep inside. And believe me, fear is pretty powerful. At a workshop I gave, one woman offered a striking description of her relationship to the scared: "I go forward, and then I come back, and then I go forward and then go around — we face each other and turn away. It's a constant dance."

I think that's an exquisite way to define our relationship with fear. She humanized it, she personified it as a human action. If we can begin to look at the dark emotions that frighten us, that seem out of control, like anger and rage; if we can see them as beautiful spiritual graces sent to propel us from a situation we should not be in, sent to give us the physical power to set boundaries, to give us the voice to say, "Enough, enough, enough," then they're not dark at all. To the contrary, they are very valuable light bringers.

The Greeks and Romans did this with their gods and goddesses. Not only did they personify them by creating recognizable statues and images of them, they gave them personalities with human quirks and strengths so that they could make a connection with them. And that's what we should try to do, too.

The image that we have of Spirit is very deeply rooted in our childhood. For example, I was raised with the idea of a punishing God, a God who looked only at my sins and not at my good points: venial sin, mortal sin, all kinds of layers of sin. I was constantly afraid of committing sins knowingly or unwittingly. I knew that some indescribable but very bad things would happen if I did sin, and worse yet, that sinning would make me a bad person.

Later in life I learned that the word *sin* comes from the Greek; it means "missed the mark." Now can you imagine how different my childhood would have been if I had been told, "When you sin you simply miss the mark of being the highest, best you that you can be." That would have put a completely different spin on it. The child who heard that would have a different perspective on her behavior and its ramifications. Perception is everything because we can flip on its head whatever is confronting us and see the choices we have made.

The gifts I took from my early background are the love of ritual and tradition. I let the other things slide away with a *Thank you. Thank you for the gifts you have given me*. Then I went on my own way, open to whatever I might find.

I have discovered beauty in many different spiritual paths. Now I realize that my authenticity brings them all together. I don't have to be labeled. Neither do you.

I recognize divinity in everything now. And that is one of the miracles for me personally about discovering the sacred in the ordinary: nothing is too insignificant. I love it all. I love the Bible. But I love it not as dogma but as wisdom. I love it as a book of stories. As a writer, I first fell in love with its language, and now I love its embrace of the human condition. There is every situation we could ever experience there — and many, please God, that we never need to experience.

As you turn to look back at your own spiritual roots, embrace its blessings that strengthen and nurture your soul and let go of the other things that keep you estranged from God.

For me, it doesn't matter what form the spiritual journey takes, what's important is the substance of the experience. If you enter the sacred place of any culture, from Muslim mosque to Hindu temple, Baptist revival tent to Jewish synagogue, Catholic cathedral to Native American sweat lodge, you'll find the same messages of truth: Cosmic, composite echoes trying to tell us that we've been looking for love in all the wrong places. We've been looking for the world to love us, when we were created by Spirit to be Spirit's beloved.

Site Report

How is Spirit measured? By attendance at mass, or temple, or week's-end services? If we don't participate in formalized religion, can we affirm that we are on a spiritual journey? Examine your answers to these questions, then write the story of your own spiritual path.

Who were you in this spiritual journey — in all the ages of your site map? What was your spiritual belief, what was your struggle? When did you discover that you love gospel music? When were you singing and loving it for the first time? When were you deeply, truly praying? Ask yourself what you were doing at these different ages and stages, and you'll get the raw material for your narrative.

FIELD WORK

 *Some Day*

It's never too late — in fiction or in life — to revise.

NANCY THAYER

I have always known that at last I would take this road, but yesterday I did not know that it would be today.

NARIHARA

What do you dream of doing some day? Taking a trip to Turkey and standing in the ruins of Troy, then watching the whirling dervishes? Planting your own herb garden? Studying Latin? Spending more time with children? Writing a novel?

Your "someday" envelope is the place to collect all those ads and mailings you've put aside for trips to the Far East, for art classes, New

England Victorian inns, tennis camp, and t'ai chi courses. As you go through those little slips of paper, are you surprised by the frequency with which some of the ideas turn up? How do you feel when you realize you've noted seven times that you heard Beethoven's First Violin Concerto on the radio, and that you'd like to own a CD of it?

Make this a fat folder; add to it and go through it regularly. Can you make some of these dreams happen now?

In his book *Late Bloomers*, Brendan Gill wrote about people who "at whatever cost and under whatever circumstances have succeeded in finding themselves. . . . to find oneself is to have been stumbling about in a dark wood and to have encountered there, unexpectedly and yet how welcomely, a second self, capable of leading one out into the safety of a sunny upland meadow. . . . for we, too, at different stages of the same journey, have our dark woods to traverse and our sunny meadows to attain. If the hour happens to be later than we may have wished, take heart! So much more to be cherished is the bloom."

Among others in the lively group Brendan Gill describes is Harriet Doerr, who enchanted thousands of readers with her first novel, *Stones for Ibarra*, published when she was seventy-four years old. "The act of writing it was in answer to a family challenge: with the death of her husband, whom she had dropped out of college to marry, her children dared her to go back to college, earn a degree, and make a career for herself." She was born in 1910 and attended Smith College in 1927. She received her B.A. from Stanford University in 1977!

"One of the best things about aging is being able to watch imagination overtake memory," she commented in an anthology in which her story "Edie: A Life," was reprinted. "A childhood once considered unremarkable is now revealed with fascinating incidents and people."

Passion, timing, accident — and luck — have enabled many late bloomers to do work they loved, to make a contribution. Still, we all need a little help. Harriet Doerr was encouraged by her children. Margaret Fogarty Rudkin (1897–1967), moved by desperate need, was encouraged by her husband, as Brendan Gill tells us: "In her middle years she found her way to great wealth as a consequence of two unrelated events that had the look of being catastrophes: her husband's financial resources were wiped out by the Depression, and it was discovered that the health of the youngest of her three sons was being endangered by an allergy that made it impossible for him to eat, among other items in his diet, commercially produced bread."

She began to make bread as she remembered her grandmother having made it, and it seemed to improve her son's health. Word that the bread was healthy and delicious spread among neighbors; finally she had to hire helpers and began selling the bread, which was called Pepperidge Farm, named for the family estate.

Her husband took loaves into New York City and persuaded a fashionable food shop to carry them. Eventually the bread began to sell widely, and the family made a fortune.

Friends and family can give us the push and reinforcement we need to take the first step. Even though we may have a marvelous idea, we all need the nurturance of support. Have you been able to find support in your circle of intimates? Who believes in you more than you do in yourself?

Site Report

What are five things you'd like to do someday? What passions did you confide to that five-year-diary from long ago? Write them by the appropriate age on your site map. Is someday today for some of those yearnings?

"It is only possible to live happily ever after on a day-to-day basis," says Margaret Bonnano. What steps can you take today to increase the chances that you'll live happily ever after? Take calcium, exercise, call a friend, pay your bills, yes. What else?

Live so that when someday comes, you'll be able to say, as Mary C. Morrison does in her wonderful book about aging, *Let Evening*

Come: "We have had our world as in our time, and if we relive it well in memory, it will bring us wisdom. We will come, each of us, to see our life as the whole that it is. Events that seemed random will show themselves to be parts of a coherent whole. Decisions that we were hardly aware of making will reveal themselves as significant choices, and we can honestly and dispassionately regret the poor ones and rejoice in the good ones. We can call up emotions that seemed devastating in their time, and recollect *them* in tranquillity, forgiving others and ourselves. When we do this, we have truly had our world as in our time, and it is in our possession from that time on, giving us its gifts of wisdom and wholeness."

Shattered

This is the hour of lead
Remembered, if outlived
As freezing persons recollect the snow —
First chill, then stupor,
Then the letting go.

EMILY DICKINSON

The House of Belonging

The blessings for which we hunger are not to be found in other places or people. These gifts can only be given to you by yourself. They are at home in the hearth of your soul.

JOHN O'DONOHUE

Almost no image holds as much sway over our romantic reveries as the dream house we will someday buy or build. "Late in life, with indomitable courage, we continue to say that we are going to do what we have not yet done," the French philosopher and poet Gaston Bachelard confesses. "We are going to build a house." From the scented linen closet to the built-in kitchen pantry, from the window seat in the upstairs hallway to the rose-covered arbor leading to the backyard, each detail of this sacred dwelling has been carefully worked out. Every woman secretly believes that someday she'll cross the threshold of her dream house, whether carried by Prince Charming or walking on her own.

It doesn't matter where you live today —

trailer, apartment, or a house. You may be rooming in a motel or seeking sanctuary in a safe house halfway between your past and your future. You may even be without a roof to call your own, camping out on a friend's couch or community cot; held hostage in a palace or pitching a tent on the dark side of the moon. It doesn't matter. If you're reading this, you're homeward bound. The blueprints of your House of Belonging exist as spiritual energy and hover over your head, ready, when you are, to be pulled down from Heaven to shelter your soul on Earth. Each day, as Emily Dickinson says, you "dwell in possibility." You must believe this because it's true.

The House of Belonging is an ancient Celtic metaphor for the human body as the earthly home for the soul; it is also used to describe the deep peace and feeling of safety, joy and contentment found in intimate soul friend relationships. This beautiful expression of connection is poetically explored in John O'Donohue's Anam Cara. "When you learn to love and to let your self be loved, you come home to the hearth of your own spirit. You are warm and sheltered. You are completely at one in the house of your own longing and belonging."

Building the House of Belonging is the soul's commitment to living a passionate life; your Authentic Self is the architect. "Can't nothing make your life work if you ain't the architect." (Thank you, Terry McMillan.) The timbers with which you build the House of Belonging are your choices; courage is the foundation stone; patience, perseverance, and permission are your bricks; faith is the mortar. "The life we want is not merely the one we have chosen and made," the poet Wendell Berry tells us. "It is the one we must be choosing and making."

Are you finding it difficult to make the choices your future is urging you toward? Is there a choice facing you this morning that's more serious than whether or not to drive an extra run for the car pool this week? If there is, will its ripples extend into next year? Are you taking into consideration the woman you'll be a year from now? "You make what seems a simple choice: choose a man or a job or a neighborhood," Jessamyn West muses (as well we all should); "however, what you have chosen is not a man or a job or a neighborhood, but a life."

If you seriously embrace the miracle of reembodiment and are making a real effort to excavate your Authentic Self, next year a more knowledgeable woman will be coping with to-day's choice. So, start thinking of yourself as only a place-holder. You might like to ask your Authentic Self what she thinks. She knows something you don't — your destiny: where you're headed, the stops on the way, and when you'll arrive. If it's time for any of the itinerary to be revealed to you, it will be. If it's not, it won't be. But you'll never know the soul's travel plans if you don't ask, "By the way, what should I pack?"

I once fell head over heels in lust with a man I knew absolutely nothing about except that he was the essence of sartorial splendor. Fell so fast, so deep, so hard, I had to call it love; completely rearranged my life to accommodate my new paramour despite intuitive misgivings. He was not an open man, and while I knew what was currently happening on the surface of his life, he kept his past very close to his chest, even while I was in his arms. Three months into the relationship, we were sitting in a restaurant and something felt strange; it was as if I were having an out-of-body experience or a dream while I was awake. It felt as though my spirit physically withdrew its presence from my body and stood at the side of the table, quietly and dispassionately observing the dynamics between these two people. Suddenly my man was nattering on like an inmate on the lam from an asylum, unpeeling his past like the layers of an onion. Mr. Romance was carrying a ton of heavy psychological baggage — phobias, paranoia, women who'd done him wrong, ancient rage toward his parents — deep-seated emotional issues that I'd worked out years before. He was rich, powerful, and successful, but spiritually he was a Neanderthal. Warning bells began to go off. I couldn't wait to get out of there; I suddenly came down with a *dreadful* headache. Once home, I snapped at my Authentic Self, "You've known this all along? Heaven knows, it would have been helpful if *I'd been clued in.* Different choices would have been made three months ago."

"Heaven *did* know," the wag shot back. "But you didn't ask."

Now, before making major decisions, I take my questions to the spiritual world for consultation. I do this by sleeping on my question for three nights. Just before I go to sleep I'll ask my question. It's been my experience that if on the fourth day, I don't wake up with clarity, during that day I'll get an intuitive hunch or a flash. Or I'll discover bits of "Isn't that interesting?" information I didn't have earlier that help to fill in the blanks. When in doubt, don't do a thing until you sleep on it.

Think of time as a long stretch on a four-lane highway. Look back over your shoulder: the past is waving good-bye. Look up ahead: the future beckons, but its form is hazy. Something's waiting, but what? Should you be exhilarated or anxious? Sometimes they feel like the same thing. "What makes us so afraid is the thing we half see, or half hear, as in a wood at dusk, when a tree stump becomes an animal and a sound becomes a siren," the Irish writer Edna O'Brien reassures us. "And most of that fear is the fear of not knowing, of not actually seeing correctly."

We are also afraid because so often we feel alone, and when we're lonely we think that we'll remain that way until the end of our days.

"Have you ever been at sea in a dense fog, when it seemed as if a tangible white darkness shut you in, and the great ship, tense and anxious, groped her way toward the shore with plummet and sounding-line, and you waited with beating heart for something to happen?" Helen Keller asks. As an infant, serious illness rendered her blind and deaf. Nonetheless, she went on to be educated at Radcliffe College and to travel the world, writing and lecturing on behalf of the visually and aurally impaired. In her autobiography, *The Story of My Life* (published in 1903), she describes the day that her great teacher and soul friend Anne Sullivan first came to her home in Alabama. Helen was six years old and did not yet know that language existed.

"I was like that ship before my education began, only I was without compass or sounding-line, and had no way of knowing how near the harbor was. 'Light! Give me light!' was the wordless cry of my soul, and the light of love shone on me in that very hour.

"I felt approaching footsteps. I stretched out my hand. . . . Someone took it, and I was caught up and held close in the arms of her who had come to reveal all things to me, and, more than all things else, to love me."

Isn't that the most beautiful description of

the Authentic Self? *She who has come to reveal all things to you.* But you need to ask for her guidance. What's ahead? What should I do? Help me to learn to trust. Teach me today in one small way that I can trust you. She will.

There are moments when we all feel little, alone, frightened, and frail, extending our hands hesitantly or using them as a shield to protect us from the unknown. We may look like grown-ups in our lipstick and high heels, but we know better. Some days I seriously wonder whether I have five restless ten-year-olds jumping up and down inside me ready to take on the world, or ten whiny, clingy, fraidy-cat five-year-olds. While it's true that we're spiritual beings with access to the same power that created the cosmos, we are enfleshed only by skin, not iron. We're so easily bruised and scraped — especially those of us who make it all seem easy. Making it look easy is the hardest thing in the world to do.

Fragile moments come to all of us — to the cashier at the grocery store who's trying to keep it all together as she rings you up (not quite as fast as you'd like); to the television superstar so wealthy and successful she's an easy target of the self-righteous; to the politician's wife ashamed by her husband's front-page peccadillos; to the domestic goddess who has to endure the embarrassment of her husband walking out on her (with her former assistant) while she's on tour promoting a book on weddings, no less. Say what you will, there but for the grace of God go we, and don't you *ever* forget it. Those public women who seem to live lives larger than our own — whether we love, admire, envy, or revile them — are more to be pitied than censured when they fall down.

So when our "little days" come, when we feel alone and helpless, we need to remember that outstretched arms are waiting to pick us up, not to make it all better for us, but to help us make it all better for ourselves. We don't have to live life alone unless we want to.

Dwelling in the House of Spirit

*Every spirit builds itself a house, and beyond
its house, a world, and beyond its world,
a heaven. Know then that world exists for you.*

RALPH WALDO EMERSON

When life was not tidy, "it was the small things that helped, taken one by one and savoured," the English writer Rumer Godden recalls in her mesmerizing memoir of passionate, authentic life well lived, *A House With Four Rooms*. Things like planting Japanese poppies, drinking very good tea out of a thin china cup, eating hot buttered crumpets, rereading a love letter. Small things savoured, even if you have to force yourself to focus on them, is how to become "happy when you are miserable." On the *Simple Abundance* journey I discovered how right she was.

One of the reasons I love Rumer Godden's writing is that she stitches the colorful thread of her extraordinary life — domestic, creative, and spiritual — with such deftness; the hem that seems to hold her life together rarely pulls, gaps, or needs staples the way mine does more often than I care to admit. Her career has spanned six decades: fifty-seven books — novels for both children and adults — nonfiction, short story collections, and poetry. The *New York Times* noted that she was a writer who "belongs in the small exclusive club of women — it includes Isak Dinesen and Beryl Markham — who could do pretty well anything they set their minds to, hunting tigers, bewitching men, throwing elegant dinner parties, winning literary fame." This sounds like the Something More club to me.

How would you describe the members of *your* Something More club?

Of all Rumer Godden's books, however, it's her memoirs that are my favorites. I am captivated by how she lived, nurtured a family, and created many homes out of shells of houses all over the world, while writing almost continuously. She is a glorious storyteller, but no story is as riveting as real life.

The soulcraft of creating and sustaining safe havens, set apart from the world, in which to seek and savour small authentic joys, is a recurring theme in the work of women writers.

Edith Wharton was in her fifties when she fell passionately in love with a house in the south of France. "I feel as if I were going to get married — to the right man at last!" She described a woman's nature like a huge house with rooms set aside for visitors and other rooms — the more comfortable ones — meant for only family and friends. "But beyond that, far beyond, are other rooms, the handles of whose doors are never turned . . . and in the inmost room, the holy of holies, the soul sits alone and waits for the footstep that never comes." Whose footsteps does your soul listen for? Another's or your own?

Rumer Godden's secret to living authentically, no matter where she actually kept house, seems to have been dwelling in the House of Spirit: "There is an Indian proverb or axiom that says that everyone is a house with four rooms, a physical, a mental, an emotional and a spiritual. Most of us tend to live in one room most of the time, but unless we go into every room every day, even if only to keep it aired, we are not a complete person."

Home Is Where Your Heart Is

There are homes you run from and homes you run to.

LAURA CUNNINGHAM

Several years ago, after her marriage ended, a good friend was forced to do the unthinkable; sell the beautifully restored, eighteenth-century farmhouse in which she had lived, loved, and raised six children over three decades. It was wrenching to watch her pack up a lifetime of memories and go through the motions of moving on.

From the outside, the small suburban town house she settled into was as unassuming and plain as her former home had been imposing and grand. I remember feeling awkward as I rang the doorbell on my first visit. Besides enduring the pain of divorce and dislocation, was my friend living each day with the discomfort of trading down?

When she opened the door, her glowing face revealed that in many ways her life had been upgraded. I hadn't seen her this happy and serene in years. Her new house radiated a warm hospitality that seemed organic: it was almost as if the walls, windows, ceilings, and floors possessed human qualities. As she led me through each light-filled room, the peace of this dear place was palpable. I had not been having a good day; but here, drinking afternoon tea and basking in the benediction of a cherry tree blooming outside her living room window, I remembered what contentment felt like.

As reluctantly I took my leave, I asked my friend to call me first if she ever wanted to sell this place. It was a ridiculous request. The house can hold only two people comfortably, and I was married with a teenage daughter and three cats. But she declared that she had no intention of ever selling. She was settled here now. She was healing.

"Besides, there isn't a man alive I'd leave this house for," she declared. If we hadn't been laughing so hard, we might have heard the angels chuckling.

That's because last year I watched my friend walk down the aisle with a wonderful man who was so much in love with her that after they were pronounced man and wife, he flashed a victory sign to the congregation. And only a few weeks before, following a legal separation from my husband, I'd moved into her old place, and set about transforming it into my own personal sanctuary.

Now, when I glance back at my gratitude journal over the last year, I'm astounded at how frequently "my beautiful home" appears there. While I was stunned to be starting over from scratch (right down to new can openers and pot holders), I now realize that my new home is coaxing me back into my own authenticity in a way I could have never imagined. As I glance around, I see glimmers of the woman I've always wanted to become expressing herself in myriad ways — favorite quotes stenciled on walls, a soothing yet surprising color palette, fresh flowers in every room. Each day, in small ways, I come home to my Authentic Self, or, to echo Edith Wharton, perhaps I am living with my true soul mate after all these years: my Self.

Heaven knows how happy I was the day I hung in my entryway a whitewashed, distressed wooden pegboard on which is carved "The House of Belonging." I'd just crossed the most important threshold of my life: the house of my own longing.

But while I had a new place of dwelling, I was sorely mistaken if I thought I'd arrived.

Crossing the threshold of my longing didn't end my sojourn to self-discovery and authenticity; it only deepened and intensified it. Suddenly there was no longer any one person standing in my way to happiness — at home, at work, or in the world. No more excuses, no one to blame. No more mitigating circumstances. No more copping a plea or copping out. No more shrugging my misery onto anybody else's shoulders. "Oh, the holiness of being the injured party," Maya Angelou admits. Amen.

The unvarnished, naked, unforgiving truth was, if I wanted Something More in my life — and I did — it was up to me to find out what it was and go after it.

A Victim of Circumstances

People are always blaming their circumstances for what they are. I don't believe in circumstances. The people who get on in this world are the people who get up and look for the circumstances they want, and, if they can't find them, make them.

GEORGE BERNARD SHAW

What is the difference between an excuse and a circumstance? This is not a rhetorical question. Here's a hint. An excuse is why you did or didn't do something: a perfectly plausible reason, a defense, a rationalization (you hope) you can live with to explain away action or inaction. *I didn't have the money. I couldn't find the time. I'm too old. I'm too tired. I don't feel well. He wouldn't let me. I've got kids.*

And circumstances? Well, circumstances are the truths that define your situation. No money? No time? Couldn't find a sitter?

Oddly enough, according to the dictionary, *circumstance* and *excuse* are not synonymous. Tell that to a hundred million women.

Is there a difference between *excuses* that stand in our way of living authentically and *circumstances* that seem to limit our choices, reduce our options, hamper our ability to be happy? According to the nineteenth-century educator and dictionary man, Noah Webster — a man who recognized his passion in *epistemology,* the science of understanding or knowing through the naming of things — to *define* is "to discover and give meaning through descriptive words."

But sometimes no noun, verb, adjective, or adverb can describe or impart the depth and breadth — never mind assess the meaning — of an experience, a feeling, a hunch, a risk, a choice, a challenge, a secret, a sensation, or a role we are called upon to play or fill. These are situations that throw our lives into chaos, confusion, or even clarity.

I believe madness escalates in direct proportion to our willful insistence on imposing meaning on the ineffable — that which defies and denies what makes sense, what seems right, fitting, and proper, what has gone before, what's familiar, what's fair.

What is. Circumstances beyond our control.

What's going on today. But not necessarily what will always be. We don't have to be, become, or stay victims of circumstances *forever* unless we choose to do so. We are meant to live through our circumstances, not stay stuck in them. "The conflict between what one is and who one is expected to be touches all of us," Merle Shain confides. "And sometimes, rather than reach for what one could be, we choose the comfort of the failed role, preferring to be the victim of circumstance, the person who didn't have a chance."

A Life of One's Own

If you do not tell the truth about yourself you cannot tell it about other people.

VIRGINIA WOOLF

In 1896, while he was gathering the raw research material destined to become the underpinnings of what is now known as psychoanalysis, Austrian physician Sigmund Freud was disturbed by a recurring pattern of remembrance among the women patients he was treating for nervous disorders and depression. He was convinced that "at the bottom of every case of hysteria there are one or more occurrences of premature sexual experiences." However, as many of his patients began retrieving their repressed memories, Freud became increasingly alarmed. So many women were naming their fathers as their seducers. In a letter to an associate, Freud confessed that the very thought that so many respectable men were sexually abusing their daughters was "astonishing." If he went public with these claims, he'd be written off as a lunatic: "It was hardly credible that perverted acts against children were so general," he rationalized.

Freud's work on forgotten psychic wounds and the use of hypnosis to recall early childhood traumas was already controversial; he could only imagine how an accusation of epidemic incest among the well-to-do would impact upon his reputation and career. There simply had to be another explanation. Eventually Dr. Freud convinced himself and the rest of the world that his female patients' memories of sexual abuse were "figments of their imaginations based on their own sexual desires," a fabricated stretch of reasoning that may have helped establish a brand-new medical discipline, but caused irreparable (and unpardonable) harm to countless women while promising to help them heal.

One of those women was Virginia Woolf, the acclaimed English novelist and critic, whose ability to conjure up the fully fleshed inner lives of her characters helped shape the contemporary novel. Through the use of imagery, symbols, feelings, thoughts, and personal impressions in a poetic stream of consciousness, she was able to give her readers insights into human nature and themselves. Unfortunately, she was unable to do that for herself.

Although she was an accomplished, well-respected, and highly prolific writer, Virginia Woolf suffered from a debilitating depression that frequently incapacitated her. It was acute self-loathing, her "looking-glass shame." From the time she was a teenager, the symptoms of what became known in the family as "Virginia's madness" were many and varied: irritability, tantrums, inexplicable mood swings, sleep disturbances, agonizing headaches, and an inability to eat properly. Virginia was a sickly child and a frail woman who experienced a series of nervous breakdowns that featured disorientation, memory lapses, and hallucinations of drowning or being subsumed by monstrous creatures. All too often she exhibited self-destructive and self-abusive behavior, including numerous suicide attempts. She also suffered from a deep hatred of her body, a fear of men, and an abhorrence of sex.

"Virginia Woolf was a sexually abused child; she was an incest survivor," Louise DeSalvo, one of the world's most authoritative scholars on Woolf, reveals in her brilliant, courageous, chilling, and unflinching book *Virginia Woolf: The Impact of Childhood Sexual Abuse on Her Life and Work*. After Woolf's death in 1941, it was discovered that she had left clues to the depth of her trauma embedded in both her private and published work. However, it was always glossed over by her biographers, who continued to perpetuate, as late as 1984, the myth of Virginia's childhood as one being "bathed in protective love." But DeSalvo couldn't figure out why the incest Virginia experienced had never been explored seriously by literary scholars as an important influence on Woolf's fictional portraits of children and adolescents. "Every secret of a writer's soul, every experience of his life, every quality of his mind is written large in his works, yet we require critics to explain the one, and biographers to expound on the other," Woolf wrote in 1928.

Virginia Woolf didn't need another biographer, she needed a kindred spirit — a soul friend across time — to bring forth her secret into the light of understanding. All writers know that the empty page conveys more than words can possibly say. It is the pauses — in life, love, and literature — that are pregnant with meaning. What's left unsaid or merely hinted at, reveals more than what's expressed. A writer's truth is always buried between the lines.

Because she was finally ready to come to terms with her own truth, Louise DeSalvo tells us in her own piercing and poignant memoir, *Vertigo*, she was ready to rediscover the depths of Virginia Woolf's life, not as a writer, but as a woman. How we are drawn to the mystery of our destiny is exquisite. She admits that when she started work on Virginia Woolf, she did not yet know how similar their stories would prove to be. DeSalvo had no way of knowing that her sister would take her own life as Virginia did; she had not yet recognized that depression was the core of her own mother's life, as it had been the core of Woolf's and Woolf's mother's; she did not realize that she too would fight depression; and she had not made the connection that both she and Woolf were abuse survivors. But most of all, Louise DeSalvo did not know that, through studying Virginia Woolf, she would learn the redemptive and healing power of writing.

Of course, we are all wounded, and not all our wounds are the same. However, there is a lesson we can take from every woman's tale. As Louise DeSalvo points out, our authentic calling, our true work in this world, becomes an outgrowth of our lives. Our work can transform and transcend whatever traumas we survive, turning them into something useful for ourselves and, we hope, for others. As she says: "My work has changed my life. My work has saved my life. My life has changed my work." It can for each of us.

In April 1939, when war clouds gathered over Europe, Virginia began to write her autobiography, *A Sketch of the Past*, which was to be an examination of the mysterious, half-hidden incidents of her life that, when re-called, triggered the eruption of powerfully dark emotions in her. At this time Sigmund Freud was living in London as a refugee; she visited him once. DeSalvo explains that Freud encouraged her to examine the root of her life-long depression by looking for "its causes in her own personal history" and in "the fractured pieces of her emotional life." Although this "was a dangerous and difficult enterprise," Virginia was ready to stop running away from her demons and engage in her own personal exca-vation process.

Born in 1882 into a dysfunctional Victorian family in which incest and abusive behavior were part of the daily round, Virginia had been molested by her two older half-brothers (as was her sister, Vanessa Bell) from the time she was six years old until she was in her early twenties. In fact, all the women in her family, including her half-sisters and her mother, were victims of some sort of abuse — sexual, emo-tional, or physical violence. Although the incest was a familiar whisper, "their stories were hidden and rationalized, revised, and recast, both in the versions which the family told themselves and each other, and in the versions of their lives that were written after their deaths," writes DeSalvo.

How many truths do we hide, rationalize, revise, recast, not only for family and friends, but for ourselves as well? "Spiritual empowerment is evidenced in our lives by our willingness to tell ourselves the truth, to listen to the truth when it's told to us, and to dispense truth as lovingly as possible, when we feel compelled to talk from the heart," Christina Baldwin tells us in her book, *Life's Companion*. She's right, of course, but that doesn't mean it's easy. Enlightenment and empowerment aren't instant. The *satori,* as the soul's awakening is called in Buddhism, usually requires an emotional investment of years of hemming, hawing, and hedging before we're even willing to stand still long enough to face the truth.

During her unraveling process, Virginia recalled many disturbing incidents that left her with feelings of rage, powerlessness, and shame — all common responses among incest survivors — for somehow "allowing" herself to be victimized. Most important, she recalled being sexually assaulted, in one case outside the dining room of the family's vacation home (which later became the setting for her novel *To the Lighthouse*). DeSalvo links the heartbreaking memory of this dining room incident and its attendant disgust and shame with the fact that Virginia had eating disorders later in life. Then, too, the assault took place near where a great mirror hung; very possibly, she watched herself being assaulted over her attacker's shoulder. Forever after, Virginia hated looking at herself in mirrors. If she subscribed to the popular Freudian theory that her memories of sexual abuse could be reduced to her own "uncontrolled urges and forces," she would have to believe that her painful memories were the result of her own unconscious "wishes." The unfairness of this distortion is soul shattering.

Even if nothing had been going on in Virginia's interior life, she was living through a very difficult and anxious era. The Nazis had invaded all of Europe during this period — bombs were falling over London and southern England; Virginia's own home had been shelled. She believed — as did many people — that the British could not hold out much longer and that invasion was imminent. Her husband, Leonard Woolf, was Jewish and they discussed taking "sleeping draughts" should the Nazis occupy England, rather than being sent to concentration camps.

Then, while reading her father's letters to her mother, from which she has hoping to glean some biographical information, she learned that she had been an unplanned child, a discovery that shocked and devastated her. Her parents, she wrote, "wished to limit their family and did what they could to prevent me."

As Louise DeSalvo sees it, this revelation was the final blow. "In reading Freud, she had been forced to question the accuracy of her vision of the past; in reading her father, she learned something new that in the best of times would be difficult to integrate." Overwhelmed by a lifetime of struggle against feelings of rejection, inadequacy, hopelessness, and fear, what Woolf wanted most was peace. As the country waited for the invasion that did not come, she could wait no longer. In the fourth week of March 1941, Virginia walked purposefully to a nearby river, weighted her coat down with a heavy rock, stepped into the water, and drowned.

What we must never forget in her tragic story, Louise DeSalvo reminds us, is that "in 1892 a terrified ten-year-old girl by the name of Virginia Stephen first picked up her pen to write a portrait of the world as seen through the eyes of an abused child. And from that time forward throughout her lifetime she never stopped examining why and how the abuse had happened, and what it had meant to her, and what it must have meant to others." Virginia Woolf "knew that behind the social masks that ordinary people wore, there were private sorrows, though to look at them, one would never guess it."

Yet in 1897, at the age of fifteen, after being brutalized for more than half her young life, she could still write: "Here is life given us each alike, & we must do our best with it. Our hand in the sword hilt — & an unuttered fervent vow!"

She determined that her destiny was going to be "very sacred" and "very important." Although ultimately she was unable to bear her burden of profound personal damage, neither *excuses* nor *circumstances* stopped her from leaving a legacy to those among us who are ready to dig deep to discover and process our truths, no matter how unfathomable they might be.

Virginia Woolf's vision for herself became at that time "an embattled one," Louise DeSalvo concludes. "She saw herself as a woman warrior, like Joan of Arc in her commitment to the cause of living her life, and possibly even killing, or dying, for her beliefs." And in many respects she was just such a warrior; her pen was her sword.

The Hour of Lead

Razors pain you; Rivers are damp;
Acids stain you; And drugs cause cramp.
Guns aren't lawful; Nooses give;
Gas smells awful; You might as well live.

DOROTHY PARKER

We cannot blot out one page of our lives, but we can throw the book in the fire," George Sand confessed in 1837. I have never hurled my autobiography into the fire, but there have been a few desolate times of impenetrable darkness and despair when I've given it a thought. Sat and stared at the flames. Cried, prayed, closed the book, gone to bed, been saved from self-destruction through Amazing Grace to awake the next morning, humbled, penitent, and grateful for another rewrite. "As subjects, we all live in suspense, from day to day, from hour to hour," the novelist Mary McCarthy tells us. "In other words, we are the hero of our own story. We cannot believe that it is finished, that we are 'finished,' even though we may say so; we expect another chapter, another installment, tomorrow or next week."

But sometimes the suspense of worrying what will happen next — or the fear that something won't — feels as though it's killing us slowly. *I want it to be over. It will never get better. You don't understand. There's no way out.* "People commit suicide for only one reason — to escape torment," Li Ang writes in her novel *The Butcher's Wife*.

And she's so right. When you're convinced that there is nothing more worth living for and that there never will be — not now, not tomorrow, not ever; when there isn't a shred of evidence that things will ever change or get better (How? Why? Says who?); when the excruciating pain — physical, emotional, psychic — is so harrowing you're on your knees begging for release, you don't want another chapter. You want to write only two words: *The End*. "They shoot horses, don't they?" Horace McCoy asks in his 1935 novel about a 1930s dance marathon that's a microcosm of human misery. In the 1969 movie of the same name, Jane Fonda plays the young, self-destructive woman who attracts her tragic destiny in the form of a drifter; she wants to kill herself, but needs another hand to pull the trigger.

"Everybody has thought of suicide and then felt: 'pushed another inch, and it could have been me,' " admits Diane Ackerman, the prize-winning poet and author, in her book *A Slender*

Thread: Rediscovering Hope at the Heart of Crisis. Having worked as a telephone volunteer in a crisis center, she meditates on the passion and pathos between those who feel unable to hold on to life any longer and those on the other end of the line who, by listening to their stories and validating their pain, are trying to help them "keep their options open" and give life another chance.

"The planet is full of hurt people, angry people, lost people, confused people, people who have explored the vast cartography of trouble, and people stunned by a sudden grief. . . . The minute one imagines oneself in the victim's predicament, and moves to save him or her, it becomes an act of self-love," Ackerman writes.

I do understand why people, particularly women, kill themselves: self-loathing. Sylvia Plath set the table for her children's breakfast, and then put her head in the oven. She'd written *the* novel of the sixties, *The Bell Jar*, which candidly tackled the reality of adolescent depression and suicide attempts. In the novel, she saved her heroine. But she was too angry, too passive, and too exhausted to save herself. Poet Anne Sexton washed down sleeping pills with a cocktail and then took a final nap in a car filled with carbon monoxide. Five years before, she'd written two poems about unrequited love that became haunting, self-fulfilling prophecies. "[I] have fantasies of killing myself," she wrote in a letter, and finally becoming "the powerful one, not the powerless one." For both of these incredibly creative but deeply troubled women, self-loathing was the common denominator. I find it heartbreaking and infuriating that, no matter how accomplished women may be, we continue to see ourselves in the diminished distortion of another's view of us, especially if that view belongs to a man with whom we are having an intimate relationship.

Ultimately life or death revolves around the power to choose your own destiny. "Choice is a signature of our species," Ackerman reminds us. Flip through the pages of world literature, and you'll be shattered by how often women write about killing themselves because they forget this all-important life-sustaining power.

Of course one of literature's most famous female suicides was conjured up by a man. In Tolstoy's *Anna Karenina*, neither Anna nor her lover, Alexy Vronsky, the dashing young army officer for whom she abandons her husband, child, and respectability, were able to stand up to the pressure when the members of their social set shunned them for their adulterous affair. Toward the end of the novel, Anna and Vronsky are living unhappily together; his love for her has diminished considerably during their social banishment; his romantic fling has reverberated with a few more serious repercussions than he'd originally expected. Anna is so unhappy she wants to die. She's sacrificed everything for him and all he's doing is sulking. *"To die! . . . Yes, that would solve everything."* Wipe out her shame and make him pay. *"If I die, he too will be sorry. He will pity me, love me and will suffer on my account."*

When you read those words, her pain sounds pretty melodramatic, doesn't it? But how many times does that thought run through a woman's mind? Even once is once too often. "Magical thinking," Ackerman observes, is "the belief that suicide will change a relationship with someone." It sure will. He'll go on to others and you won't.

"The beginning of things . . . is necessarily vague, tangled, chaotic and exceedingly disturbing," especially for Edna Pontellier, the beautiful, bored, and tragic heroine who swims in the nude to her death in Kate Chopin's novel *The Awakening*, published in 1899. But when you're miserable and see no way out, so is the end: vague, tangled, chaotic, and exceedingly disturbing. It is the same for those left behind, especially the children of suicides; eighty percent of them will also attempt to kill themselves, and many will succeed. I also know that none of us has any idea of the countless lives we touch and change for the better in the course of our lifetime — or of the lives we're shortchanging, including our own.

"No grief, pain, misfortune, or 'broken heart'

is an excuse of cutting off one's life while any power of service remains," Charlotte Perkins Gilman wrote in 1935. Unfortunately, she wrote it in her own suicide note. It seemed to be the only option when Charlotte sadly came to the conclusion that her "usefulness" was over. Perhaps that was because she'd spent her entire life living for others, never for herself. Life's sorriest victim is the martyr.

We'd like to think that we're insignificant, but the truth is that each one of us has enough power embedded in our being to set the world on fire; instead, all too often, self-loathing singes our soul, until, like a match thrown on a mattress, we burst into flames.

A friend of mine was once engulfed in despair over a situation that seemed so completely out of her hands that she seriously considered taking her own life. She went so far as to make plans, right down to checking into a hotel so that her family wouldn't find her body. Although we'd had many conversations about her problem and her deepening ordeal, I had no idea just how hopeless she'd been feeling until after she'd made the decision to live and go back into therapy. When she admitted to me how close she'd come, I told her I wished I'd known how distraught she had been.

"No, you don't. If I'd said, 'Sarah, I'm so unhappy I'm going to kill myself,' what do you think you would have said?"

"Probably, 'Don't even think about it!' Or

'Don't talk like that!' "

"Exactly. Which is why I didn't say anything."

Of course, she's right. Which is a very sad commentary on the concept of unconditional love. We can't bear to think that someone we care about is so distraught that they'd rather not be living, or that we can't help them, so we hush them up.

I asked my friend what brought her back from the brink. She said she'd made a list, weighing the pros and cons. Then she wrote out the names of all the most important people in her life: family, friends, colleagues. She had thought about each one and assigned a potential response to her suicide:

Sorry/Disturbed
Grief-stricken/Get over it
Devastated/Never forgive themselves or me

To her great surprise, most of the people on her list fell into the last category. She decided not to kill herself when she realized she'd leave a trail of devastation in her wake. "I wasn't willing to face that karma," she says with a smile. Now she volunteers as a suicide hot-line counselor. When a voice on the other end of the line says, "I want to die," my friend says, "Tell me all about it. Tell me why," and then lets the caller ramble on for as long as it takes. But she makes the person write out a list while

314

still on the phone with her.

Suicide is the ultimate eviction from the House of Belonging. "I've never quite believed that one chance is all I get," Anne Tyler thinks. She's right, but you've got to be here to get it.

Making the Best of It

I read and walked for miles at night along the beach, writing bad blank verse and searching endlessly for someone wonderful who would step out of the darkness and change my life. It never crossed my mind that that person could be me.

ANNA QUINDLEN

It was as though his tears could wash away her hurt. " 'Oh, Jesus,' he whispered, 'I am so god-damned sorry.' And I cried, too. When I cried in those days it was for his pain, not for mine." This is how Fran Benedetto, the heroine in Anna Quindlen's powerful novel, *Black and Blue*, begins to explain to us her unconscious, insidious, surreptitious descent into self-loathing's purgatory: becoming and remaining a victim of domestic violence. Year after year, she would tell their son — and herself — that the bruises and broken bones were the result of accidents, and they sure were: "The accident was that I met Bobby Benedetto in a bar, and fell crazy in love." The hitting was there from the first; then the hitting turned into humiliation and then into hatred — but not for him, for herself, "the cringing self that was afraid to pick up the remote control from the coffee table in case it was just the thing that set him off."

According to Catholic teaching, those who have died in the state of grace but not sinless, not completely without blame, expiate their unforgiven transgressions by undergoing punishment before being admitted to Heaven in a place called purgatory. The Buddhist's purgatorial equivalent is called Yama, where good karma and bad karma are calculated. How long a soul remains in purgatory is anyone's guess. As a little Irish Catholic penitent child, I remember feeling as if the destinies of all the lost souls in purgatory were dependent on my prayers alone to get them out. I don't worry about the souls in purgatory these days; now I pray for battered women.

At one point, Fran likens her situation to one she'd read about in the newspaper, in which a custodian secretly kept a woman imprisoned in his building's basement and, whenever the mood struck, went down to the cellar and had his way with her. "Part of me had been in a cellar, too, waiting for the sound of footfalls on the stairs. And I wasn't even chained. I stayed because I thought things would get better, or at least not worse. I stayed because I wanted my son to have a father and I wanted a home. For a long time I stayed because I loved Bobby Benedetto. . . . [But] he made me his accomplice in what he did, and I made [our son] Robert mine."

And finally, this realization becomes Fran's turning point. She recognizes that her son has become a fearful, secretive, distrusting child. Fran comes to see the destruction in the secret lies she's told Robert about accidentally walking into doors in the dark; in the diversions she's created, such as turning on the bathroom taps full blast to mask the sound of her sobbing; and in the stories she's made up for him about the terrifying noises and slamming sounds at night being from the television in the next room. "But in some closed-up-closed-down corner of his mind" he knows the truth, and Fran knows that "the secret was killing the kid in him and the woman in me, what was left of her. I had to save him, and myself."

Why hadn't she grabbed her son and left sooner? "It's hard to understand, for a woman who had never had it happen to her, never watched her husband sob in contrition with those choking sobs that sound like he's swallowing glass." First Fran stayed because they were starting a family, and then she stayed because she was unwilling to mess up her child's formative years; and then, when that was no longer a factor, she stayed, even after the end of the school term, because leaving meant messing up the holidays. "So I stayed, and stayed, and stayed" — even as she came to understand that her husband's surest expression of love came with the bowl of soup he brought her after breaking her collarbone.

For leaving means leaving it *all* behind, the good as well as the bad. It's not just leaving behind the horrendous arguments, or even the "stretches of tedium" that lazily connect our married days together, but also leaving a life that feels larger than the one we'll live on our own, even if, as Fran comes to know, it's actually a life that's "been whittled way down to its essentials."

In the first few months after I separated and was living on my own, the things I missed so acutely, the recollections that seared my soul, were the little, barely recognized moments of rhythm and reassurance in my daily round: feeding the cats in the morning while the water boiled for tea, setting the table at night, watching movies together as a family, and eating hamburgers every Saturday night.

As Fran tells us, "Whenever I thought about leaving, as much as leaving Bobby I thought about leaving my house. Balloon shades and miniblinds and the way I felt at night sleeping on my extra-firm mattress under my own roof . . . all of it helped keep me there. And if that sounds foolish, just think about the solid feelings you get when you open your cabinets and there are mugs for the coffee that have held the coffee day after day, year after year . . . Small things: routine, order. That's what kept me there for the longest time. That, and love. That, and fear. Not fear of Bobby, fear of winding up in some low-rent apartment subdivision with a window that looked out on a wall. Fear of winding up where I came from . . ."

For a long time that was enough to overcome the constant anxiety of not knowing when or where his hand would find her again — and how close to killing her he might get the next time. "It took me a dozen years of house pride and seventeen years of marriage before I realized there were worse things than cramped kitchens and grubby carpeting."

In the end, Fran doesn't leave for herself, she leaves for her child, thank God. "I'm not real good at doing things for myself. But for Robert? That was a different story."

This is a wonderful, moving, wounding book with a message for all of us. Franz Kafka believed that writing was praying. Anna Quindlen's passionate devotional leaves you shaken even if you've never had a man lift his hand in anger toward you. But sometimes, as Kafka explains, we "need the books that affect us like a disaster, that grieve us deeply, like the death of someone we loved more than ourselves, like being banished into forests far from everyone else, like a suicide." There are many ways of killing yourself. No one knows this better or hides it worse than a battered woman.

Giving Sorrow Words

Sorrow fully accepted brings its own gifts.
For there is alchemy in sorrow. It can be
transmuted into wisdom, which, if it
does not bring joy, can yet bring happiness.

PEARL S. BUCK

Several years ago I gave a Simple Abundance workshop for the mothers of my daughter's schoolmates. As I always do, I spoke about looking for the sacred in the ordinary. So often we move through our days in a fog or a frenzy — until Spirit startles us with a cosmic wake-up call, a profound awareness of how much there is in our lives to be grateful for. How much we have, but also how much we have escaped.

These luminous moments are *everyday epiphanies*. "The beauty of the world has two edges, one of laughter, one of anguish, cutting the world asunder," Virginia Woolf tells us. She could have been describing those transformative moments that can be joyful, sobering, or both, such as the overwhelming relief you feel after a child who has wandered off, even for a few minutes, is found safe and unharmed. With so much tragedy in the world, I told the women, if we can tuck our children in at night, go to sleep knowing that they are safe and sound, and wake up with them the next morning, blessed are we among women. All the workshop participants nodded their heads in agreement. During a break afterward, one of the mothers, a lovely woman I'd often wished I'd known better but with whom I had only a nodding acquaintance, came over to me and said that what I'd said about everyday epiphanies resonated with her.

Two weeks later, on a beautiful Monday morning in October, the telephone rang. It was a friend calling to tell me that one of our first graders, Alison Sanders, had been killed in an automobile accident. Oh, God, no. "You know her mother, don't you? Beth Sanders. She took your workshop." Oh, God. Beth had been the woman I'd spoken with during the break. Tragedy had a beautiful face.

As a parent, it is the wounding we fear most. It is the nightmare you pray will never befall you, if you can even bring yourself to articulate that prayer. It is the phone call you pretend you'll never receive. It is the unthinkable. But the unthinkable happens every day to some woman somewhere. "Mothers put God on trial daily as they see their children suffer, and daily God is found guilty," Mary Lee Wile writes in *Ancient Rage*, a thought-provoking biblical novel about the understandable anger the mother of John the Baptist felt toward God after her son was murdered.

When the unthinkable is reported in the newspaper, you can turn the page. On the six o'clock news? Turn it off. But when the unthinkable happens to someone you know, you're forced to think, and then you become terrified. Women whose children have died often feel betrayed by other women; it seems as if we avoid them (sometimes we do) and even stop mentioning their dead child. (We're silenced by guilt and unnameable fear.) It's not that we're like Job's friends, who concluded that he brought his misery on himself. We're the friends of Job's wife. The Bible doesn't tell us what they said, but I'd be willing to bet it wasn't what they said that mattered, it was what they thought. *If it can happen to you, a woman who is so good, kind, and loving, what can happen to me and mine?*

That afternoon, as mothers arrived at school to pick up their children, women talked quietly among themselves and cried in each other's arms. After they wiped their tears, each one said in her own way, "What can I do?" Preparing food, getting the house in order, organizing and anticipating the needs of others is how women grieve, especially when it is a sorrow mourned in the realm of the unspeakable.

I asked about the arrangements. Alison was being brought home, I was told, and her family would be receiving visitors from three to nine over the next few days. I was quite surprised. Like many people, I was familiar with (and repulsed by) the American artifice of death: funeral parlors, gaudy satin-lined coffins, embalmed grief in two-hour intervals — even when it is a death in the family. Although I had longed for some special quiet time with both my parents after they died — for a last moment to try and say all the things I couldn't while they were alive — I could barely bring myself to stay longer than a half hour. Twenty years before, I had attended a home wake in the West Country of Ireland and been moved by the intimacy of the Irish way of death. But I had never attended a home-centered death before in this country. I was told that some of the women were organizing a vigil. Would I like to participate? Of course. I would be called later with the details.

"A vigil is an act of devotion — a time set aside for watching and waiting," Noela N. Evans explains in *Meditations for the Passages and Celebrations of Life*. While vigils — readings, prayers, meditation, chanting — are part of the rhythm of life in a religious community, most of us are not familiar with the practice as part of our daily round. I had been expecting that a group of mothers would gather and silently pray for Beth, Alison, and her family; instead, I was told that individuals would be keeping watch throughout the day and night in the child's bedroom where she lay. The purpose of the vigil was to offer prayers and readings to guide her on her journey as she crossed the threshold between life and death. Rudolf Steiner, a German philosopher of the early twentieth century who created the Waldorf school system that both Beth's children and my daughter Katie attended, believed that our spiritual essence (which I call the Authentic Self) disengages slowly from the body. For three days the soul of the deceased hovers nearby, gathering together what it needs from the lessons of this life to carry into the next.

Steiner also believed that, before we are born, the soul and God agree on when it shall be called Home after this lifetime's lessons are completed. What we call Life is really only a spiritual foreign-exchange program; Earth is like a junior year abroad. But just as few high school or college students want to hop on the first plane after the school term is completed in London, Paris, Rome, or Madrid to reunite immediately with their parents, the soul needs encouragement to leave the *joys* of Earth behind. The ties that bind must be loosened gently. Our regrets hold our loved ones back, for they feel our pain at their departure. That is why, when we're in the presence of someone who is preparing to cross the threshold, it's imperative that we reassure them that it's all right for them to leave us and return Home.

I felt very uncomfortable when I arrived at Beth's home. How would I ever be able to sit in the room with her dead child? I barely knew Beth; the vigil was being conducted by her intimate friends and family members. Really, I should remain downstairs with the others; I'd just come to offer my sympathy from a respectful distance. But a close friend reassured me that Beth wanted me to sit with her and Alison. As I passed through her kitchen, I noticed she had written some thoughts from the workshop and posted them on the refrigerator; our lives were meant to cross in this mystical way. My invitation to bear witness to the saddest farewell in the human experience was a soul-directed event.

Beth's small house was filled to the rafters and beyond. There was a continuous procession of food, friends, families, flowers. All the human senses mingled among the crowd: sight, sound, taste, touch, scent and knowing. Life's major and minor chords could be heard: crying, conversation, children's noises — even laughter. Strangers embraced family members, comforted each other, helped each other, served each other. "The closest bonds we will ever know are the bonds of grief," the writer Cormac McCarthy has observed. "The deepest community [is] one of sorrow."

The intimacy was palpable. Real. Authentic.

"This *is* how we're supposed to live, isn't it?" I said to a woman I'd just met a few minutes before. "Yes," she said softly. "Isn't it beautiful?" You would have thought we were alien visitors to a strange planet at the further reaches of the galaxy, and in many ways we were.

Upstairs it was the same. Death was the host, but Life was the guest of honor. Alison lay in a beautiful, simple pine casket lined with her colorful play cloths, the ones she'd created houses out of and worn as fairy *king* capes. She wore a flower wreath in her hair and was surrounded by her stuffed animals, toys, and love offerings from her brothers. Grace and Grief were her attendants. The room was illuminated with candles, aromatic with the fragrance of flowers and beeswax. Handmade decorations from schoolmates decorated the walls. In the corner was a chair with a small light for the person keeping vigil to read by. There was a slow, steady stream of visitors bringing Beth their love and support. Both adults and children entered the room shyly, but Beth immediately put everyone at ease. The children asked questions, from the prosaic to the profound. Why did Alison feel so cold? Because her body lay on dry ice to preserve it. Could she hear them talking? Yes, her mother said, she was sure of it. Their first glimpse of death was not frightening. Alison looked different from the Alison they had seen just a couple of days before, and they were trying their best to understand (as were their parents), but it was . . . *it was*, that's all. Could they leave a picture or a note for her? Could their mother tell Beth a story about when Alison did this or said this or played this game with them? What would happen to Alison's pumpkin for Halloween; would it still get carved? This was a cause for great concern. Yes, her mother said. It would still get carved. She wanted it to be a scary face. Yes, her mother reassured them. It will be. (And it was.)

In the hallway, two boys huddled together, whispering.

"What do you think? Does she look like Alison?"

"Yeah. But not really. You know."

"Yeah."

"She's not fooling around."

"Yeah. But it's only her *dead* body. It's not Alison."

"Yeah. Her *dead* body. Where do you think she is?"

"Betcha she's in the backyard on the trampoline."

"Yeah. Let's go find her."

The vigil keepers came and went quietly, keeping watch all through the night and into the next day.

Life After Loss

Loss as muse. Loss as character. Loss as life.

ANNA QUINDLEN

If we are alive, we cannot escape loss. Loss is a part of real life. "Have you ever thought, when something dreadful happens, a moment ago things were not like this; let it be *then* not *now,* anything but *now?*" the English novelist Mary Stewart asks. "And you try and try to remake *then,* but you know you can't. So you try to hold the moment quite still and not let it move on and show itself."

There is a story of a woman who lost her only child and was bereft, inconsolable, and alone. She went to the Buddha to ask his help in healing her wounded spirit. If he couldn't, she would follow her child to the grave and forgo her destiny. Karma be damned. She would not, could not continue to live this way. The Buddha agreed to help but told the mother she must first bring him back a mustard seed from a house that had never known sorrow. And so the woman set out to find one.

Her search took her a long time. She went from house to house all over the world but there was not one that had never entertained grief as a guest. However, because every house knew what her pain felt like, they wanted to give her a gift to help ease her anguish. It could not make it go away, but it might help. When the woman returned home she opened her heart and showed the Buddha what she had been given: acceptance, forbearance, under-standing, gratitude, courage, compassion, hope, truth, empathy, remembrance, strength, tenderness, wisdom, and love. "These gifts were given to help me," she told him.

"Ah, they were? And how do you feel now?" he asked the woman.

"Different. Heavier. Each gift comforts me in its own way, but there were so many I had to enlarge my heart to carry them all and they make me feel sated. What is this strange full feeling?"

"Sorrow."

"You mean I'm like the others now?"

"Yes," said the Buddha softly. "You are no longer alone."

Sacramental Possibilities

All our acts have sacramental possibilities.

FREYA STARK

I have known many sacred moments in my life, but the two holiest encounters I have ever been blessed to know and shall ever know were bringing my child into this world and helping another woman's child leave it. Ancient memory tells us that humans cannot look into the face of God and survive — the power of the Light would sear flesh, which is why Spirit appeared to Moses in the burning bush. Today, Spirit appears visible to us cloaked in the veils of life, death, and love.

I don't think anyone present during Alison's threshold parting will ever think about death in the same way. Don't misunderstand me; I still fear the death of my own child, the agony of finality, the enormity of loss, *the being left behind*. But I do not fear my own death any longer, and that at least is a beginning. I have Alison and Beth to thank for teaching me this major life lesson. "It is the denial of death that

330

is partially responsible for people living empty, purposeless lives . . ." Elisabeth Kübler-Ross tells us, "for when you live as if you'll live forever, it becomes too easy to postpone the things you know that you must do." There was nothing Beth could do to alter her child's destiny or her own, but she could honor her daughter by taking charge and taking care of her in death with the same love, respect, and devotion she had known in life. When it was determined that Alison was brain-dead, Beth asked that Alison be kept on life support through the night; she crawled into the hospital bed and cuddled her baby the way she had for seven years. In the days that followed, she did everything in her power to continue to serve the spiritual needs of her child during this most profound passage, and discovered in so doing, that while she was powerless in the face of death, life needed her to become a powerful woman. Life needs women who will claim their power, own their power, and use it well for all of us. That is Everywoman's destiny. Yours and mine, as well as Beth's.

Authentic choices require that we push past our comfort zone. It's easier for us to do that when we realize we have been given power for a purpose. To change the world for the better. Divinely inspired, soul-directed choices only happen when we follow our intuitive heart. Because Beth did, an entire community learned more about life and death in one week than most people learn in seventy years. Though there were tears, there was also a certain magic in what transpired, a timelessness and a palpable presence of Spirit — both God's and Alison's. The Irish poet W. B. Yeats called the renting of the heart through revolution "a terrible beauty." What is the death of a child if not a revolt against the natural order of the universe? But there is no other way to describe Alison's gift other than a *terrible beauty*. The paradox of children playing in the backyard below her bedroom, their laughter punctuating the silence of shock, brought home in a deeply personal way the immediacy of life, the sanctity of all our loving relationships, and the eternal continuum.

Alison was killed by an airbag in a low-speed accident while riding in the passenger seat of her father's minivan. It was an accident from which she should have walked away. Alison's father, Rob Sanders, formed *Parents for Safer Airbags*, a group of bereaved parents dedicated to preventing other families from experiencing this needless tragedy. Their work has brought public awareness to this issue and has certainly saved the lives of many children. Their work continues.

So does Beth's. She has focused her inner life energies on staying connected to her child (not just to her memory, past tense) and by giving birth to a unique resource center in this country, *Crossings: Caring for Our Own at Death*.

She would like to help others learn how to honor their natural, authentic, sacred impulses during those first critical days after the death of a loved one. Forced by circumstance to create her own rituals for grief, Beth found that the soul-directed decisions she made as a mother at the time of Alison's passing enabled her family and friends to experience a meaningful and sacred encounter with death at a time usually marked by chaos, confusion, disconnection, and the feeling of powerlessness that leaves behind regrets that last a lifetime. *"Be careful, then, and be gentle about death. / For it is hard to die, it is difficult to go through/ the door, even when it opens,"* D. H. Lawrence begs the living in his poem, "All Souls' Day." *"Oh from out of your heart/ provide for your dead once more, equip them/like departing mariners, lovingly."*

Beth's life is different from the one she thought she would be living. But it has a beauty, passion, and fierce reality to it that is, believe it or not, enviable because it is the essence of Something More. Once I asked her how she continues to go on after the unthinkable. She smiled and said, "I just keep trying to walk through my karma with as much grace as possible." She believes that before we live our earthly lives, we choose our lessons. For her, our karma is really our decision, once we're here, whether we will or will not honor our soul's journey to authenticity.

And that is about the best definition of karma I've ever heard.

We are born to love certain souls into full being, unconditionally. Certain souls are born to love us the same way. Some we give birth to, others we meet on the playground, at a workshop, in the office, on a blind date. We turn toward some, we turn away from others. Our choice — to walk toward or turn away from — becomes our destiny, our deeply personal love story. But in the end there is really only one history or *herstory*, and it is the heart's. "The beginning of my history is — love," Marie Corelli wrote in 1890. (Haven't women been wise for a long time?) "It is the beginning of every man and every woman's history, if they are only frank enough to admit it."

Sometimes it's very difficult to know which choice to make to move toward your destiny, especially if it involves an upheaval in your life and the lives of those you touch. When that happens, perhaps you're not the one meant to make the decision. Which is why I ask, "What would Love do?"

And do you know what? She always knows.

FIELD WORK

 *The House of Belonging*

Think of the inside of your house as your soul and the outside architecture as something like your bone structure, your genetic inheritance. . . . Our true home is inside each of us, and it is your love of life that transforms your house into your home.

ALEXANDRA STODDARD

Where do you feel at home? We can't always be in the geographical area we yearn for "in the heart's deep core," as W. B. Yeats wrote in his poem, "The Lake Isle of Innisfree." But wherever we are, we can create a cozy home for ourselves and our families.

Sometimes, as a child, I would take the laundry sheet I used to become a princess, throw it over a card table in the living room, and, voila! create a little house all my own. It was a safe place where I belonged, and I could invite others in if I chose.

So we practice and hone our home-building skills when we play as children, acting out the primal urge to build a nest, as birds do, as other mammals do. The boy in his fort learns to do this, the girl in her playhouse. Can you recapture that joy of discovery and invention in your own home today?

How about this old yellow and green box of Crayolas? Now why did you save *that?* Are you surprised by the rush of joy and freedom surging through you when you unearth it?

Do you ever use the crayons now — maybe just to doodle? When a friend was very young she colored the living room wall with crayons. When her mother saw her artwork, she shrieked, and made my friend throw the crayons away, one by one. She never colored another wall. Or anything else. I have urged her to tape a large sheet of paper to the wall and color it, using crayons, watercolors, or colored pencils. As a child, I was always admonished for drawing outside the lines. These days, when I'm feeling pretty sassy, I buy myself a kids' coloring book, color anywhere I want, and hang the picture over my computer. You might like to treat yourself to a new coloring book and the deluxe box of crayons — the kind filled with *all* the colors and the sharpener in back. Revel in the bounty of color, and use them all!

Which flowers and herbs do you love? Do you have them in your garden or your home? There is nothing so soothing, nothing that gets you into the rhythm of life more readily, than working in a garden, whatever its size, and pruning, plucking off dead leaves, watering, whispering encouragement to your plants. Then snipping off some basil, parsley, or chives to use for dinner.

Gertrude Jekyll (1843–1932) is one of the *Late Bloomers* that Brendan Gill describes in his attractive little book by that name. She moved beyond "the conventional Victorian garden, with its beds of flowers set out in geometric shapes. . . . With her own garden serving as a testing ground, she launched an attack upon the laborious artificiality of gardens then in fashion." She and the young architect Edwin Lutyens worked together, he designing "many of the handsomest country houses ever built in the British Isles," and she laying out the accompanying gardens. "Her purpose was always to make a strong plan and then have it appear to be entirely natural, with an abundance of native plants and herbs, their colors blending together and their fragrance an element more important than mere large, showy blooms."

What was in your first garden? Carrots? String beans? Impatiens? Sweet peas? You can satisfy many cravings with a garden — not only a hunger for food, but a hunger for color. You can create a masterpiece of color with your garden just as much as you can with a paintbrush.

At the farmers' market, when you see a fresh eggplant or sweet potato or mushrooms, do you wonder, "What can I cook with these?" Why not?

What was the first thing you learned to cook? Bacon and eggs? Mashed potatoes? French toast? Do you still love to cook, even though you've done it thousands of times? An actress must bring freshness and enthusiasm to her role in the theater even though she has rehearsed it hundreds of times, she must perform every time as though she is doing the scene for the first time. Can you bring back to your cooking some of the enthusiasm you had when you were a child banging pots together in the kitchen, struggling to create something new?

Today gather some fresh herbs and use them in a salad or omelette — or just put them in a jar and inhale their fragrance deeply.

Site Report

How do you define *comfort?* List five things that represent comfort for you.

Is your home as cozy as you would like it to be? Does it reflect who you and your family are? What images have you been collecting in that manila envelope — tile floors, chintz-covered chairs, simple maple desks, elegant dining room tables? What fabrics do you love? Can you get new pillowcases in a favorite fabric, or tack up a liner made from it, along your closet shelves?

List the dwelling places of your life, according to the age groupings on your site map. What did you love about them? In whose home did you and your friends congregate as youngsters? What was it about that home that drew you in and embraced you? Can you recreate that feeling in your home now?

Sensing

Nothing can cure the soul but the senses, just as nothing can cure the senses but the soul.

OSCAR WILDE

Sensing That There's Something More

I am not afraid. . . . I was born to do this.

JOAN OF ARC

If Joan of Arc could turn the tide of an entire war before her eighteenth birthday, you can get out of bed.

E. JEAN CARROLL

Once upon a time, a young woman left her home, family, and everything she thought was holding her back from being happy (such as finishing school and marrying the perfectly nice boy with bad breath from next door) in order to search for her soul mate. She was fiercely determined — she'd go around the world if she had to. She'd keep at it until the end of time, if it took that long. Well, a year, anyway — the window of opportunity ordained by her round-trip excursion fare ticket.

But, that wasn't what she told her horrified parents, who thought very little of "this setting out business," as it was snidely called during heated late-night arguments around the kitchen table. Instead, she told them she was going abroad to seek her fame and fortune. She wanted Something More than the life her mother had settled for. By God, *she* was going to make something of herself, she declared defiantly, with the unshakable conceit and certainty one possesses only between the ages of eighteen and twenty-seven.

And finally, after many tears and hugs and promises to write often, find a church as soon as she found lodging, and never go out with strange men without money in her pocket, they had to let her go.

Of course, she didn't write home, or even think about looking for a church. And she always went out with strange men without pocket money because most of the time she didn't *have* any pocket money. Perhaps this is why, three decades later, she shudders with disbelief to think of all the heartache she caused, all the tears and recriminations that bore her name, all the harm she escaped, all the adventures she survived, all the stories she could tell. She *knows* it's the reason she frequently finds herself checking her teenage daughter in the middle of the night, as if vigilance alone could postpone the inevitable — the day her daughter announces she wants Something More than the life her mother stumbled upon.

Making the Connection

Connections are made slowly, sometimes
they grow underground.

MARGE PIERCY

Can you think back to the best moments of
your life? Moments of clarity and commitment? Moments of transcendence and transformation? Moments of exhilaration and engage-
ment? Those Kodachrome moments, when you
felt so incredibly alive you actually offered
thanks without prompting. Remember? Revisit
those moments of profound pleasure when
every beating pulse echoed James Joyce's Irish
heroine, Molly Bloom, in her flowing surrender
to passion: *"And yes I said yes I will Yes."*

What's the first memory that comes to mind?

During those indelible moments, Spirit was
a palpable presence, bearing witness to the
extraordinary awakening that is the miracle of
authenticity. If you were actually aware of
this numinous presence, then these moments
became everyday epiphanies — those "ah-*ha*"
transmissions, when the static of the world

345

suddenly clears through Divine Intervention. It's at these times that the soul's Morse code — the dots and dashes of our daily round, so often dismissed as meaningless — not only connect, but resonate on the deepest level.

Spirit is also present during life's inescapable moments of denial, depression, and despair. When faith falters. When we erupt in rage. When we feel betrayed, abandoned, and bereft. When we prefer to be left alone. As flawed as we are, our instincts are unshaken: at least we know what's fair and what's not. And this — whatever *this* might be — is not fair. But during those interminable dark nights of the soul, we're not, thank God, left to our own devices. Angels are ready to extend a hand to help us back to our feet or carry us off the battlefield of disbelief. But we must ask for help, even if we can only articulate our SOS through cries and whispers. We are never alone on our journey toward Wholeness, from our first breath until our last — and beyond.

The Sentient Soul

It is human longing that makes us holy.

JOHN O'DONOHUE

It is hard for us to believe, when we feel lonely and long for Something More, no matter how much or how little we have, that we are echoing our origins.

It was spiritual longing that made us human. Longing and loneliness. Spirit wanted to fall in love.

And so Divinity's desire and dreams roused from the clay of the Earth, a being of fragrance and breath, vision and voice, to taste and touch, to know and be known: the beloved.

You.

From ancient times we have been told that we were created in God's image. If we believe this, that we mirror Divinity's nature, then this reflection must include what we deny — our own insatiable longing. Holy hints of our true identity are encoded in everything that surrounds us; everything that triggers our desire for Something More. The German poet

Rainer Maria Rilke believed, "God speaks to each of us as he makes us, then walks with us silently out of the night. These are the words we dimly hear:

You, sent out beyond your recall,
Go to the limits of your longing.
Embody me."

The Secret Language of the Soul

Sensuality, wanting a religion, invented Love.

NATALIE BARNEY

From the beginning we were meant to experience, interpret, revel in, and unravel the mysteries of this gift — Life — through our senses. Luckily, most of us are born fully sentient beings, able "to perceive the world with all its gushing beauty and terror, right on our pulses," as poet and naturalist Diane Ackerman tells us in her exquisite evocation, *A Natural History of the Senses*. Still, all too often, we journey through our days in a dull trance, asleep to the magic of everything about us.

Did you know that, of all human activities,

making love is the only one that engages and excites all our senses simultaneously: sight, taste, smell, hearing, touch and intuition? (Sex uses only five. Guess which one is missing.)

This is because our senses speak the secret language of the soul. Eastern spiritual traditions have always recognized the sacredness of our sexuality and have honored the realization that our senses are pathways to the soul. Each day, in myriad ways, Spirit attempts to restore the Divine Connection through our sensory perceptions. It doesn't matter how depressed we are, when we explore and exult in the sacredness of what we dismiss as "ordinary" — the aroma of homemade spaghetti sauce simmering or the exquisite sensation of freshly laundered linen against bare skin, we are restored to Paradise through peace and pleasure. And if you don't believe me, change the sheets and begin chopping tomatoes, onions, and garlic.

"The senses don't just *make sense* of life in bold or subtle acts of clarity," Ackerman explains. "They tear reality apart into vibrant morsels and reassemble them into a meaningful pattern."

Making Sense of It All

The need to find meaning . . . is as real as
the need for trust and for love,
for relations with other human beings.

MARGARET MEAD

If we could only understand. If we could only make sense of it all. And yet, even at our best, after a good night's sleep, we can't take in half of what's happening around us. George Eliot believed that "if we had keen vision and feeling for all *ordinary* human life, it would be like hearing the grass grow and the squirrel's heart beat, and we should die of the roar which lies on the other side of silence. As it is, the quickest of us walks about well wadded with stupidity."

The only way that I've been able to break through the cotton batting of my own bafflement is to trust the wisdom of my intuition — my capacity to know something without rational evidence that proves it to be so. Intuition has been called our sixth sense, and like our imagination, it's a spiritual gift.

Wild animals rely on their intuition to stay

alive; we need to hone ours to thrive. "It is only by following your deepest instinct that you can lead a rich life and if you let your fear of consequence prevent you from following your deepest instinct then your life will be safe, expedient and thin," Katharine Butler Hathaway wrote in 1946.

This marvelous power is available to each of us every day. Unfortunately, we often dismiss it. Except when we are in or on the verge of falling in love. The English writer D. H. Lawrence, who spent his entire life writing about women in love, was convinced that the intelligence that "arises out of sex and beauty" is intuition, and he was right.

When we are in the throes of romantic love, when the lilt of our laughter is the epitome of sex and beauty, we live by and through our senses. If we don't exactly hear the squirrel's heart beat, at least when we are besotted with another's beauty our sensory perceptions soar. "The flesh of a peach, the luminosity of early morning, the sound of distant church bells — the pleasure the lover takes in all the small experiences is heightened by love, suffused with special meaning," Ethel S. Person tells us in *Dreams of Love and Fateful Encounters*. We become magnets drawn ineluctably to the meaning of life because love initiates us "into the divine mysteries."

But how many times in our lives do we know the heart's high season? How many times do we savour the ripeness of flesh? Surely each summer the peach grows heavy and hypnotic in the fragrance of its own fruitfulness. Did you let the juice run down your chin this summer? If not, why not? Does convention hold you captive? Must the arbor be another ark, to be entered into only two by two?

And if the fruit is not chosen as a love offering, if the peach falls to the ground weighted down not only by its own sweetness, but by the weary waiting to be singled out; if the succulent moment of its perfection passes with no appreciative mouth to bear witness to life's goodness, tell me, who is the spoiler? The lover who chose not to take a walk in the orchard because she was alone, or the lover who chose to sample another's offering?

A Woman with a Past

Women . . . are born three thousand years old.

SHELAGH DELANEY

During my twenties I lived in England, Ireland, and France. My primer on authenticity began when I had the good fortune to cross paths with

352

an amazing person who became my first mentor, a Renaissance woman who showed me the extraordinary hidden in my ordinary.

When I first encountered Cassandra, I was painfully trapped in an impenetrable shell of self-consciousness. Whenever I found myself lured by her gracious hospitality to dinner parties or country weekends, I would politely excuse myself after being introduced and seek refuge in an empty room far from the crowd. Eventually she'd come looking, only to discover me happily settled in a soft armchair before a cozy fire, my head buried in a book. One night, after taking the book from my hand and before leading me back to the dining room, she drew out my social discomfort. I confessed a terror of exposing myself, of risking ridicule in even the most casual conversations. Cassandra promised me that I need never worry about being uncomfortable in social situations again, as long as I could regale strangers with stories of daring, folly, and risks.

"Well, there are some wonderful books about Victorian women explorers in your library," I told her. "I'll see what I can find."

"Find?" she teased with me with mock horror. "Sarah, you can only *borrow* other people's stories after you've started *living* your own. You must become your own heroine. Most people have lives crowded with incident but without purpose. You must start seeing each day as a blank page waiting to be filled up with amusing anecdotes, profound turning points, provocative choices, and pursuits of passion. The world adores storytellers, but deplores those who refuse to live their own stories."

The Great Escape

The day you were born, a ladder was set up to help you escape from this world.

RUMI

Children begin to leave their mothers the moment we first lay them in the cradle. Do you think that baby is struggling with all the determination of a Seminole alligator wrestler to lift his sweet, downy head just to get a closer look at a stupid stuffed animal? Think again. The child is getting the lay of the land. Scouting out the territory. Measuring the cubic inches of the bassinet walls he'll be scaling before you can turn around to tuck him in for the third time tonight.

One of the sweetest men I've ever known has spent years trying to understand why his parents didn't love him enough to lock the kitchen door. By the time he was three, he'd had more nocturnal feedings with the local sheriff than at home; every night after the house was asleep, he'd make another attempt to escape. The *why* of a little boy too young even to speak, repeatedly tottering down a dark country lane in his Dr. Denton's seemed unfathomable to me at first. Then one day, the answer appeared out of nowhere with startling clarity. "You had to find your people," I told him. "And your parents, even if they brought you into this world, are not your people."

Who among us hasn't felt so disconnected and out of sync with our blood family that we didn't wonder at one time or another if the nurses had switched babies at the hospital? Surely your real family would understand the real you. Wouldn't they?

Hide-and-Seek

Let us not fear the hidden. Or each other.

MURIEL RUKEYSER

Every moment of every day, consciously or un-consciously, we all seek *our people* or hide from *our familiars*. Some of us, like my friend, start sooner rather than later, but eventually one day we all wake up to find we're players in the cosmic game of hide-and-seek. Those who pos-sess good listening skills, who are naturally curi-ous, or who are simply open to life's possibili-ties get to join the game the easy way: announcing to the Universe, *"Ready or not, here I come . . ."* The rest of us numbskulls opt for the hard way, and find ourselves pushed kicking and screaming all the way to enlighten-ment: *"Ready or not here you go . . ."*

Our people should never be confused with *our familiars*. Unfortunately, we mix up the two all the time, which causes us enormous emotional distress and disillusion. *Our people* are our *spiritual* family, the kith and kin we've unconditionally loved and been loved by since the beginning of time. Sometimes we are connected by blood ties. But not always.

Our familiars are those individuals whose lives intersect with ours in order to play a role crucial in helping us manifest our Divine Destiny. They can be in our lives for an hour or for what seems like an eternity — however long it takes for us to "get it," whatever life lesson the "it" may be.

Distinguishing between *our familiars* and *our people* tries and tests our souls because it's supposed to. Our familiars push all our buttons and set off every sensor around the perimeter of our sanity. A good tip-off is that you don't particularly *like* your familiars. Did you ever hate someone on sight? She's one of your familiars. This person is a mirror reflecting a major flaw in our own perfect personalities that requires immediate attention. Those we hate make us certifiable in the same way that we, unfortunately, secretly drive our own selves crazy.

But, our familiars are shapechangers. More often than not we love, not hate, our familiars. In fact, we can be so attracted and attached to these catalysts for celestial metamorphosis that our relationship becomes obsessive and destructive. This is what happens when we love a bad man.

Bad Men

A woman has got to love a bad man once or twice in her life, to be thankful for a good one.

MARJORIE KINNAN RAWLINGS

A man does not have to be a drug king, gangster, pimp, slumlord, philanderer, rapist, murderer, or child pornographer to earn the adjective *bad*. A bad man is *any* man who repeatedly (as in more than twice) behaves badly toward you or makes you feel bad, either while you're in his company or without him. Especially without him. You'll recognize the scoundrel because the odor of something sweetly rotten lingers in his wake.

A bad man can be a sage or a saint. A bad man can be a priest, poet, philanthropist, or politician. A bad man can win the Nobel prize for medicine or the Oscar for best director. A bad man can feed the hungry or save the whales. A bad man can be someone else's perfect husband; he just shouldn't be yours. As Anna Quindlen so succinctly points out, "Testosterone does not have to be toxic." This, of course, is the lesson we have chosen to learn in this lifetime if we were born women.

I hope you're reading this book sitting down.

Bad men are spiritual graces sent in disguise to teach us, through torment, to love ourselves.

Even Bad Men Bring Gifts

It is tragic that some gifts have to be made so costly.

BERTA DAMON

It goes without saying, doesn't it, that I fell desperately in love with a man who was hopelessly in love with Cassandra. She was twenty years older than he and dismissed his romantic overtures as if he were a cute but naughty and untrained puppy constantly trying to climb up her leg. From behind the veil of romantic intoxication, I thought Richard was divine — handsome, wealthy, educated, witty, and charming in a scruffy, Oxford University way. I treated him like a god, which he thought he was, and which, after our mutual admiration for Cassandra, turned out to be our largest area of common ground. Eventually, when I could no longer deny the obvious, I shakily asked Cassandra why she wasn't interested in him. "Because Richard is so enamored with Richard that there isn't enough room in a romantic relationship for anyone else. I've made it a guiding principle to love only men who love me first, second, and third. I deserve nothing less, and so do you. The only difference between us, Sarah, is that I know this and you don't. Yet. It's sad that we have to become the authors of our own misfortune before we can realize a happy ending is always the writer's creative choice. I told you to become the heroine of your own stories, darling, not the sacrifice."

Her words stung. I felt naked and ashamed. I hated her for ridiculing both Richard and me and consigning our feelings to that vast and imprecise void of unworthiness. I walked out the door enraged and swore I would never see her again. Of course now, as I excavate this uncomfortable memory, I realize that all that Cassandra did was speak the truth to me with love. That night I told Richard of our conversation. He listened silently and then a look of incredible sadness came over him. "Of course, I'll never be able to look her in the face again," he said softly. My heart leaped. Could it be true? I had vanquished my rival? I thought my prayers had been answered.

But months later, Richard still didn't love me. Instead, he was passionately in love with the memory of the man he might have become if Cassandra had loved him. The last time we were together I asked him why she was so un-forgettable. "Because she's *a woman with a past*," he said simply. "A woman who capti-vates you because she insists on cherishing her-self above all others, including you."

It's the Thought That Counts

*Love is short, forgetting is long,
and understanding longer still.*

MERLE SHAIN

I've *thought* about Richard's observation for the last twenty-five years, because to be perfectly honest, I wasn't capable of *understanding* it. That is, until I began to understand myself. Forget the old adage, "Understanding is the beginning of knowledge." It's the reverse. Knowledge is the beginning of understanding. I had to get to know myself — who I'd been, who I was, who I was meant to be — before I could ever begin to understand a concept as sweeping as cherishing myself.

Now I have come to recognize that Richard, in his hapless way, gave me a gift too. Cas-sandra was different from younger women because she was able to wear proudly her passion for life, instead of her heart, on her sleeve. I was throwing myself at Richard, as we all do at men; but she knew to hold back because she valued herself. She knew her price — *priceless*. She knew that the kind of love she gave was only going to go to somebody worthy of it. When you're young, your self-worth comes from being loved by other people; but by the time you become a woman with a past, you know your value, and you love yourself. That's where your self-worth comes from. *No man can ever give you your self-worth, but you can let plenty of men rob you of it.*

On the surface it would seem that what Richard was saying was that Cassandra was self-centered, which she was. But self-centered in the best possible way: *being centered in the truth of who she was.* Her Authentic Self.

A woman who knew she deserved nothing less than to be loved, truly, madly, deeply. Unconditionally. Devotedly. Exclusively. A woman who would not settle for anything less. Because that was the only way she knew how to love.

Earthly Tutorials

Now for some heart work.

RAINER MARIA RILKE

It has occurred to me that, for at least half this book, I've been writing about the negative components of relationships. Pain. Bad men. Wrong choices. This isn't a coincidence. Love relationships are where we women take our Earthly tutorials in spiritual growth. As Kathleen Norris, a 1930's novelist, wryly observed, "There are men I could spend eternity with. But not this life."

That's because women are heart-centered creatures. We live in our hearts. Oh, we often visit our heads during the day; women do run corporations, launch banks, publish magazines, travel to outer space, trade securities on Wall Street, close million-dollar movie deals, get elected to national office, anchor the news, write Supreme Court decisions, and win Nobel prizes. But after all is said and done, women wake up and go to sleep in their hearts. The heart is the Sun of their own private solar system. Everything else — their children, job, home, family, friends, and need for creative self-expression — are the planets that revolve around the heart and depend on its energy to give them heat and light.

How many times must we stop whatever we're supposed to be doing at home, at work, or with our children, how many times must we cancel an appointment, miss a deadline, let something slide that we were going to do for ourselves, out of a driving need to sort, share, ponder, discuss, and dissect with a close friend the vagaries of an intimate relationship? One minute we're projecting profit-and-loss estimates and the next (either internally or in a quick telephone call to a pal), we're analyzing ways to respond to yet another unconscious slight, another missed anniversary, another hurtful silence. And it's only after we've aired these emotional issues that we can get back to crunching numbers before that big afternoon meeting. Peace at any cost, until we're physically bankrupt and need to file either for divorce or a Chapter 9 reorganization of the relationship to balance love's ledger.

We can't help ourselves. Getting to the heart of the matter is a soul-directed impulse. Getting to the heart of the matter is a sacred imperative, as pure as prayer. When a woman's heart isn't at peace, she can't invest her time, creative energy, and emotion in anything else. She can't focus. Since there's plenty swirling around her, impatiently awaiting the attention she doesn't have — because she's struggling to hold the center of her universe together with her bare hands — she becomes conflicted, confused, annoyed, scattered, depressed, and often testy.

All of a woman's spiritual, creative, and sexual drives — her power — emanates from her heart. When the heart is in danger, her Authentic Self is simply following its prime directive: get rid of the blockages, get the heart open to receive and send out love, get the heart centered and in alignment with what's truly important, and then get on with it. Real life. Nothing is more important to a woman than healthy intimate relationships — with her lover, partner, children, parents, siblings, and friends.

You might find it helpful, as I did, to understand the anatomy of a woman's heart. The heart is a hollow muscular organ that circulates blood to the body by swishing it through its chambers. Now, think of the blood as love. A woman's hollow heart is constantly filling and flowing with circulating love energy. When there is a spiritual blockage in the heart, a hardening of the arteries through the constricting emotions of anger, frustration, and resentment, love cannot flow freely and her heart hurts. Have you ever felt so sad, lonely, or upset that the middle of your chest hurt? Heart-ache is real.

Can we stop pretending that these things don't matter? When you have a fight or are frozen out by someone you love, getting to the heart of the matter is the only damn thing that does matter.

In the chest cavity, the anatomical heart is held in place by muscular attachments of veins and arteries. Mystically, a woman's heart is held in place by her attachments to those she loves. A woman's heartbeat — anatomically and mystically — is regulated by a unique nervous system that either accelerates or depresses (speeds up or slows down) the sending and receiving of messages by impulses, tiny electrical shock waves that "travel along a slender bundle of neuromuscular fibers, called the bundle of His."

I swear I did not make this up. (See the "Heart" article in the *Microsoft/Encarta Encyclopedia*.) I'm struggling to make sense of it.

The bundle of His. His needs. His wants. His confusion. His preferences. His priorities. His problems. His pain. His hang-ups. His stress. His fear. His disappointments. His expectations. His phobias. His stuff. Have I left anything out?

Whenever we're successful at fixing or patching whatever needs to be repaired in our important, intimate relationship, when the rift is healed — or better yet, when we've been able to recognize that "his" mean-spirited, rude, obnoxious, inconsiderate, or selfish behavior has absolutely nothing to do with us (a lifelong curriculum in human behavior) — women focus with amazing speed. When we're at peace, when we feel loved and are loving properly in return, we're back on track, saving the world with a smile. It's been said, and I agree, that there is *nothing, nothing, nothing* that two women cannot accomplish before noon, if left alone to figure it out. That is, of course, unless one of them is upset with her husband or lover.

Becoming a Woman with a Past

We find what we search for — or,
if we don't find it, we become it.

JESSAMYN WEST

There is nothing more alluring, intriguing, and romantic than being perceived as *a woman with a past*. Except, of course, knowing that you are one, which makes you glorious. Magnificent. Powerful. But, *every* woman is a woman with a past because every woman's destiny is to love and be loved truly, madly, deeply. Each of us loves or has loved passionately. Annie Dillard believes that each of us was created to give expression to our "own astonishment." A woman with a past has done just that with her life. She celebrates her quirks, exults in her extravagances, feels secure in her own skin, faces down her fears, and cherishes her foibles. Because of that, she's grounded in the soul knowledge that there is no other woman like her. Never has been. Never will be.

A woman with a past. Past history. Past lives. Past loves. Passion — past, present, and in her future.

Unlike the rest of us, a woman with a past does not secretly mourn a love lost, a love that could have defined her but a love that she denied. I believe that the rest of us do mourn such a love: the love that couldn't be returned, the love that frightened us, the love that challenged us, the love that would cost more than we were willing to pay, the love that bankrupted us, the love that was unconventional, so we turned away.

Who was your lost love? No, not that one. Not lost causes, though God knows we've loved more than our share. Try again.

All right, I'll give you a hint.

Who *is* this lost love? You feel the loss of this incredible presence in the absences of each day. It's *You.*

Yes, I mean you. The excited and enthusiastic *you* who was killed off (or so you thought) and then buried long ago under the refuse of other people's opinions, preferences, prejudices. The *you* entombed by the impossible expectations of others and the destructive ones of your own. The *you* buried alive beneath your own personal sinkhole of self-loathing. The woman with your past. Your Authentic Self. The woman you long to become. The woman Spirit created you to be.

The Holy Longing

It seems to me we can never give up longing and wishing while we are thoroughly alive. There are certain things we feel to be beautiful and good, and we must hunger after them.

GEORGE ELIOT

The only thing more irresistible than telling the truth is listening to it. Like moths drawn to the flame, we flit through our entire lives secretly searching for stolen moments when we can allow ourselves to be swept away by something larger than the life we've settled for. Our restless hearts possess a "holy longing," as the nineteenth-century author Johann Wolfgang von Goethe so beautifully describes it. This holy longing is to live passionate, rather than passive, lives.

> *In the calm water of the love-nights*
> *Where you were conceived, where you have*
> *conceived,*
> *A strange feeling comes over you*
> *When you see the silent candle burning.*
>
> *No longer caught up in the obsession of*
> *darkness,*
> *A desire for higher love-making*
> *Sweeps you upward.*
>
> *Finally distance does not make you falter,*
> *Flying, soaring, arriving in magic*
> *And insane for the light,*
> *You are the moth,*
> *And you are gone.*
>
> *And so long as you do not accept this truth*
> *And be willing to die, so that you might live,*
> *You will always walk this dark earth*
> *A troubled guest, alone.*

Passion is truth's soul mate. And whether or not we are comfortable with this spiritual truth makes a tremendous difference. The moth was born with flight as her destiny. Wings repeatedly singed and scorched because she resisted her fate become blackened and blistered and begin to shrivel. Unable to live, caution pulls her down to a painfully slow and excruciating death. But the little moth who embraces her inescapable fate and finally summons the courage to break free from indecision's orbit, soars to her destiny illuminated, transfigured in a brilliant burst of heat and light; at last true to her passionate nature, for once and always, authentic.

The Karmic Clock

There comes a time when we aren't allowed to know.

JUDITH VIORST

A woman found herself ensnared and enslaved in an impossible, loveless marriage that looked to all the world to be a match made in Heaven. It was the kind of marriage every little girl dreams of, which is why she dug her moat wide and deep even before she said "I do" to her Prince of Darkness.

Hers was a public marriage and the woman and her movie star husband's ideal life — complete with gorgeous homes and beautiful children — seemed to all the world to be picture-perfect. It certainly appeared that way on the glossy pages of the high-style magazines in which they appeared.

Her husband did not beat her with his hands but with his tongue. And while the wounds of psychic abuse are far easier to camouflage than the bruises of the physical batterer, this makes them even more dangerous. What is hidden cannot be healed. And although the woman was beautiful, kind, generous, clever, smart, and savvy, a devoted mother, and accomplished in her own field, nothing she did pleased the man she married, who belittled and berated her for her inadequacies every single day of their life together. Her mystified circle of intimates were mesmerized by this tragedy, transfixed and rendered mute, much like morbid strangers who chance upon a terrible accident. They were at a loss to explain it, except that the woman's husband was gorgeous (in that disturbing way that upsets the natural order of things). But her friends knew that the woman hadn't known her husband's kiss for years and that she basked in his charm only in public. Still, the woman remained faithful to her own self-abuse, as well as to her marriage-in-fame-only.

Then one day, without warning, two decades of public devotion and private torture came to an abrupt halt. The woman discovered that her husband had been having an affair with her children's nanny for ten years. Finally, for the first time, the humiliation was more than she could bear. Four hours after she confronted him, on her twenty-first wedding anniversary, she filed for divorce.

Not long after she ended her marriage, the woman went to have an astrology reading, which she did every year around the time of her birthday. The woman and her husband shared one of the most loyal, loving, and relationship-centered signs in the zodiac. But, the couple were as opposite in temperament as two people could possibly be, something the woman had found curious but had never investigated further, despite the fact that she believed in astrological guidance, had had birth charts done for her children, and often gave readings to her friends as gifts. Trying to make sense of her disastrous and self-destructive marriage, she asked the astrologer to do a birth chart for her husband and give her an assessment of their compatibility.

The woman was completely unprepared for what the astrologer told her. In forty years, the astrologer had never seen a more incompatible relationship chart. "I have to tell you," she told the woman, "the incompatibility is so strong — violent — I thought I'd made a terrible miscalculation, so I did the chart twice. If you'd only stayed together for a week, I'd have been surprised at your staying power; these are the charts of mortal enemies. How you lived together for twenty years and had four children and survived, I can't imagine. The psychic cost you paid had to be enormous. But what you've gained spiritually is beyond measure. Your husband does not share your astrological sign; he was born on the cusp. You're complete opposites. Light and darkness. You're loyal; he's faithless. You're passionate; he's cerebral. You're a giver; he's a grabber. I've never seen anything like it."

The woman was stunned. How could this be?

"I can only guess that your soul kept this knowledge hidden from you because your union was karmic. If you had known, you would have ended the relationship as soon as you found out. But, you couldn't end the relationship. You needed to be together to work through the three most important spiritual lessons all of us must learn: passion, betrayal, and forgiveness."

The Essential Union

*The strongest, surest way to the soul
is through the flesh.*

MABEL DODGE

Anaïs Nin believed that "we travel, some of us,
forever to seek other lives, other souls." Most
of the time we think that the other we so desperately seek is our soul mate — the person we'd
instantly recognize and feel completely comfortable with if our paths chanced to cross.
The one who'd give us the opportunity to say *I
feel as if I've known you my whole life.* How we
long for this one soul who loves us unconditionally — a startling assumption, since presumably this other one knows and loves us
better than we know ourselves. Like many
women, I have spent half a lifetime in a restless
and relentless search for this elusive presence,
believing that I could not become complete
without such a union. I was right. But, only
now do I realize that the other essence, the other
being I have been seeking is not another person.
To my great astonishment, I have discovered

375

that I have been seeking another *me*. My Authentic Self. And so have you. Why else, when we feel lost, confused, and alone, do we say, "I'm struggling to find myself"?

FIELD WORK

 *Relationships*

The word intimacy comes from a Latin root that means innermost.

SUSAN WITTIG ALBERT

In our most precious relationships, we trust the other person enough to reveal our innermost selves. And we can provide that safety and nourishment for others, too.

The psychologist Carl Jung said, "The meeting of two personalities is like the contact of two chemical substances: if there is any reaction, both are transformed." In what ways have relationships transformed you?

Digging carefully at our site location, we seem to have uprooted your old jewelry box, containing the ankle bracelet your first boyfriend gave you and the letters you wrote and received from family and friends in college.

Which of these people represent your own inner circle — the soul friends with whom you truly belong and feel safe? The ones with whom you feel that your Authentic Self can emerge, be appreciated, and be loved? Which friends have been the true ones, the ones who cared about you and were happy to see you flourish?

Reread the letters that were written to you. Who is the person your mother, your girl-friend, and your boyfriend, were writing to — remember her and describe her. Read the letters you wrote in college. What was on that girl's mind? Does anything about the letters surprise you?

Reach out now to someone you want to be closer to. Write him or her a letter.

Site Report

Select photos of the people you love and make a photocopy of them for your discovery journal. Or sketch them. Or draw a symbol that represents them.

How would you define a good relationship? What elements does it include?

Trace your concept of a good marriage, a good love affair. Let's look for the good — we all know the bad. Visualize yourself in the future, in your cheerful home — who would you like to have there with you?

The poet Adrienne Rich says, "The most important thing one woman can do for another is to illuminate and expand her sense of actual possibilities."

Whose life have you expanded?

Who has lit up *your* life?

FIELD WORK

 *Entertainment*

The creation of something new is not accomplished by the intellect but by the play instinct acting from inner necessity. The creative mind plays with the objects it loves.

C. G. JUNG

We're back at the sacred site of your soul. It's time to play. Have you unearthed some childhood toys from that trunk? Are these your old jacks and rubber ball? Hold those metal jacks in your hand and feel their spikiness. Toss them into the air and flip your hands palm-side down — receive the jacks on the back of your hands. Isn't that what you used to do? Don't you marvel at the confidence and dexterity of the nine-year-old girl who could swiftly move her hand across the floor, sweeping up exactly the right number of jacks? Where is she now?

I'm convinced that some of those old games from childhood were as pleasing for their sense of touch as anything else. In this excavation, you are reawakening your tactile sense as well as your memories.

What's this? An old key chain? Was this what you used for hopscotch? What was it called? A charm? Token? Marker? Pick it up; be aware of the pleasant heft of it. Do you feel like tossing it? What does it give you the urge to do today? Toss bread dough? Throw a pot and fire it? Jump rope?

Why not bring some of these playful artifacts into your life now? You could set out a small box on your coffee table. I have one — it contains twenty beautiful marbles from my childhood. My friend and I used to collect them in the vacant lot near us. Someone was shooting them out of guns for target practice, but we didn't know that; we thought they grew in the lot like weeds. She and I made "plays" with them, turning them into domestic characters. The bigger ones were the mother and father, the tiny ones the babies. I still admire their beauty, the ones with stripes of blue and green, the clear liquid topaz one, the smooth white one that looks like a bubbly soda drink.

I marvel at the rich imaginations we had, my friend and I. There's a wonderful passage in

Ntozake Shange's novel *Sassafrass, Cypress & Indigo*, when one of the girls is admonished for her rich imagination. "Indigo, I don't want to hear another word about it, do you understand me. I am not setting the table with my Sunday china for fifteen dolls who got their period today."

Who did you like to set the table with the Sunday china for?

Site Report

What are your favorite books from childhood? Arrange a get-together with a friend; each of you bring books that you loved, and read from them aloud together. Better yet, do this with some children. But if you've been yearning to read Dr. Seuss all by yourself, go ahead! Add to your journal quotes from authors who have affected you.

Start a reading group, or a tennis group, or a hiking group. Gather a few friends together and set up a schedule so that you can regularly pursue this activity you love and also see each other.

Take those old home movies and get them converted to a video cassette for easy watching and for sharing.

What is your favorite hobby? Your favorite actor? Actress? Artist? What music do you prefer listening to? What are your favorite films, playthings, vacations, holidays, comforts, comic strips, fantasies, music, and magazines. Describe them in your journal.

Something More

But we're not satisfied with what we ourselves have learned about the world and ourselves. We're always waiting for a stranger to come and tell us something more. And "something more" means "the rest of it," and that's what we need most; we miss it. So, go ahead, stranger! . . . tell her what she herself is, beyond what she herself already knows she is . . . her life, her years, her great expenditures of self, what of herself is honey and what is gall on her tongue, the hunger she has, and the hunger she sees.

ELIO VITTORINI

The Queen of Sheba

Solomon had three hundred wives and seven hundred concubines. But there was only one woman at whose feet he lay, the Queen of Sheba. And she was neither one nor the other, for she was the King's match. And so, fittingly, he gave her everything she asked of him and much, much, more. She in turn, gave herself to him. And their rapture knew no bounds and their love for each other never betrayed them.

My favorite love story is that of King Solomon, whom the ancients considered the wisest person in the world, and the Queen of Sheba, who knew better.

Before Helen of Troy, before Cleopatra, before Catherine the Great, there was Sheba — history's first recorded woman with a past. Not too much is known about her — biblical reports are sketchy — except that she was so alluring, so beguiling, and stunning that she inspired Solomon to pen the most passionate love poem ever created, the *Song of Songs*. That says it all to me. Actually all we really need to know about the Queen of Sheba is that she was such a savvy babe she managed to accomplish what a thousand other women couldn't. She brought the most powerful biblical King to his knees, and he was smiling all the way down.

Exactly how did the Queen of Sheba accomplish this? By being her gutsy, glorious, Authentic Self. Solomon's equal. The King's match. She knew it, he knew it, and she never let him forget it in subtle but unmistakable ways. She was the first woman not to bow down to him. *She* knew who should be receiving the adoration. So she looked him straight in the eye, probably flashed him a sly and knowing smile, then turned and slowly sashayed away into her tent to wait for him to bring her love offerings. She let Solomon give her everything she wanted and much, much more *before* she even turned in his direction. Why?

Sheba knew the happiness she could bring into Solomon's life. She wanted to see if he deserved her love. She wanted to see how he'd enhance the quality of *her* life before she let him in.

Sheba longed for a soul mate; she wanted a companion who could meet her as an equal on every level — intellectually, emotionally, and passionately. She had been lonely for too long, but she was still the Queen of Sheba and would not settle for less than her equal. She knew that for a woman there was something worse than being alone: being with a man who doesn't deserve you and doesn't know it. Was

386

Solomon her match? King or not, she would have to test him.

Now, the Queen of Sheba was a very generous woman. In fact she was known for her generosity; her people lived very well, which is why they adored her. When Sheba arrived at Solomon's court for the first time, she brought him the most beautiful objects from around the world as tokens of esteem. The King was overcome with her largesse.

But material objects were not what Sheba wanted from Solomon; she already had everything. She wanted to see if the wisest man in the world knew what a woman truly wanted: gifts tied with heartstrings. Unconditional love, selflessness, support, loyalty, enthusiasm, attention, thoughtfulness, devotion, romance, constancy, caring, emotional primacy — these were the love gifts fit for a Queen.

From the moment Solomon laid eyes on the Queen of Sheba, he knew this was a woman unlike any other in the world. And, as a man, not just as the greatest King in the world, he wanted her to be his and his alone. Because she was his equal, he knew what he had to do, and he had never done it before. He would have to open his heart to her and place her happiness and well-being before his own in every situation. He would have to discover what delighted her and then plot and plan her pleasure. Solomon knew he was Sheba's passionate, generous match; he would prove it.

And he did: from sharing his favorite wine and fruit to personally selecting flowers and fragrant incenses, from putting the affairs of state on hold in order to spend time with her to providing for her entertainment when the kingdom couldn't wait.

For those of us in search of Something More, meditating on the Queen of Sheba's considerable gifts, talents, and wisdom can be a wellspring of inspiration.

Sheba knew that when a new man comes into your life — whether he's a king or a carpenter (the two are not mutually exclusive), if he can't match your generosity of spirit and meet your emotional needs, you'll *never* be happy together. When you yourself are rooted in *abundance* consciousness (and hopefully by now you're a good part of the way there), and the object of your affections (whether you've known him for a week or been married to him for twenty years) is rooted in *lack,* the two of you will always feel frustrated and continually clash.

Nothing else matters. Not your astrological signs, not the way he makes you laugh, not the kisses that make you swoon. If you two aren't generous, demonstrative, and emotional equals, you'll always feel that you aren't getting the love you deserve, and you'll be right.

My devotion to the Queen of Sheba increased one day after I overheard a priceless and very instructive exchange between two young women working behind a department store cosmetic counter. I had been waiting for someone to help me, but became so mesmerized by their discussion of the romantic trials and tribulations of a third woman that I didn't want to interrupt. It seems their mutual friend's boyfriend was a loutish brute and had been from the get-go. Him, they wanted to skin alive. Her, they wanted to thrash. Enough was enough. The patience, love, and forbearance of our soul sisters goes only so far, thank God, when we are hell-bent on self-destruction. Angels don't always wear wings.

"I just want to grab her by her shoulders and scream, 'Girlfriend, pull your pathetic self together. Stand tall to your man. Don't you go giving up your throne. You have forgotten your birthright. You are the daughter of the Queen of Sheba. Now start acting like it.'"

"Amen," said the other woman. "The man *hasn't been born* that I'd let treat me that way."

"That's because we know we're royal blood."

"That's the truth. You know, when a man says to me, 'What do you want from me?' you know what I tell him? Everything you got, mister. Everything you got and then some. Keep on giving me everything you got and I'll let you know if you're giving me enough. If it's not, I'll tell you, and then you can give me more."

The women started to laugh and so did I.

"Now that's what *that girl* needs to do. She's giving us all a bad name."

"Can I help you?" one of them asked me.

I said they already had. I'd come for a lipstick, but was leaving enlightened and didn't want to break the spell. I know the truth when I hear it, and that day I was ready for my next lesson. Spirit speaks to us in many ways.

"Women who set a low value on themselves make life hard for all women," Nellie McClung wrote in 1915, and those two young women knew that. Quite frankly, I'd never thought about it before. But now, suddenly, that very simple truth became pregnant with possibilities for some powerful pondering.

Practically every woman I know personally suffers, in varying degrees, from the Queen-of-Sheba-deficiency, an imbalance affecting communication between the brain and the soul. Sheba-deficiency symptoms include distortion, disorientation, and confusion similar to that exhibited by members of deposed royal families who find themselves living in exile. In other words, people who have lost their inner and outer bearings. Those of us who suffer from this mystical malady, which comes and goes depending on our emotional wellness, self-confidence levels, and relationship resilience, keep forgetting who we are. We misplace our crowns.

When we lose touch with our true natures, we become unable to create boundaries that protect, nurture, and sustain our self-worth — which is worth a Queen's ransom. We forget that we're first-rate women and try to play down to the rest of the world so that we'll be accepted. But if you want to be admired, adored, and loved, you're going to have to hold out. One thing's for sure: the Queen of Sheba did not suffer from self-loathing.

"What is terrible is to pretend that the second-rate is first-rate. To pretend that you don't need love when you do; or you like your work when you know quite well you're capable of better," Doris Lessing admonishes us. "There is only one real sin, and that is to persuade oneself that the second-best is anything but the second-best."

And you're not second-best. You're descended from an ancient, sacred lineage: the daughters of Sheba. Stand tall. Girlfriend, the man hasn't been born whose love is worth throwing away that throne.

Soul Mates

Two are born to cross their paths, their lives, their hearts. If by chance, one turns away, are they forever lost?

MICHAEL TIMMINS

Yes, in a very real and deep sense they are lost, but not forever. Just in this lifetime. What is lost is the *they* that the two would have become together. The *they* that could have set the world on fire with their passion and purpose. The *they* that could have ransomed and returned a portion of the world's lost heart together, just as they were intended to ransom and return a portion of each other's lost heart. The *they* that would have proved absolutely, positively, beyond a shadow of a doubt, that true love is the grand Divine Design for each of our destinies.

But that's not all — something else is lost as well. In the ancient Celtic mystical tradition, it's believed that when two people born to cross paths, lives, and hearts do embrace each other, a third entity comes into being — a

Spirit companion that watches over the two souls to help them love each other into fullness. If they choose to turn away from the labyrinth of their life together, that Spirit companion will not hover over their human hearts. Divine Mission aborted.

So let there be no misunderstanding: our choices concerning love are sacred. When one heart *consciously* turns away from the caresses and challenges of the holy other — whether it's you or him — much of what was meant to be is lost.

We are meditating upon soul mates here — "the Beloved," as Solomon called the Queen of Sheba. *My Beloved is mine and I am hers.* Love as ancient reunion and recognition, not as acts of intent, will, fantasy, or fling. *My Beloved is mine and I am his.* Some call this authentic love the One and Only. My soul feels more comfortable speaking about the love of this life as the Other.

The Other.

That other soul, John O'Donohue explains, lay next to your clay in the earth "millions of years before the silence of nature broke." Then came the separation, and you both rose up into "distinct clay forms each housing a different individuality and destiny." But over the history of the world, "your secret memory" has mourned "your loss of each other. While your clay selves wandered for thousands of years through the universe, your longing for each other never faded."

O'Donohue writes that "the Celts had a refined and beautiful notion of friendship. In the early Celtic church, a person who acted as a teacher, companion, or spiritual guide was called *anam cara,* the Gaelic words for 'soul friend.' The *anam cara* was the person to whom one confessed, revealing confidential aspects of one's life, one's mind, and one's heart. This person had a special intimacy with you, and your friendship was an act of primal recognition. It cut across all barriers of convention, morality, and religion. The *anam cara* could see you from an eternal perspective."

But how do you know whether someone you love is your soul mate, your *anam cara?* I mean, if you're in love, he's bound to be, right? Not necessarily. There are a lot of people we can be happy with, but these relationships don't all feel as if there is an *inevitability* about them. With soul mates, the feeling of inevitability is potent. This is often very difficult because acknowledging this inevitability makes you vulnerable in ways you never knew existed. Those of us for whom control is a major part of our modus operandi will find this enormously discomforting.

"All enduring love between two people, however startling or unconventional, feels unalterable, predestined, compelling, and intrinsically normal to the couple immersed in it," observes Lillian Ross, who chronicled her forty-year love affair with *The New Yorker* editor William Shawn in her memoir about their relationship, *Here But Not Here.*

How many loves in our lives feel unalterable, predestined, compelling, and inevitable? Finding your soul mate often sends your world into an initial tizzy, because it can mean the rejection of some of the systems and relationships you've come to count on to give your life strength, stability, and structure. I don't think there is a more frightening feeling in the world than the moment before surrendering to one's destiny when it involves another. There is a lovely film by Henry Jaglom called *Déjà Vu* that "raises uncomfortable questions about making compromises in life that many happily mated couples over thirty would rather not ponder," Stephen Holden noted in the *New York Times.* Does one just scrap everything if true love happens to present itself at your door? Good Lord, *there's* a provocative question that had practically everyone at the screening I attended sitting silently in their seats for several long minutes after the credits ended. "Well, that was an interesting film," the woman sitting next to me said to her husband. "Yes, it was," he said. "I'm just grateful you're my soul mate."

The One Who Loves
Your Pilgrim Soul

Whatever our souls are made of,
his and mine are the same.

EMILY BRONTË

I have felt his numinous presence for over a year now, in my solitude and half sleep. The Other. But I have not yet seen his face in this lifetime. Several months after my marriage had ended and I was living alone, William Butler Yeats woke me up. He was sitting at the foot of my bed. For the last thirty years in my dreams, Willie's been my spiritual mentor and messenger, but that, as they say, is another story for another day.

"Yes, Willie."

"Sarah, it's time."

"Yes, Willie. Time for what?"

"Sarah, he's waiting for you."

"Who, Willie? Who's waiting?"

"The one who loves your pilgrim soul. The one who cherishes the joys and sorrows of your changing face."

"I thought that was you, Willie."

"I do, pet, but there is another. The Other."

"How will I find him?"

"Follow your heart."

"How will I know him?"

"Open your eyes."

"What does he look like?"

"The reflection of your soul."

"Could you be more specific? Could I have a little something more to go on?"

"Exactly. You'll find him on the other side of Something More."

And he was gone. The whole celestial conversation took a few heartbeats. I didn't know what it meant. I seldom do. That doesn't stop me anymore.

The reflection of my soul.

The Other Side of Something More.

You wonder how books and personal journeys come into being? I started the *Simple Abundance* journey by sitting at my dining room table one ordinary morning and writing out a list of all the things I had to be grateful for. I wanted to stop focusing on what was missing in my life because I was sick and tired of living in lack.

On this particular morning, I was tired of being lonely. So I sat down and wrote a spiritual personal ad for my *anam cara,* my soul mate, and described him — his soul qualities — in minute detail. I don't know his name, his age, the color of his eyes or his hair (or even if he has any hair), but I do know 104 marvelous things about him. When I shared it with a close woman friend, she said, "He sounds just like you."

Isn't that interesting?

The reflection of your own soul.

When I shared it with a close man friend, he said, "My God, Sarah, will you settle for half that list?"

"Why should I?" I heard myself asking. Why should any of us settle for anything less than the meeting of Heaven and Earth? I've spent my whole life settling and stumbling and barely surviving. I've been shattered and now in the middle of my life, have to start over again from scratch. Well, if I have to start all over again, this time I'm going to get it right. Whatever "it" is. I refuse to settle for anything less than Something More than I've had before. Because it wasn't enough.

To Know and Be Known

You can live a lifetime and, at the end of it, know
more about other people than you know about yourself.

BERYL MARKHAM

"The human journey is so short. We no sooner realize that we are here than it is already time for us to be leaving. The brevity of life gives a subconscious urgency to our desire to know ourselves," John O'Donohue reminds us. "Perhaps this is what a friendship gives us. The real mirror of your life and soul is your true friend. A friend helps you to glimpse who you really are and what you are doing here."

Just as we look for our worth in the eyes of others, so do we look for our definition. We think our definition is found in the roles we play in the lives of others. Who are you? Are you a wife? A mother? A teacher? A bookkeeper? These are roles. Some are more long-playing than others, but they are still roles.

Who are you?

How about a mystery? That is your reality. That is your truth. That is your Something

More. It isn't another person. It isn't true love. True love is found only on the other side of Something More. "When one is a stranger to oneself, then one is estranged from others, too," Anne Morrow Lindbergh believes. So do I.

But sometimes, inexplicably, we'll meet someone who is a kindred spirit, whether platonic or passionate. And for a little while, in their company, we don't feel alone, we don't feel like a stranger. This person seems to know us so well — our interests, concerns, values. He or she shares our passions. There's a *simpatico* there, an easy familiarity, an intimacy in an hour that takes years with others, if it's ever achieved at all. We've met one of *our people*, and he or she is a friend to our soul. A pal so fabulous that we feel like twins separated at birth. Another like us, but not necessarily the Other.

"A soul mate is someone to whom we feel profoundly connected, as though the communicating and communing that take place between us were not the product of intentional efforts, but rather a divine grace," Thomas Moore tells us in his *Soul Mates: Honoring the Mysteries of Love and Relationship*. "We may find a soul partner in many different forms of relationship — in friendship, marriage, work, play and family. It is a rare form of intimacy, but is not limited to one person or to one form."

400

And so for a little while we are happy. Content. Satisfied. Then you know what? We stop looking for our Authentic Self. Don't need to anymore. A buddy with flesh and bones has come along, thanks very much. We were lost. Now we're found.

But life, even at the best of times, is completely unpredictable. Lovers leave us. Friends move away. Friends and lovers die. Love affairs go awry, friendships are altered by circumstances. Then we find out, in our forties and fifties, that our friends can't save us any more than we thought love alone could save us in our twenties and thirties.

Has anything so great ever happened to you that you wanted to share it immediately, but no one you wanted to call was home? Or your heart is breaking and there's only one friend who will understand, and she's left the machine on? You feel as if there's no one in the world you can talk to.

You're right.

There is no one who can save us from the emptiness, the estrangement that comes with the lonely desperation of wanting to be known before we die. Wanting to know who we are. For better, for worse, because we haven't a clue, we call this the search for Something More.

The Heart Grown Brutal

We fed our hearts on fantasies
The heart's grown brutal from the fare,
More substance in our enmities
than in our love. . . .

W. B. YEATS

Yeats wrote these lines about his beloved Maud
Gonne, the famous Irish beauty who tortured
him with a romantic dance of intimacy that was
never physically consummated. (It's from a
poem called "Meditations in Time of Civil
War," but the "meditations" in question in-
volved the wrenching of his soul, not just Ireland's political destiny.)

The love affair in his mind lasted thirty
years. She called it "a spiritual marriage." Poor
Willie, the fever didn't break for him until he
was an old man. So desperately did he love
Maud, he even tried (and failed) to marry
her daughter to be close to her. Life and love
didn't seem very generous to this beautiful,
sensitive, spiritual, and evolved soul, if you take
away the fact that he was one of the world's

greatest poets. His destiny was to be something other than a *They* with Maud. William Butler Yeats was meant to be a *They* with Life. And because of that, he's a *They* with me, and maybe you, but we're not Maud.

But what if it wasn't *your* soul, but your mate's that turned away from your destiny? Are you alone forever, never to become a *They?*

No. Love's not that cruel. Life's not that stingy. You may feel that way today but you won't forever.

This is what I believe happens when one of the two who were born to cross paths, lives, and hearts turns away. His karma continues, as he chooses. But I promise you that his future does include the harrowing and heartbreaking moment when he realizes that you were the love of his life and he threw away his chance for happiness.

Granted, your destiny changes, too. You are left, but you are not meant to be alone, which is why your soul still hungers for Something More. You now have two options. Chase this Something More in a series of unfulfilling repeat-and-return relationship reruns with bad men until the day you die. Or, you can stop running. You can stand still for a moment, long enough to swear to God that you'd rather be alone for the rest of your life than endure one more minute of a destructive, unhealthy relationship with a man who does not deserve you. You decide to try a turn on the dance floor with the One that brought you, baby, here to Earth.

Spirit.

You ask Spirit to love you into full being. When you do, you begin the reembodiment process of the ages. You become your own Beloved.

"The beloved is one who nurtures you, trusts you, supports you, encourages you, loves you without conditions," Iyanla Vanzant tells us. "That's you."

Me, myself, and I?

That's right. You.

You and Spirit. The dream team. The perfect couple. A match made in Heaven to better the Earth. Something better than the lover who left you. Something More. You fall in love for the first time and discover that your soul mate is Life. "For me, nothing is so exciting as to imagine that *life* is my lover — and is *always* courting me," Julie Henderson writes in *The Lover Within*. "To relate to life in that way is a challenge and a surrender that invites me deeper into being alive in every moment that I can manage it."

When you fall passionately in love with Life — despite all its complexities, compromises, and contradictions — Life falls passionately in love with *you,* in spite of *yours*. Trust me, you will never find a lover who will adore, desire, embrace, and delight you more than Real Life. This is a relationship of equals.

"What if," Willa Cather asks, "what if Life's meant to be our sweetheart?"

What if, indeed.

Something More

Each relationship you have with another person reflects the relationship you have with yourself.

ALICE DEVILLE

Ralph Waldo Emerson believed that no one could be considered a success until they had survived the betrayal of someone they loved and trusted.

I disagree. I think authentic success is something much, much more: surviving the betrayal of someone you loathed and tormented. Yourself.

And how do you do that? By stopping it, that's how, just stopping it. Today. By praying right this moment for the courage to learn how to transform the self-loathing into self-loving every day through your passionate choices.

By now you realize that Something More is not money, or fame, a home featured in *Architectural Digest,* or a love affair with a movie star.

Something More is repose of the soul. Something More is self-worth.

Something More is self-knowledge. The knowledge that your passion is holy and that the only way you'll be able to live authentically is to be true to your passions.

But the only way you or I can be true to our passions is to swear never, ever to betray ourselves again.

Because Something More is the certainty that no one in the world can betray me except me. Other people, those I love and trust, can and will disappoint me, fail me, and hurt me, because they are human. I will disappoint, fail, and hurt those I love because I am human. Human beings disappoint, fail, and hurt each other, even those we love with all our hearts.

But no one else in the world can betray me.

Thank Heaven. I wouldn't want it any other way. Neither should you.

Our hopes begin to resemble regrets, and our regrets begin to resemble our hopes when we betray ourselves. When we stay put even though we know we should push past. When we stumble but don't get up. When we deny what and who we love. When we let others choose for us.

Living Something More will require courageous choices every day, and our ability to make choices is inextricably linked to our self-worth. Do I deserve to be happy? Damn right I do. Am I ever going to be unhappy again? Not if I can help it.

If you can say that about yourself, then the reembodiment process is well under way. No longer do you have to accept the world as it exists because now you can reshape, reclaim, and re-create the world in your own image.

But in order to do that you have to realize that you have found your life's work — excavating your buried dreams. That's because only the archaeologist of your Self can crack the soul's code: your authentic needs and wants. You have to know what you need and want out of life before you can make the choices necessary to honor them.

Your authentic needs and wants are encoded in those dreams, in the trace memory of your deepest longings. Keep shoveling away the dung of the world's disbelief as you uncover the shards of purpose, peace, and pleasure that bring you joy.

The heart of Something More is knowing that your choices — and from now on, only yours — must be the ones that come first. And if that makes you the most self-centered woman in the world, then you can stop your restless searching for Something More because you already possess it.

Something More is caring, communion, companionship, connection, commitment. Something More is the giving and receiving of unconditional love. For at the end of the day, or at the end of a life, all we truly have is ourselves and love. And if we love our selves — truly, madly, and deeply — all we have is all we'll ever need.

For the sake of all that is holy, believe that you deserve nothing less than Something More.

With Thanks and Appreciation

As for me, I know of nothing else but miracles.

WALT WHITMAN

Being an Irish writer, I trust the unseen more than the visible, which is why I have come to rely on the spiritual secret that "The Book" always knows more than I do, thank God. So let me begin with the acknowledgment of my collaborator — the Great Creator — in whom I move, write, live, love, find my being and my meaning. That I was graced with bringing *Simple Abundance* into the world is a source of continuing amazement; that I was blessed with the gift of *Something More* could be viewed as an embarrassment of riches, except that I am very proud of this book. It is the miracle I prayed for my entire life.

I'm grateful I no longer need to solve this mystery, I'm just extremely happy these books have my name on them. Perhaps it is because I agree with Franz Kafka that writing is the most personal form of prayer. Once I accept an assignment, my job, as I see it, is to

409

simply show up, try to get out of my own way, and work with Spirit. When I do, the impossible happens on every page and every day. Nowhere is this miracle more apparent to me than by the caliber of the extraordinary people who seemed to be mystically drawn to help shepherd my work into the world with as much devotion as if it was their own. Blessed am I among writers, and I know it.

There were many times during the writing of *Something More* when my faith faltered but my colleagues, friends, and family's generosity of spirit never wavered. They believed this book into being.

Maureen Mahon Egen, President of Warner Books, understood that I wanted to write more than just a coda to *Simple Abundance* and graciously gifted me with all the love, latitude, and largesse necessary to let the book that begged to be written emerge on its own terms, and she was genuinely thrilled (which genuinely thrilled me) that the one we ended up with bore absolutely no resemblance whatsoever to the one promised. Maureen is not just Warner's chief operating officer, she is their visionary and a kindred spirit. I look forward to our continuing creative collaboration.

Caryn Karmatz Rudy started out as my editor but ended up as the midwife to *Something More*, and it was a breach birth all the way. Her calm, confident reassurance and repose of the soul led this book out of the daunting darkness of creative confusion into the light of publication. Why do I love her? Let me count the whys, especially her courage under fire. For all the times she cheerfully and convincingly answered "Beautifully!" in response to "How's it going?" from the powers-that-be, I owe her a tremendous karmic debt (if not a long weekend at Canyon Ranch). All's well that ends well is all well and good, but a savvy co-conspirator is not a bad backup. I pray paying her back will be a lifelong pleasure.

Heartfelt thanks to my other benefactors at Warner Books: Managing Editor Harvey-Jane Kowal was the essence of elegant restraint, proving again that less is more, especially her choice of only two words of encouragement: "No Pressure"; Jamie Raab, Warner's hardcover publisher, cares as much about the writer's process as the product, a rare and greatly appreciated benediction. Thanks again to copy editor Ann Armstrong Craig for continuing to perpetuate the illusion that I have command of the English language, and to copy chief Ann Schwartz for her sleight-of-hand skills that enable her to magically describe books that have yet to be conjured up.

Kudos to the repeat performance of the Warner design and production team: Diane Luger, Thom Whatley, and especially Flamur Tonuzi for the lovely cover design; Margaret Chodos-Irvine again created our charming cover art, which proves once more that a picture is worth a thousand words.

A nod, a wink, and a hug to all those who toil so tirelessly behind the scenes in order that my books are so enthusiastically received: Publicity diva Emi Battaglia sings my praises and always hits the high notes. Jennifer Romanello, my Warner publicity maestra, blends the flats of everyday with the sharps of the extraordinary to create one harmonious symphony. Take another bow, ladies. Susan Richman's energetic verve is contagious, and Jimmy Franco's mere presence is cool water when the fever runs high. The subsidiary rights team — director Nancy Wiese, Tracy Howell, Julie Saltman, and Sarah Telford — have spread my words from China to Croatia; and thanks to Chris Barba, vice president of sales at Warner, for taking *Something More* under her personal wing — every book dreams of such a godmother.

A glass of good cheer is lifted for a toast to Time Warner Audio's Judy McGuinn, who should win a Grammy for graciousness. Maja Thomas is the alchemy of creativity and kindness; she makes my spoken words soar and even transforms the toughest recording session into a few days of playing hooky; John Whitman's erudite abridgments are much applauded.

Simply abundant thanks to Letty Ferrando, Jackie Joiner, Carolyn Clarke, and Lissy Katz for always making me feel as if I am the only author published by Warner Books.

Many others bless me enormously every day with the gift of their time, creative energy, emotion, loyalty, friendship, support, and unconditional love. In Washington — Dawne Winter, Beth Sanders, Jane Parker, and Jennifer Page are Simple Abundance, Inc. The solace and sanity they bring to my daily round is priceless. Whoever said that no one is irreplaceable never met these women.

Kathy Schenker, Sally Fischer, Nancy Hirsch, and Yael Schneiderman in New York make sure that no one loses sight of the woman behind the book or forgets that the Simple Abundance Charitable Fund is the cornerstone of my House of Belonging. And bless Stacey Bosworth, my personal assistant in New York and special projects coordinator, for always bringing the party with her.

Margaret Gorenstein and Katie Maresca made sure I could sleep at night by taking care of permissions; they have my undying gratitude for taking on a thankless job, which is why I want to thank them here.

My sister, Maureen Crean, and brothers, Pat Crean and Sean Crean, shelter me with their steadfast loyalty and unwavering support. I'm grateful that three of my people are blood-related. Thanks to Maureen for being the brains behind my being coaxed into the twenty-first century with a Web site, and to Pat for holding my hand on a moment's notice.

Jonathan Diamond intuitively knows my needs. Before I ask, he's already answered. He is and will always be my Prince Charming.

Two accomplished women and gifted independent editors assisted me in countless ways during the writing of this book; their steady assistance was a net underneath me as I leaped on the page, and their never-ending flexibility, insights, and detective skills were a source of constant inspiration. Thank you, Sally Arteseros, for the private tutorial in archaeology, for personally excavating the lost library of the ancient Assyrian king Assurbanipal on my behalf and for delivering some of his 30,000-volume clay tablet stacks to my desk every week, as well as for tying up loose ends and staying unflappable. You helped me in so many ways, I know I'm forgetting something. I also know that making it look easy is the hardest job in the world. Thanks for making me appear brilliant.

A bow to Susan Leon for creatively and cheerfully brainstorming with me about pivotal points in women's lives, whether she was in London or L.A. When I was stuck, Susan made sure I didn't come unglued. Her gifted ability to find women's stories that poignantly brought this book's truth home to me personally was matchless and her contribution invaluable.

Finally, there are no words to convey my gratitude and love to my daughter, Katie Sharp, and my dear friend Chris Tomasino, who is not just my literary agent and business manager, but my sword and my shield. I could dedicate every book to Katie and Chris. That says it all. They are not just child and friend, but *anam caras,* and their presence in my life is my greatest blessing.

But the soul of this book's inspiration is expressed in my dedication. Two years ago I met Katie Brant and Larry Kirshbaum, and the trajectory of my life changed in profound ways. Katie's beauty and bravery embodies the essence of *Something More.* Her gentle but passionate perseverance and unflinching belief that we could convince the corporate world to look beyond the bottom line was the spiritual catalyst for my new imprint at Warner Books, The Simple Abundance Press.

And Larry Kirshbaum, Chairman of Time Warner Trade Publishing, taught me how to turn a publishing pipe dream into a beautiful reality. When *Simple Abundance* was "coming out" into society, he was the suave gentleman who made sure that a shy debutante became the belle of the ball, and a gal never forgets the guy who brings her to her first big dance.

I only pray that they can read the love and gratitude in my heart between every line.

Sarah Ban Breathnach
July 1998

Continued from p. 4.

Selected Bibliography

She is too fond of books,
and it has turned her brain.

LOUISA MAY ALCOTT

My sources for the quotes have been rich and varied. My favorite collections of quotations are: *The New Beacon Book of Quotations by Women,* compiled by Rosalie Maggio (Boston: Beacon Press, 1996); *Bartlett's Familiar Quotations,* Sixteenth Edition, edited by Justin Kaplan (Boston: Little, Brown and Company, 1992); and *The Columbia Dictionary of Quotations,* compiled by Robert Andrews (New York: Columbia University Press, 1993).

Ackerman, Diane. *A Natural History of the Senses.* New York: Random House. 1990.

——— . *A Slender Thread: Rediscovering Hope at the Heart of Crisis.* New York: Random House, 1997.

Albert, Susan Wittig, Ph.D. *Writing from Life:*

Telling Your Soul's Story. New York: Jeremy P. Tarcher/Putnam Books, 1996.

Ang, Li. *The Butcher's Wife and Other Stories.* Edited and translated by Howard Goldblatt. Boston: Cheng and Tsui, 1995.

Anthony, Evelyn. *The Avenue of the Dead.* New York: Coward, McCann & Geohegan, 1982.

Bagnold, Enid. *National Velvet.* New York: Avon Books, 1991.

Baldwin, Christina. *Life's Companion: Journal Writing as a Spiritual Quest.* New York: Bantam Books, 1991.

Bowen, Elizabeth. *To the North.* New York: Viking Penguin, 1997.

Branden, Nathaniel. *The Psychology of Self-Esteem.* New York: Bantam Books, 1983.

Brown, Molly Young, Editor. *Lighting a Candle: Quotations on the Spiritual Life.* New York: Hazelden/Harper Collins, 1994.

Buck, Pearl S. *To My Daughters, With Love.* Cutchogue, New York: Buccaneer Books, 1992.

Cameron, Julia, with Mark Bryan. *The Artist's Way: A Spiritual Path to Higher Creativity.* New

York: Jeremy P. Tarcher/Putnam Books, 1992.

Ceram, C. W. *Gods, Graves, and Scholars: The Story of Archaeology*. Translated from the German by E. B. Garside and Sophie Wilkins. Second, Revised and Substantially Enlarged Edition. New York: Vintage Books/Random House, 1986.

Chopin, Kate. *The Awakening*. New York: Avon Books, 1982.

Christie, Agatha. *An Autobiography*. New York: Berkley, 1996.

Conway, Jill Ker, Editor. *Written by Herself: Autobiographies of American Women: An Anthology*. New York: Vintage Books/Random House, 1992.

Davis, Rebecca Harding. *Life in the Iron Mills and Other Stories*. Edited by Tillie Olsen. Second Edition. New York: Feminist Press, 1985.

Davis, Dr. Avram, and Manuela Dunn Mascetti. *Judaic Mysticism*. New York: Hyperion, 1997.

Deetz, James. *In Small Things Forgotten: An Archaeology of Early American Life*. New York: Anchor Books/Bantam Doubleday Dell, 1996.

DeSalvo, Louise. *Vertigo: A Memoir.* New York: NAL-Dutton, 1996.

————. *Virginia Woolf: The Impact of Childhood Sexual Abuse on Her Life and Work.* Boston: Beacon Press, 1989.

Evans, Noela N. *Meditations for the Passages and Celebrations of Life.* New York: Crown, 1994.

Fagan, Brian M., Editor. *Eyewitness to Discovery: First-Person Accounts of More Than Fifty of the World's Greatest Archaeological Discoveries.* New York: Oxford University Press, 1996.

Ferrucci, Piero. *Inevitable Grace.* New York: Jeremy P. Tarcher/Putnam Books, 1990.

Fraser, Kennedy. *Ornament and Silence: Essays on Women's Lives from Edith Wharton to Germaine Greer.* New York: Alfred A. Knopf, 1996.

Gibran, Kahlil. *The Prophet.* New York: Alfred A. Knopf, 1996.

Gill, Brendan. *Late Bloomers.* New York: Artisan/Workman, 1996.

Godden, Rumer. *A House with Four Rooms.* New York: William Morrow, 1989.

Gunderson, Edna. "The New Madonna." From

USA Today, March 3, 1998.

Henderson, Julie. *The Lover Within: Opening to Energy in Sexual Practice*. Revised Edition. Barrytown, New York: Station Hill Press, 1997.

Ibsen, Henrik. *A Doll's House*. Translated by Peter Watts. London: Penguin Books, 1965.

Jong, Erica. *Fear of Fifty*. New York: Harper-Collins, 1994.

Keller, Helen. *The Story of My Life*. New York: Bantam Books, 1990.

Kipfer, Barbara Ann. *The Wish List*. New York: Workman, 1997.

Lawrence, D. H. *All Souls' Day*. From the complete poems. Collected and edited with and introduction and notes by Vivian de Sola Pinto and Warren Roberts. New York: Penguin Books, 1993.

Linfield, Jordan L., and Joseph Krevisky, Editors. *Words of Love: Romantic Quotations from Plato to Madonna*. New York: Random House, 1997.

McCoy, Horace. *They Shoot Horses, Don't They?* Cutchogue, New York: Buccaneer Books, 1993.

McIntosh, Jane. *The Practical Archaeologist: How We Know What We Know about the Past*. New York: Facts on File®, 1986.

McMillon, Bill. *The Archaeology Handbook: A Field Manual and Resource Guide*. New York: John Wiley and Sons, 1991.

Microsoft Encarta Multimedia Encyclopedia (CD-ROM). Redmond, Washington: Microsoft, 1998.

Miller, Sue. *The Good Mother*. New York: Harper & Row, 1986.

Moffat, Mary Jane, and Charlotte Painter, Editors. *Revelations: Diaries of Women*. New York: Random House, 1974.

Moore, Thomas. *Soul Mates: Honoring the Mysteries of Love and Relationships*. New York: HarperCollins, 1994.

Morrison, Mary C. *Let Evening Come: Reflections on Aging*. New York: Doubleday, 1998.

Myss, Caroline. *Spiritual Madness: The Necessity of Meeting God in Darkness*. (Audiotape; 2 cassettes). Boulder, Colorado: Sounds True, 1997.

Norris, Kathleen. *Amazing Grace: A Vocabulary*

of Faith. New York: Riverhead Books/Penguin Putnam, 1998.

O'Donohue, John. *Anam Cara: A Book of Celtic Wisdom*. New York: Cliff Street Books/HarperCollins, 1997.

Olsen, Tillie. *Silences*. New York: Seymour Lawrence/Delacorte Press, 1978.

Person, Ethel S. *Dreams of Love and Fateful Encounters: The Power of Romantic Passion*. New York: Viking Penguin, 1989.

Quindlen, Anna. *Black and Blue*. New York: Random House, 1998.

Renfrew, Colin, and Paul Bahn. *Archaeology: Theories, Methods, and Practice*. New York: Thames and Hudson, 1991.

Rilke, Rainer Maria. *Rilke's Book of Hours: Love Poems to God*. Translated by Anita Barrows and Joanna Macy. New York: Riverhead Books/Putnam, 1996.

Rose, Phyllis, Editor. *The Norton Book of Women's Lives*. New York: W. W. Norton, 1993.

Ross, Lillian. *Here But Not Here*. New York: Random House, 1998.

Rumi. *The Illuminated Rumi.* Translations and commentary by Coleman Barks. Illuminations by Michael Green. New York: Broadway Books/Bantam Doubleday Dell, 1997.

Sark. *A Creative Companion.* Berkeley, California: Celestial Arts, 1991.

Selznick, Irene Mayer. *A Private View.* New York: Alfred A. Knopf, 1983.

Shain, Merle. *Some Men Are More Perfect Than Others.* New York: Bantam Books, 1973.

Shange, Ntozake. *Sassafras, Cypress & Indigo.* New York: St. Martin's Press, 1996.

Sheehy, Gail. *New Passages: Mapping Your Life Across Time.* New York: Random House, 1995.

Sleigh, Julian. *Crisis Points: Working Through Personal Problems.* Floris Books, U.K.; distributed by: Hudson, New York: Anthroposophic, 1990.

Steinem, Gloria. *Revolution from Within: A Book of Self-Esteem.* Boston: Little, Brown & Company, 1992.

Stoddard, Alexandra. *Creating a Beautiful Home.* New York: William Morrow, 1992.

————. *Making Choices: The Joy of a Courageous Life.* New York: William Morrow, 1994.

Thurman, Judith. *Isak Dinesen: The Life of a Storyteller.* New York: St. Martin's Press, 1982.

Tolstoy, Leo. *Anna Karenina.* Translated by David Magarshack. New York: Signet Classic/ New American Library of World Literature, 1961.

Tyldesley, Joyce. *Daughters of Isis: Women of Ancient Egypt.* New York: Penguin Books, 1995.

————. *Hatchepsut: The Female Pharaoh.* New York: Viking, 1996.

Tyler, Anne. "Still Just Waiting." From *The Writer on Her Work*, Edited by Janet Sternburg. New York: Norton, 1992.

Waller, Robert James. *The Bridges of Madison County.* New York: Warner Books, 1992.

White, Kate. *Why Good Girls Don't Get Ahead but Gutsy Girls Do.* New York: Warner Books, 1996.

Wile, Mary Lee. *Ancient Rage.* Thorndike, Maine: Thorndike Press, 1996.

Williamson, Marianne. *Illuminata: Thoughts,*

Prayers, Rites of Passage. New York: Random House, 1994.

——————. *A Return to Love: Reflections on the Principles of a Course in Miracles.* New York: HarperCollins, 1993.

Woolf, Virginia. *Orlando.* New York: Harcourt Brace & Company, 1928.

——————. "A Sketch of the Past." From *Moments of Being.* Edited by Jeanne Schulkind. Second Edition. New York: Harvest Books/ Harcourt Brace & Company, 1985.

—————— . *A Room of One's Own.* New York: Harcourt Brace Jovanovich, 1929.

Yeats, W. B. "The Stare's Nest by My Window," *Meditations in Time of Civil War, The Tower* (1928). New York: Macmillan, 1933.

For Further Information

SARAH BAN BREATHNACH would like to hear from you about your search for Something More. Please contact her at the addresses below. And if you'd like information on her forthcoming newsletter, *Something More*, please let us know.

Sarah has prepared a *Something More* readers' circle study guide. If you would like a copy please send a stamped, self-addressed envelope to:

Sarah Ban Breathnach/Something More
Post Office Box 11123
Takoma Park, Maryland 20913
(301) 320-1791

To reach Elizabeth Sanders' resource center, *Crossings: Caring for Our Own at Death*, please write to P.O. Box 721, Silver Spring, Md. 20918. Telephone (301) 593-5451.

About the Author

Sarah Ban Breathnach's work celebrates quiet joys, simple pleasures, and everyday epiphanies. She is the author of the #1 *New York Times* bestseller SIMPLE ABUNDANCE and THE SIMPLE ABUNDANCE JOURNAL OF GRATITUDE.

Sarah Ban Breathnach is the publisher of The Simple Abundance Press, an imprint of Warner Books. She is also the founder of the Simple Abundance Charitable Trust, a non-profit bridge group between charitable causes and the public, dedicated to increasing awareness that "doing good" and "living the good life" are soul mates.

Sarah Ban Breathnach lives outside of Washington, D.C., with her daughter.